National Institute of
Economic and Social Research
Economic Policy Papers 3

BRITAIN'S TRADE AND EXCHANGE-RATE POLICY

Edited by
ROBIN MAJOR

 Heinemann Educational Books · London

Heinemann Educational Books Ltd

LONDON EDINBURGH MELBOURNE AUCKLAND TORONTO
HONG KONG SINGAPORE KUALA LUMPUR NEW DELHI
NAIROBI JOHANNESBURG IBADAN
KINGSTON

British Library Cataloguing in Publication Data

Britain's trade and exchange-rate policy. –
(National Institute of Economic and Social
Research. Economic policy papers; no. 3).
1. Great Britain – Foreign economic relations
I. Major, R L   II. Series
382.1′0941   HF3506.5

ISBN 0-435-84467-9
ISBN 0-435-84468-7 Pbk

Published by Heinemann Educational Books Ltd
Filmset by Northumberland Press Ltd
Gateshead, Tyne and Wear
Printed in Great Britain by Richard Clay (The Chaucer Press) Ltd
Bungay, Suffolk

Foreword

The conference whose papers are here collected was the third in the series – I was privileged to help to organise the first, to write a paper for the second and to take the chair at the third. It was to my mind both the most friendly and the most successful of the three discussions and I now believe that this series of conferences can become one of the established features of British discussions on economic and social policy. There was the same spirit of shared knowledge, of differing theoretical presuppositions, but of insistence on rational choice in decision-making, which characterises the best of the American discussions in similar fora that I have attended.

Whereas the public impression of economists is that they speak in closed logico-deductive systems, never emerging from their own frameworks to argue rationally with opponents, this meeting exemplified the sort of discussion which policy-makers could have listened to with profit. I would particularly draw attention to the approach to unity on the analytical description of the relative effects of exchange-rate changes and the imposition of trade controls. But light, rather than heat, was also spread in the discussion of the availability of exchange-rate policy as one of the weapons in a government's armoury – the theme which has recurred in all three conferences.

One percipient journalist asked after the first conference whether anybody had changed his mind in the course of discussion. This is a harsh test to apply. But at least there has been a greater willingness to believe that the views of others merit serious attention. This is an important part of the battle.

Michael Posner
Social Science Research Council, London
Pembroke College, Cambridge
July 1979

Contents

Contributors and Participants

Chairman
M. V. Posner, Chairman, Social Science Research Council.

Contributors
C. Allsopp, Fellow of New College, Oxford.
M. J. Balfour, Chief Adviser, Bank of England.
M. Beenstock, Senior Research Fellow, London Business School.
S. J. Brooks, Research Officer, National Institute of Economic and Social Research.
T. Burns, Senior Lecturer, London Business School.
V. Cable, Director, Overseas Development Institute.
M. Emerson, Director, National Economies and Economic Trends Division, European Communities Commission.
J. H. Forsyth, Chief Adviser, Morgan Grenfell & Co. Ltd.
D. Lal, Lecturer, University College, London (on leave at World Bank, Washington).
R. L. Major (*Editor*), Senior Research Fellow, National Institute of Economic and Social Research.
Professor R. R. Neild, Fellow of Trinity College, Professor of Economics, Cambridge.
Mrs S. A. B. Page, Research Officer, National Institute of Economic and Social Research.
L. Turner, Research Fellow, Royal Institute of International Affairs.
G. D. N. Worswick, Director, National Institute of Economic and Social Research.

Other participants
F. T. Blackaby
Professor W. M. Corden
S. Dell

J. Dixon
W. A. H. Godley
C. Johnson
H. H. Liesner
Sir Donald MacDougall
G. Maynard
P. Oppenheimer
T. M. Rybczynski
J. R. Sargent
A. Singh
Professor J. H. B. Tew
W. Wallace
D. Watt

1 Introduction

by R. L. Major

The conference held at Bretton Woods in July 1944 inaugurated a new era in international trade and payments with the establishment of the International Monetary Fund (IMF). Among the Fund's declared purposes were to promote international monetary cooperation and exchange-rate stability, to facilitate balanced growth of international trade and the correction of maladjustments, and to shorten the duration and lessen the degree of disequilibrium in the international balance of payments.

For several years after the war international trade was severely restricted by controls, imposed mainly on balance of payments grounds. But from 1948 to 1973 trade increased ninefold in manufactures and nearly fourfold in primary products. It would obviously be wrong to attribute these developments to the IMF alone. Even if we consider only the role of international organisations, it is clear that the GATT, OEEC (later OECD), EEC, EFTA and other preferential systems all played important parts in trade liberalisation. But as the source of the financial framework within which an unprecedented expansion of international transactions was accommodated Bretton Woods must be considered an outstanding success.

The same accolade cannot unfortunately be awarded for achievement of balance of payments equilibrium, at any rate if this is interpreted to mean the avoidance of persistent surpluses and deficits in the current accounts of the major countries. There has been continuing maladjustment in this sense and in the first quarter of a century of its existence the system to which the name of Bretton Woods was popularly attached was subjected to mounting criticism because of the excessive rigidity in respect of exchange rates which was attributed to it and which was blamed for the apparent inadequacy of the adjustment mechanism. The attribution was in a sense unfair, as the Bretton Woods system did in fact provide for changes in rates 'to correct a fundamental disequilibrium'. But after the general realignment of

1949 changes as between the industrial countries were rare and came to be regarded as entailing a loss of face for the government concerned even, in the case of Germany in 1969, when the direction of change was upward. Disequilibria tended if positive to remain uncorrected and if negative to be corrected only temporarily by periodic recourse to contractionary policies which adversely affected levels of trade and national standards of living. A further weakness was the position of the dollar as the currency to which other currencies were pegged and in which other countries' reserves came to be held. This meant that other countries depended for growth of reserves on a deficit in the United States balance of payments, which, however, weakened their confidence in the very currency they were acquiring.

Generalised floating of the currencies of the industrial countries came in March 1973 less by international agreement than as the culmination of a process of drift as one major country after another abandoned, at least temporarily, the 'fixed but adjustable peg' adopted nearly thirty years previously. Nevertheless high hopes were held that under the new regime capital flows would become equilibrating, rather than disequilibrating as in the past, and that the problem of surpluses and deficits would largely disappear, if at some cost in terms of uncertainty for the international trading community.

Unhappily these hopes have not been fulfilled. Central bank intervention in the foreign-exchange markets has increased steadily during the past six years and even so the scale of OECD countries' imbalances on current account has been rising in relation to their GDP – a point which remains valid even if adjustment is made for the development of an aggregate deficit as the counterpart of the OPEC countries' surplus. A concomitant of increased freedom of exchange rates has been diminished freedom of trade and other aspects of the world economy have become markedly less favourable. The extent and even the existence of any causal connection with the change in the exchange-rate regime are, however, matters of debate, particularly as this change broadly coincided with a dramatic rise in the prices of commodities and of oil in particular.

It would probably not be disputed that the oil price rise of 1973–4 and the resultant transfer of purchasing power from private consumers in oil-importing countries to public authorities in OPEC played a major part in 1974–5 in the price explosion and the recession in the industrial world, nor that the recession has contributed in turn to the adoption of increasingly protectionist policies. What is more disturbing is that neither the subsequent revival of economic growth nor the slowing down of inflation has been adequately sustained, while greater restriction of imports threatens to become permanent even in countries where the balance of payments problem is one of surplus rather than deficit.

The United Kingdom's position is particularly unsatisfactory. North Sea oil has brought a temporary improvement in the balance of payments and, at the time of writing, a marked strengthening of the rate of exchange. But the non-oil balance of trade has sharply deteriorated and inflation has been accelerating rapidly, though the underlying rate of growth of output appears to be relatively low and unemployment is still high.

It was against this gloomy background (some aspects of which are delineated in greater detail in the papers by Brooks, Mrs Page and myself which constitute Chapter 7) that external authors were invited to prepare their papers for the conference which the National Institute recently organised. The purpose of these papers was to provide a basis for discussion of the policies which the United Kingdom should pursue domestically and advocate in the international arena, and they appear in the book in pairs. The first paper in each case puts forward propositions which in the second are subjected to critical analysis.

The first pair of papers (Chapter 2) deals with trade between industrial countries and in particular with the Cambridge Economic Policy Group's case for protectionist policies; the second pair (Chapter 3) is in the main critical of such policies in the general context of trading relationships between the industrial countries and the third world. The third and fourth pairs (Chapters 4 and 5 respectively) are concerned with questions of exchange rates; one discusses the European Monetary System (EMS), presenting cases for and against full United Kingdom participation; the other is mainly concerned with the results of simulations carried out at the London Business School of the potential effects on other key variables in the British economy of a higher rate of exchange for sterling such as EMS membership might entail. A final pair of papers (Chapter 6) discusses the problem of persistent surpluses in the balance of payments of certain countries, the first paper suggesting that this is heightened, and the difficulties of the deficit countries aggravated, by the policies towards capital flows which the two groups have respectively followed.

The book concludes with an account (Chapter 8) of the discussion at the conference. To minimise delays in publication the length of the book has been severely restricted and the account of the conference proceedings is correspondingly summary. It has also been necessary for purposes of publication to reduce the length of the original papers, and I am grateful to the authors for accepting cuts which in some cases were very substantial. Thanks are due also to Miss Little for her hard and skilful work in preparing the book for the printer.

2 Managed Trade Between Industrial Countries

by R. R. Neild*

This paper considers the 'management' of trade between industrial countries, how it is related to the recession and whether in the period ahead more management (or organised free trade) is likely or desirable. The object is to find a coherent explanation of current trends based on realistic assumptions and to consider its implications for policy.

Definitions

'Management' is defined as any action designed to cause a deviation from international free trade. This definition seems to fit what people have in mind when they talk about intervention. All government economic measures will have indirect effects on the level and pattern of production and trade. But here it seems best to consider only those measures other than changes in the exchange rate which may influence foreign trade independently of demand management and monetary policy – that is measures which change trade flows at a given level of demand. This definition includes taxes, subsidies or quotas applied to exports or imports, state purchasing policies, tax concessions and subsidies to particular industries or to foreign enterprises and nationals, trade deals where strategic or state financial leverage is used to promote trade, other industrial policies and similar measures. We consider trade in manufactures on the grounds that it is with respect to manufactures that increased management of trade between industrial countries is, or could be, most important.

* In preparing this paper I have drawn freely on the published work of colleagues in Cambridge and on the many discussions I have had with them about this subject. I owe a particular debt to Francis Cripps and Terry Ward who commented on a draft and to Noxy Dastoor who prepared the figures.

The Problem of Bias

The subject matter is as strongly value-loaded as any in economics, particularly if one uses the traditional terms free trade and protectionism. Yet to try to avoid these terms for the sake of neutrality is so awkward, and probably ineffectual, that it seems better to use them.

The positions taken today by participants in the free trade versus protection debate are no different from those taken by their predecessors long ago.

On the free trade side, belief in free international trade is part and parcel of a general faith in the price mechanism. Thus Marshall, in assessing Adam Smith's contribution to economics nearly a hundred years ago (see Marshall [8], p. 627), used the term free trade in its widest sense:

> He developed the Physiocratic doctrine of Free Trade with so much practical wisdom, and with so much knowledge of the actual conditions of business, as to make it a great force in real life; and he is most widely known both here and abroad for his argument that Government generally does harm by interfering in trade. While giving many instances of the ways in which self-interest may lead the individual trader to act injuriously to the community, he contended that even when Government acted with the best intentions, it nearly always served the public worse than the enterprise of the individual trader, however selfish he might happen to be.

And an American professor of economics, in a book published this year (Krauss [5], p. 36) writes, 'The emergence of the new protectionism in the Western world reflects the victory of the interventionist, or welfare, economy over the market economy.'

On the other side, there is the view that free trade is a doctrine used by strong countries to justify commercial conquest of the weak. Thus Frederick List writing in the 1830s (List [7] p. 131) accused England in the following terms of first using protection (the 'political system of commerce') to foster industrialisation and then espousing free trade (the 'cosmopolitical principle') to conquer others:

> It would be most unjust, even on cosmopolitical grounds, now to resign to the English all the wealth and power of the earth, merely because by them the political system of commerce was first established and the cosmopolitical principle for the most part ignored. In order to allow freedom of trade to operate naturally, the less advanced nations must first be raised by artificial measures to that stage of cultivation to which the English nation has been artificially elevated.

And recently the French Prime Minister, M. Barre, in calling for new rules of the game of international trade, argued that without proper rules 'free trade is nothing more than a pretext for the strongest and least scrupulous as well as being a trap for the weakest' (Kaldor [4]).

The question whether or not some degree of intervention in trade is desirable is separate both from the question whether one uses the price mechanism or direct controls and from the question whether one uses general or selective measures. For example, a general *ad valorem* tariff on manufactures uses market prices almost as much as devaluation – though, as we shall see, it is significantly different in other respects.

Facts

My impression is that there has been an increase in the management of trade by industrial countries, directed against developing countries more than industrial countries. But when one reads reports about actual and proposed acts of management one can easily forget that these acts may not be introduced or may be ineffective, that some acts go unreported and that there are continuing policies which open up or ease trade (directly as in the Tokyo round or indirectly by standardising units, specifications, etc.). The reading of reported actions is not a very reliable guide to the true change in obstacles to trade – which is an elusive concept at best.

An alternative procedure, which has its limitations too, is to inspect the relationship of the growth of trade in manufactures with the growth of production. Since 1950 the volume of exports of manufactures by industrial countries has grown substantially faster than their industrial production. In recessions the growth of trade has been checked. In the present recession the movement of trade relative to production scarcely appears to be exceptional, allowing for the fact that the recession has been deeper and more prolonged than any since the last war.

These developments stand in contrast to what happened in the interwar period. From 1923 to 1929 exports of manufactures rose faster than output of manufactures, but the difference in the two growth rates was by no means as marked as in the period since 1950. Between 1929 and 1932 output fell by 29 per cent and exports by 44 per cent, but that differential cannot be taken simply as evidence of protection, since it was associated with a huge improvement in the terms of trade: to obtain the imports needed to sustain a given level of activity industrial countries needed to export a third fewer manufactures. On the other hand, in the recovery from 1932 to 1937 most of this change in the terms of trade was reversed, yet exports of manufactures grew much more slowly than output. That, pretty surely, is evidence of protectionism, which we know was increasing strongly in the 1930s.

For the period since 1960 the figures for trade in manufactures can be subdivided to distinguish exchanges among industrial countries from their trade in each direction with developing countries. From 1960 to 1973 exports of manufactures from one industrial country to another and exports of manufactures from developing countries to the industrial countries both rose by about 300 per cent. Exports of manufactures from the industrial countries to the developing countries increased by only about 130 per cent, having slipped behind mainly in the early 1960s.

Since 1973 there has been a striking change in the pattern of growth of trade in manufactures. While trade between the industrial countries, which dipped sharply in 1975, has recovered and shows a stronger increase than industrial production from 1973 to 1977, it has been far outstripped over that period by the growth of exports of manufactures both to and from the developing countries. This can be seen in Table 2.1.

Table 2.1   Pattern of trade in manufactures, change 1973–7

	Change in volume 1973–7 (percentages)	Value 1977 ($ billion)
Industrial production	+5	—
Exports of manufactures		
Between industrial countries	+11	381
Industrial to developing countries	+63	143
Developing to industrial countries	+32	35

Sources: United Nations, *Monthly Bulletin of Statistics*, June 1979 and earlier issues.

The rapid growth in exports of manufactures from the industrial countries to the developing countries is not surprising, since relatively little of the dramatic worsening in 1973 and 1974 of the terms of trade between manufactures and other products including oil had been reversed by 1977. But the increase in exports from developing countries to industrial countries is a different matter. It looks as if it must reflect greater movement of advanced but labour-intensive production to low-wage countries in order to supply advanced countries as well as local markets. While the absolute size of exports of manufactures from developing countries to the industrial countries is not large, its rapid growth during the recession no doubt helps to explain the increase in protection and demands for protection against the products of developing countries.

On the basis of this limited evidence, I shall proceed on the assumption that the increase in protection in trade in manufactures has so far been quite limited; what is important is to look to the future and consider how trade management may affect recovery from the recession, the restoration of full employment and the achievement of price stability. Before one can judge what has happened or what should be done, it is necessary to find an analytical framework in which to explain satisfactorily the relationship between the current recession, the imbalances in trade that go with it and the various steps that have been taken, or might be taken, to manage trade.

The Determinants of Trade

Conventional trade theory is not much help here, since it rests on unrealistic assumptions about the perfection of markets and the conditions of production and addresses the question of what determines the pattern of trade and output in a setting where there is full employment.

An alternative approach, derived from Lord Kaldor, is to start by considering the laws of production and conditions of trade in the three sections – primary, secondary, tertiary – into which an economy is conventionally divided. From the evidence around us we can classify the sectors as: (a) primary, with decreasing returns to growth of output and perfectly tradeable products; (b) secondary, with increasing returns to growth of output and imperfectly tradeable products; (c) tertiary, with mixed returns to growth of output and products with limited tradeability.

In the case of primary products, the finite endowment of natural resources of any nation or region means that, once it has been fully explored and opened up, there will be decreasing returns to the application of extra resources. This may be relieved by technological progress, but that will be largely the result of advances in the secondary and tertiary sectors where new inputs and techniques are developed. Primary products are perfectly tradeable in the sense that, apart from perishable goods, they are transportable and usually homogenous, so that the buyer is indifferent between the produce of competing suppliers.

In secondary industry, of which manufacturing is the largest part – the rest consists of public utilities and the like – there are increasing returns, internal, external and dynamic: the costs per unit of a given manufactured product diminish with the scale of output of a firm; the growth of firms causes growth of the market, of ancillary firms and of skills and other assets in the nation of area where they are located, and the leading producer is better placed than others to develop new products and new production techniques. Manufactured products are imperfectly tradeable in the sense that, although transportable, they are differentiated, so that buyers are not indifferent between the products of competing suppliers. Moreover, precisely because of diversity and change, buyers cannot be perfectly informed about the relative merits of these products. Increasing returns mean that in manufacturing we are faced by 'circular and cumulative causation', as one manufacturing nation after another assumes the lead and enjoys a virtuous circle, while others suffer a vicious circle. We cannot explain why a nation assumes the lead, nor predict who is going to do so next. We can use biological analogies, referring in loose, Darwinian terms to a growth process with unpredictable properties, rather as Marshall referred to trees in a forest as an analogy for the representative firm without being too precise about what determined the birth and death of individual trees.

Tertiary industry is a murky area, because the products are so hard to measure and various. For present purposes the important point is that production of services of most types is essentially a complement to rather than a substitute for the production of goods. Demand for a large part of services, notably transport and distribution, derives from production of goods in the primary and secondary sectors, with the result that in the long run higher output depends heavily on higher output of goods. Another large part – health, education and public services – has to be viewed as a social charge on the production of goods, not as an alternative form of wealth creation; a nation cannot live by producing only health services and education, except to the limited extent that these can be exported. If services can be sold internationally they can be substituted indirectly for production of goods, but only a few can in practice be exported on a significant scale.

The Consequences of Trade

Given these conditions, there is the possibility that when one country, gaining the benefits of increasing returns, encroaches on the markets for manufactures of another, the latter, because of diminishing returns in agriculture and the non-tradeable nature of most services, may have difficulty in maintaining employment and may lose from trade.

Kaldor [4] illustrates how these conditions of production undermine the basic case for free trade by taking Ricardo's classic example of the exchange of cloth (which can be taken to represent manufactures) for wine (representing primary products) between England and Portugal, and introducing the assumption that there are increasing returns in cloth production and decreasing returns in wine production, instead of constant returns to both. His example is roughly as follows. Portugal has land well suited to wine growing but not enough to employ the whole labour force at a living wage. In the absence of international trade, the remainder are employed in making cloth by traditional means, one yard being exchanged for ten litres of wine. On the other hand, in England, where the cloth industry enjoys a superior technology and larger output, one yard of cloth is exchanged for one litre of wine. The opening of trade – assuming that as it occurs the Portuguese are not able quickly to emulate the technology and industrial practices of the English cloth trade – will mean that the price of cloth will fall so much in Portugal that it will no longer be profitable to produce cloth there. If the workers released from making cloth could all be employed in making wine at constant returns Portugal would be better off, but the limited supply of land prevents that. And it may be impossible to save the Portuguese cloth trade by reducing wages if there is a minimum wage in terms of wine below which cloth-workers could not subsist. Hence, the result may be that, while Portugal exports more wine and exchanges it for cloth on more favourable terms than before, this gain is outweighed by the loss of cloth production. Portugal's real national income falls while England gains.

The crucial assumptions are the minimum wage in terms of wine, decreasing returns in wine production (which limit Portuguese employment possibilities in that sector) and the productivity gap which prevents the employment at a minimum wage of Portuguese workers in cloth production. These assumptions, which appear historically realistic, suffice to explain why, as List [7] tells us, the Methuen Treaty of 1704 made Portugal poorer than before. A modern instance where protection has been used for a long time to prevent an outcome of this kind is New Zealand.

An analogous process may obtain in developed countries such as Britain and the United States, which are losing out today in competition in the market for manufactures. In their case it is the tertiary rather than the primary sector which is the main alternative to manufacturing as a source of employment; the floor to the real wage in manufacturing is set not by a subsistence quantity of primary produce, but by an achieved wage level comprising a mixed basket of goods and services, or an expected level which is a function of the achieved levels of previous periods. Their problem can best be understood as a variant of the Portuguese case as follows:

(a)   These countries have been unable to retard the increase of the real wage in manufacturing, either by reducing the growth of money wages relative to other countries or by devaluation, to the point where they can compensate for their non-price disadvantages in the market for manufactures.

(b)   They may have experienced a relative shift of labour from manufacturing into the tertiary sector over and above the normal trend associated with growth as foreign competition has squeezed manufacturing employment. The facts are hard to establish, but because tertiary products have such limited tradeability, a shift of resources into this sector cannot contribute greatly to performance in foreign trade.

(c)   Faced by this impasse and by the evidence that the main effect of devaluation has been to aggravate inflation, the reaction in Britain has been to tighten fiscal and monetary policy, so as to eliminate the foreign deficit and hold up the exchange rate. The United States is now beginning to follow the same course.

(d)   The second reaction has been to take piecemeal steps to protect, often indirectly, industries where the threat to employment has been strongest or politically most awkward. Systematic and explicit protection is avoided because it runs counter to the formal and self-imposed code of free trade, the foundations of which are not examined.

Many industrial countries whose manufacturing industry has not been left as far behind as Britain's have reacted to the international depression, which emanated temporarily from the Organisation of Petroleum Exporting Countries (OPEC) and more persistently from the creditor positions of Japan, Germany and a few other countries, by adopting policies of this kind: they have deflated to the point where their payments are balanced or in surplus and they have taken a few steps one way or another to stave off the pressure of foreign competition while still espousing the virtues of free trade.

This explanation of recession and of the pressure to protect pre-supposes that the imbalance between strong and weak industrial countries is not corrected by movements of labour, capital, entre-preneurship and technology. This seems to fit the facts. Even when migration is unrestricted, labour is plainly rather immobile inter-nationally; it will not move much until wage differentials are wide. (Whether this reflects the net social advantage or constitutes grounds for subsidising emigration is a question which does not seem yet to have been addressed in Britain.) Financial capital is not scarce. Newspaper reports suggest that Japanese and German firms get good results here, so that one might have expected imports of foreign entrepreneurship and technology, whether by British firms hiring foreign managers and technologists or by a movement of foreign firms into Britain. The trouble presumably is that British firms cannot easily recruit and assimilate foreigners and, if foreign firms want to shift managers, technology and machines abroad in pursuit of cheap labour, they are likely to go where it is really cheap, not to the United Kingdom or the United States, so long as there is free trade.

Adjustments to the Exchange Rate

A second assumption is that the imbalance between strong and weak countries cannot be corrected by exchange-rate adjustments; if de-valuation were effective no country could suffer a balance of payments constraint – each could choose its level of employment. The problem with devaluation is that, in the imperfect market for manufactures, the benefits are so slow to emerge and the effects on inflation are so strong that it is very difficult, if not impossible, to achieve an enduring gain to trade. 'Real-wage resistance' stands in the way.

Revaluation by the few strong countries, notably Germany and Japan, would be likely to produce results if those countries would allow it to go far enough – the contribution of the main surplus countries to total supplies of manufactures and to demand for primary products in the rest of the world is small enough that a revaluation by them is unlikely to have its effects nullified by inflation in the rest of the world. Nor is revaluation by those countries likely to be nullified by its dampening effect on their own wages and prices, for at some point this would require absolute cuts in money wages which are likely to be resisted.

Thus the strong countries, unlike the weak, enjoy freedom as regards exchange-rate adjustment, but they resist revaluation as a matter of choice because of industrial opposition to the squeeze on profits that it entails and because they fear losing the economic–political strength that stems from a strong foreign balance and from export-led growth. Germany's aim in promoting the EMS was clearly to insulate herself from revaluation and so protect her competitive advantage *vis-à-vis* her EEC partners – an advantage which, at a given exchange rate, will tend to increase if Germany's inflation rate remains lower than that of her neighbours.

The policy followed in Britain of holding up the exchange rate in order to check inflation appears to offer little hope for a country with such a weak industrial position; unless it produces a marked short-run fall in the rate of inflation below that of other countries, in which it seems to be failing, it can work only if higher unemployment in the long term reduces inflation to a rate similar to that of other countries and the exchange rate can then be brought down without causing inflation to accelerate.

Import Protection versus Devaluation

The potential attraction of import protection for an industrial country faced by unemployment is that, whereas devaluation immediately causes a rise in prices and a reduction in the real wage and so generates inflation, protection (whether by tariff or quota) permits an immediate reduction in prices, an improvement in the real wage and hence the possibility that inflation will be eased. Because economists are brought up to consider protection on the basis of models which assume the existence of full employment – odd since protection has usually been adopted as a reaction to unemployment – the proposition that with unemployment protection might have these advantages over devaluation is unfamiliar. The proposition has been explored and rigorously set out in Godley and May [2].

The reasons why protection offers these short-term attractions over devaluation are shown summarily in Table 2.2. Retaliation is assumed not to occur with either devaluation or protection; the economic attractions of protection compared with alternative policies must be explored before one can address such questions as whether retaliation

Table 2.2   Short-term effects of devaluation and protection

	Devaluation	Protection
Effect on:		
Terms of trade	Deterioration	Quotas – no change Tariff – improvement
Distribution of income	Shift to profit	No general change
Taxes (with autono- mous public expenditure constant)	Raised to prevent balance of payments deteriorating	Cut to prevent balance of payments improving
Real wages	Fall	Rise

is justified, likely or worth risking. It is assumed that a given balance of payments must be maintained with both devaluation and protection, that in the case of protection a tariff or quota system is applied across the board and (unrealistically) that the money wage is given.

The column showing the effects of devaluation will be familiar: it causes a deterioration in the terms of trade and a shift to profit incomes. Since the volume responses are slow and the terms of trade are worse, it is necessary to raise taxes in order to keep the balance of payments constant. The real wage declines on all three scores – worse terms of trade, the shift to profits and the increase in tax rates.

With protection the terms of trade do not deteriorate. There is no general change in the distribution of income with a tariff nor with quotas so long as pricing behaviour is the same as with a tariff. (If that is not so, countervailing taxes could be applied.) Since the propensity to import is reduced, tax cuts are necessary if the balance of payments is to be kept constant. Moreover the required cuts will be bigger than might appear at first sight since, with income rising as a result of the lower import propensity and lower tax rates, the revenue yielded by any set of tax rates will rise strongly and outlay on unemployment benefits will fall. For example, it has been estimated that if unemployment in 1978 had stood at $2\frac{1}{2}$ per cent instead of nearly 6 per cent, tax rates (or expenditure) could have been reduced by 6 or 7 per cent of GNP (approximately £10 billion at today's values) with the same *ex post* budget balance. However, it is not intended to assert that an immediate return to that level of unemployment is possible, nor that it would necessarily be appropriate to maintain the same *ex post* budget balance as in 1978 (see Ward and Neild [10]).

The Godley–May analysis suggests that for these reasons the difference between the effects of devaluation and protection on the real wage is large over quite a long transitional period. The important implications are:

(a)   that protection will *reduce* inflation if the dampening effect on money-wage increases produced by the rise in real wages is stronger than any stimulating effect of higher employment;

(b)   that consumers will be better off to the extent of the increase in the supply of home-produced consumer goods less any decrease in the supply of imported consumer goods. In the short run, in which exports and other foreign income are assumed in the absence of retaliation to be constant, the supply of imported consumption goods will be reduced only to the extent that the composition of imports shifts to purchases of primary products and other inputs to sustain the higher level of domestic output. Since the diminution in the supply of imports of manufactured consumer goods on this account will be a fraction of the increase in the supply of domestically produced consumption goods, there can be little question that consumers would be substantially better off;

(c)   that as compared with continuing recession, which appears to be the alternative since devaluation has been found wanting, protection would seem capable of helping rather than hindering efficiency. It expands demand for manufactures, which is the prerequisite of industrial growth and, if a general *ad valorem* tariff is used, it may be better for efficiency than piecemeal interventions to support employment in the face of continuing depression.

Protection, World Trade and Output

If protection is adopted only by those industrial countries where the level of output and employment is constrained by inability to pay for imports and, if those countries use protection as a means of raising output and employment whilst maintaining imports at the maximum level they can afford instead of using it as a means of reducing imports absolutely and acquiring international financial assets, there is no reason why the level of world trade should be reduced by their action (Cripps [1]) and the level of world output will rise.

The difference between constrained and unconstrained countries is illustrated in Table 2.3. Japan and Germany enjoy such strong balances of foreign payments and have such large reserves that they can choose fairly freely their levels of unemployment and the levels chosen are relatively low. On the other hand, the United Kingdom and the United States have weak external positions – in spite of oil in the former and partly because of it in the latter. Their reserves are low and with present policies their unemployment is high.

Table 2.3   *Unemployment and balance of payments positions in selected OECD countries, 1978*

	Unemployment rates[a] (percentages)	Current balance (US$ billion)	Change in reserves 1977–8[b] (percentages)	Ratio of 1978 reserves to imports[c]
Japan	2.4	+ 16.6	+ 44.8	4.8
Germany	3.5	+ 8.2	+ 33.7	4.9
France	5.4	+ 1.6	+ 43.3	2.0
USA	5.9	– 16.4	+ 28.2	1.3
UK	6.8	+ 0.2	– 18.9	2.6
Italy	7.1	+ 5.0	+ 24.8	3.2
Total OECD	5.3[d]	– 1.0	+ 28.0	3.0

Source: *National Institute Economic Review*, no. 87, February 1979, pp. 39, 45, 46 and 83.
[a]Percentages of total labour force standardised to international definitions.
[b]Reserves of gold, foreign exchange holdings and SDRs at end-years.
[c]Monthly averages for the calendar year, valued f.o.b. for United States, Canada and Australia.
[d]Represents about 90 per cent of OECD, including Australia, Canada, Finland, Norway, Spain and Sweden as well as countries listed above.

World trade will be reduced if, as they adopt protection, constrained countries increase the proportion of their imports which come from unconstrained countries (for example, Germany and Japan), because the latter can be presumed to have chosen the level of activity they want and to be unlikely to respond to extra foreign sales by letting activity (or exchange rates) rise, so that their imports move *pari passu* with their exports. Such a shift might occur if protection were non-discriminatory and inputs required for higher activity came disproportionately from unconstrained countries. There is no obvious evidence that this is so, except perhaps in the case of oil and OPEC, but since OPEC countries appear to adjust their spending to their income quite rapidly, this may scarcely be a valid case. If a switch to imports from unconstrained countries does occur, the difficulties of constrained countries will increase as one reduces imports from another; an increase in their total output will require a stronger reduction in their import propensities, and hence in world trade, and the gain to welfare from higher output will be qualified to a greater extent than otherwise by diminished gains from trade.

Conversely, world trade will be increased if constrained countries, as they protect, increase the proportion of their imports that comes from other constrained countries, for each of them can be assumed to raise activity and imports in response to an increase in its export income. If that happens, they relieve one another's constraints, facilitate the increase in output and minimise the reduction in trade relative to output. The case for discrimination against surplus countries found expression in the 'scarce currency' clause of the IMF statutes, but that clause has remained a dead letter.

In short, if the strong industrial countries do not revalue sufficiently to take the competitive pressure off the manufacturing industry of the weak industrial countries, protection is the only way for the weak to raise demand and employment and try to revive their manufacturing industry. And if they do protect, it will not reduce the exports of the strong industrial countries, which are constrained by the payments those countries make to other countries.

The Precedents

The United States, as has been pointed out elsewhere (Cripps [1] p. 41), provide an example in the postwar period of virtuous behaviour by an industrial country that had risen to dominance in world markets and a persistent creditor position: she encouraged imports, she permitted discrimination against her exports while encouraging liberalisation of trade within Europe, she permitted other countries to devalue against the dollar and she provided a flow of aid and investment.

In the interwar period, on the other hand, the United States provided an example of how not to behave. As Hal B. Lary showed in his brilliant study produced during the Second World War (Lary [6]), the United States achieved a dominant industrial position during the First World War and in the 1920s, while her industry was so highly protected that her imports consisted largely of food and raw materials. In the 1930s the huge United States depression and the reversal of capital flows caused an astonishing collapse in the supply of dollars to the rest of the world; in 1932 United States imports had fallen to 30 per cent of their 1929 value (with both prices and volumes down). And shortly after Britain and other countries devalued the United States followed suit and nullified their action. It is little wonder that, in the absence of a coherent strategy to meet the depression, countries resorted to bilateralism as a defensive policy, summed up in the phrase 'buy from those who buy from us', and that in 1953 someone as cautious as Dennis Robertson should have spoken of 'a quasi-revolution in United States policy' as one of the conditions for a successful restoration of convertibility (Nurkse [9], pp. 44–5). It is remarkable that such a revolution occurred and has gone so far.

I do not wish to suggest that the situation is anything like as grave today as that in the 1920s or 1930s. The contractionary pressure which Germany and Japan now inflict on others stems not from a major collapse of demand within their economies, but mainly from their competitive lead in the world markets and their policy of limiting revaluation. Nevertheless, the example of United States policies in the two periods points up the choices that are open today.

Alternative Forms of Protection

The question whether in the present international economic situation management of trade in the form of protection by the weak is either likely or desirable can be answered by the statements that: (a) It is likely, except in so far as weak countries regard unemployment as an acceptable or desirable means of trying to reduce inflation or influence industrial relations. (b) It is desirable as the best available policy in a world where full exchange-rate adjustment is resisted by the strong and is not a feasible policy for the weak, and, in the case of Japan, import promotion is resisted too.

Protection can, however, be made more or less desirable according to the form it takes. The argument for discrimination against countries in surplus has already been considered. (A combination of discriminatory and non-discriminatory protective measures may sometimes make sense. For example, all constrained countries might apply a

common discriminatory tariff against Japanese and German goods
sufficient to balance trade at full employment between the two groups,
yet the weakest, say Britain, might still not be able to reach full
employment unless in addition to the discriminatory tariff it added a
general one.)

There remain many important questions. First, should protection –
and the same arguments apply to export restraint – rely on market
mechanisms or be selective between products? The answers are very
much matters of faith. My own instincts are to go for market mechanisms and the minimum of selection, because I would like to see the
windfall gain from the greater scarcity of imports appropriated for the
community and the risks of corruption, lobbying and perverse
selection, which go with the allocation of quotas, avoided. From a
macroeconomic point of view a general *ad valorem* tariff would be
sufficient. But in Britain a flat-rate tariff on manufactures and semi-
manufactures could be better, since there is no point in protecting
primary production and raising the price of food further.

The *long-run* effects of this policy would resemble the *long-run* effects
of a maintained *real* devaluation, plus a system of food and raw-
material subsidies financed by a tax on exports. The important point
is that there is no resemblance between protection and a devaluation
that is *not* accompanied by a tax on exports and a subsidy on food and
raw materials. Without these, the two policies are crucially different in
the short run, the period which determines whether either is to be
successful. The adverse effects of devaluation on prices and real wages
and hence inflation, noted above, could only be mitigated by food and
raw-material subsidies to the extent that they were financed by taxes
which redressed the shift to profits.

An alternative suggested by Lord Kaldor is to set aside the surplus
of foreign-exchange receipts over and above that needed to buy
materials and food and to auction to that value import licences which
were valid for all but exempt goods (food and basic materials). The
result would be tantamount to a varying tariff on manufactures plus
a subsidy to all exports; it is half-way to a devaluation. The system
avoids the problem which arises with tariffs of deciding in advance how
high to set the tariff. Discrimination between supplying countries
could be achieved by requiring, say, double licences for imports
against surplus countries or half licences for imports from others. A
market in licences could be permitted, in which the authorities might
intervene.

Whatever system is used a number of issues need consideration. (a) Should there be exemption (or reimbursement) for imports that are re-exported? And should semi-manufactures imported for home use be taxed? Theoretical considerations suggest that, in order to keep the degree of effective protection as uniform as possible, the answer to both questions is yes. But what are the costs and benefits in practice? (b) How should the exchange rate be managed? (c) How open should the system be to international capital flows? (d) How far should differential support to industries with special problems, some of which is desirable and some inevitable, be given through differential tariffs or differential quota or licence arrangements rather than by subsidies or other forms of protection? (It can be argued that subsidies are subject to more scrutiny by Parliament and so are less likely to become entrenched – though tariffs might be scrutinised too. The costs of tariffs and subsidies may be borne by different people.) It would seem desirable that whatever system was adopted should be transparent, so that it could be monitored and coordinated internationally.

The Alternative to Organised Protection

If protection were adopted by the weak countries along the lines suggested here, there is no reason to believe that they could not move progressively to higher employment plus external balance. There is clearly spare capacity and labour in Britain, though the precise amounts are not known. (In the United States the problem is to avoid deflationary action to correct the foreign balance and to hold the exchange rate.) If there were a world constraint on primary products it would still be appropriate for weak countries to protect if they were not to constrain demand and output more severely than other countries.

It is possible that, once the case for protection was developed, the strong countries would respond to a greater extent, by letting their exchange rates rise or, in the case of Japan, by opening up their markets and being more hospitable to imports, and it is in this context that the retaliation argument needs to be considered, for the strong countries need to be confronted with the alternatives open to the weak countries and to them.

If protection is not adopted on a coherent basis and the strong countries do not relieve the competitive pressure on the weak, a continuing drift into recession seems likely, at least in Britain, accompanied by piecemeal indirect measures to prop up and modernise industry and possibly by more international measures of the same kind. Management of trade is likely to occur through indirect protection; Britain, being one of the weakest countries, is no doubt an extreme case, but the extent of indirect protection – though it is hard to measure – seems considerable. 'A businessman's guide to government handouts' (*Investors Chronicle* [3]) showed a remarkable array of subsidies to all kinds of industries. The scale of outlay has presumably increased since 1977.

Management in a Growing System

If economic growth were restored by macroeconomic actions of the kind suggested above, there would still be demands for protection by particular industries where employment was sharply threatened by new competition. The argument that short-run protection is justified if labour mobility is low and the alternative is wasteful unemployment has been recognised even by Professor Haberler (Nurkse [9], p. 312). The problems of ensuring that protection is only temporary are familiar. What is very difficult to know is whether the frequency with which legitimate cases for transitional protection come along has increased because, say, technology is moving more rapidly or multinational firms are moving new technologies to areas of low-cost labour more jumpily than before, or whether conditions in that respect are broadly the same as before, but the recession has made each microeconomic move appear a problem because alternative employment opportunities are not readily available. I guess the latter to be the main explanation: if the macroeconomic conditions were corrected, for which broad forms of protection appear to me to be necessary, the microeconomic problems would be much diminished. For example, the Japanese invasion of the markets for motorcycles, cameras and cars is part of the earning of a huge surplus by Japan; if Japan had been stopped or deterred from earning such a surplus by the application or threat of protection those markets would not have been invaded to anything like the same extent.

Summary and Conclusion

So far protection does not appear to have reduced trade in relation to production substantially, but the recession persists. The continuing cause of the imbalance in trade and the international recession associated with it is the cumulative tendency towards differential rates of progress in manufacturing industry in different industrial countries in a period of inflation and real-wage rigidity. The losing countries cannot protect their position by devaluation, but could do so by protection; the gainers could take the pressure off the weak by revaluation and import stimulation, but are reluctant to do so. Unless the gainers change their ways and adopt policies which are calculated to promote growth, continuing recession and a piecemeal drift to protection in manufacturing seem likely, but if a coherent strategy of protection, preferably with discrimination against the gainers, were adopted, unemployment could soon begin to be reduced. If balance in trade and hence the possibilities of growth were restored by general measures along these lines, it is an open question how far there would be pressure for intervention in trade between industrial countries in specific types of manufactures and how far such intervention would be desirable.

References
[1] Cripps, F., 'Causes of growth and recession in world trade', *Economic Policy Review*, no. 4, March 1978.
[2] Godley, W. A. H. and May, R. M., 'The macro-economic implications of devaluation and import restriction', *Economic Policy Review*, no. 3, March 1977.
[3] *Investors Chronicle*, 18 March 1977.
[4] Kaldor, N., 'The foundations of free trade theory and its implications for the current world recession' in Proceedings of a Conference of the International Economic Association at Obernai, 1978 (publication forthcoming).
[5] Krauss, M. B., *The New Protectionism*, Oxford, Blackwell, 1979.
[6] Lary, H. B., *The United States in the World Economy* (for US Department of Commerce), Washington (DC), US Government Printing Office, 1943.
[7] List, F., *The National System of Political Economy*, London, Longmans and Green, 1885.
[8] Marshall, A., *Principles of Economics* (8th edn), London, Macmillan, 1952.
[9] Nurkse, R., *Equilibrium and Growth in the World Economy*, Cambridge (Mass.), Harvard University Press, 1961.
[10] Ward, T. S. and Neild, R. R., *The Measurement and Reform of Budgetary Policy*, London, Heinemann Educational Books, 1978.

Comment

by Deepak Lal*

Introduction

Professor Neild suggests: 'Because economists are brought up to consider protection on the basis of models which assume the existence of full employment ... the proposition that with unemployment protection might have these advantages over devaluation is unfamiliar.' But at least among development economists concerned with international trade his arguments for protection are neither new nor unfamiliar, and my critique will merely reiterate obvious and well known counter-arguments. It is important to emphasise that Professor Neild is wrong in saying that these counter-arguments, which are now part of conventional trade theory, are vitiated because this 'rests on unrealistic assumptions about the perfection of markets and the conditions of production and addresses the question of what determines the pattern of trade and output in a setting where there is full employment'. Perusal of the classic paper by Haberler [15], followed by the work of Meade [26], Johnson [16], Bhagwati and Ramaswami [5], and Corden [9], will show clearly that modern trade theory is concerned in particular with providing rigorous rankings of alternative policies (including protection) when one or other of the perfectly competitive assumptions (including full employment) breaks down. This by now is conventional trade theory and bears little resemblance to the old-fashioned theories which Professor Neild presumably thinks are still conventional.

I could discern four major strands in Professor Neild's arguments concerned with:

(a)   the existence of increasing returns in modern manufacturing industry;

(b)   the existence of real-wage rigidity in labour markets in the United Kingdom and possibly other OECD countries;

(c)   the alleged ability of import restrictions to raise domestic employ-

---

* The views expressed are the author's and should not in any way be associated with those of the World Bank.

ment and real income (welfare) levels above those realisable through devaluation in an economy with money-wage rigidity;

(d)   supposed deleterious effects on 'weaker' deficit countries of the failure of surplus countries to follow expansionary policies.

I shall discuss each of these four strands in the following sections.

As a preliminary it may be useful to reiterate the essentials of the modern theory of trade and welfare for second-best economies, that is those in which one or more of the conditions for perfect competition do not hold, so that the market and shadow prices of goods or factors diverge. The major result is that the correction of such *domestic* distortions requires a tax or subsidy on domestic consumption, production or factor use and not on international trade. Secondly, use of protection will reduce the level of economic welfare below the feasible maximum and possibly below the level under free trade. Thirdly, the only infallible case for protection is the so-called 'optimum tariff' argument, when a country has monopoly or monopsony power in *foreign* trade and a tax or subsidy on foreign trade which equates the domestic prices facing consumers and producers to the *marginal* rates of transformation of the relevant commodities in foreign trade is optimal for national economic welfare. Finally, for any given domestic divergence alternative interventions can be ranked in terms of their effects on national economic welfare. In assessing these effects one can use either a well-ordered social utility index (which implies cardinality) as in Samuelson's social indifference curves [29] or, if inter-personal comparisons of utility are eschewed, Samuelson's device of the utility possibility locus [30].

We can now apply these principles to Professor Neild's arguments.

Increasing Returns

It is well known that increasing returns, at least when they are large relative to the size of the economy (see Arrow and Hahn [1]), lead to a breakdown of perfect competition. But that in itself does not provide an argument for protection. Professor Neild invokes increasing returns of all sorts 'internal, external, and dynamic' and cites a numerical example due to Professor Kaldor which he says 'undermines the basic case for free trade'. A number of points need to be made on this particular argument, which is hardly new (see Graham [14], Tinbergen [32] and Viner [33]).

First, as my numerical counter-example in Table 2.4 shows, any mild decrease in costs in the two-commodity spirit of Kaldor's example will not controvert the case for free trade. The important point is whether or not increasing returns in the cloth industry offset decreasing returns in the wine industry sufficiently strongly to lead to

Table 2.4   Feasible combinations of output under varying returns to scale

Point[a]	Wine		Cloth	
	Output (decreasing returns)	Change in output	Output (increasing returns)	Change in output
I	140		0	
		− 20		+ 5
II	120		5	
		− 30		+ 6
III	90		11	
		− 40		+ 7
IV	50		18	
		− 50		+ 8
V	0		26	

[a]Point I is for the case where all resources are in the wine industry and point V where they are all in the cloth industry. The intermediate points are derived for equal movements of resources from the wine to the cloth industry, each having the same factor intensity.

non-convexities in the economy's production possibility frontier. In my example, which shows the outputs of the two goods available when equal amounts of the primary factors are shifted between the industries (which are assumed to have the same factor intensities, in order to enable us to talk of a shift of equal amounts of resources and also abstract from the bias towards convexity of the production possibility curve which differing factor intensities could entail) the production possibility curve remains convex. As by hypothesis there are no other domestic distortions, then opening up to foreign trade cannot reduce welfare, as the trade plus production possibility frontier will contain within it the purely domestic production possibility frontier to which the country would be confined under autarky.

Secondly, even if the economies of scale are big enough to lead to non-convexities in the production possibility frontier and there are no other distortions, but the increasing returns are international in the sense that average cost depends on the size of the international market, then, as Ethier [12] has recently shown, each country gains from foreign trade irrespective of its size as long as there is average-cost pricing in the industry with increasing returns.

Thirdly, even if the increasing returns are purely 'national', then, as Kemp and Negishi [17] have shown in a model where there are any arbitrarily chosen number of industries with decreasing costs, constant costs and increasing costs, welfare will not be reduced in an autarkic country opening up to trade if this results in no expansion of any increasing cost industry and no contraction of any decreasing cost industry.

Finally, even if none of the above cases applies, so that, at least in principle, in the presence of national increasing returns, the opening up of an initially autarkic country to foreign trade could reduce welfare, the optimal policy will still not be protection. Provided lump-sum taxes are available it will be an 'optimal' subsidy to the increasing returns industry to enable it to produce at the optimal scale with marginal-cost pricing of its output. If it is not feasible to finance the subsidy in this way (as is likely) only a second-best welfare level can be attained, where the gains from a marginal increase in the subsidy are equated with the welfare costs of the marginal increase in distortionary taxation required to finance it. Clearly the optimal subsidy, and hence the second-best level of output of the increasing returns industry, will be lower where distortionary taxation has to be used. This policy, moreover, would be preferable to a tariff, which would be equivalent to a subsidy financed by taxing consumers of the product. The reason is that a tariff, in addition to its distortionary effect on consumers, will entail another distortion cost, namely a bias against non-protected industries, whose relative prices will be lowered. Thus, it is only if for administrative or political reasons a policy of domestic tax and subsidy is ruled out that protection *may* (not will) improve domestic welfare as compared with free trade. In this sense most valid arguments for protection (apart from the optimum tariff argument) must be based on considerations of public finance (see Little [23]).

Finally, and more importantly, purely static economies of scale which require expansion of domestic demand (assumed to take place over time) will not (in the absence of other domestic divergences between social and private costs) require government intervention (see Corden [9], pp. 272 ff.); the increasing returns have to be due to external economies or dynamic factors like Arrow's 'learning by doing'. For the latter, as Bardhan [2] has shown, the optimal policy will be a domestic tax and subsidy policy altering over time. We can therefore put the increasing returns argument aside as probably a red herring in Professor Neild's 'case for protection.

Real-wage Rigidity

Professor Neild is therefore right to emphasise that in his numerical example the minimum real-wage assumption is crucial to the demonstration that free trade may decrease welfare. The case for protection in an economy with real-wage rigidity has been analysed rigorously in the professional literature, with Haberler's classic article [15], followed by Bhagwati [3], Johnson [16], Lefeber [21] and most definitively by Brecher [6] and [7]. With real-wage rigidity and even without increasing returns, the opening of trade by an autarkic country with full employment *could* lead to unemployment and welfare loss, as was shown by Haberler [15]. But again the alternative policies can be ranked, as was done by Brecher [7]. If the real-wage rigidity is the only distortion, the optimal policy would be a general wage subsidy (financed through lump-sum taxation) equating the actual rigid real wage to the lower shadow wage (which in this case would be the notional perfectly competitive wage). If lump-sum taxes were unfeasible, the second-best policy would still be a general wage subsidy (though lower than in the optimum case) financed by distortionary taxation. The height of the subsidy would be such that the divergence between the (notional) perfectly competitive wage and the actual rigid wage would be offset only up to the point where the marginal welfare benefits were equal to the marginal welfare costs of the distortionary taxes required to finance the subsidy. Or, to put it differently, the shadow wage rate would be higher than in the optimum case and as a result (because of the restrictions on lump-sum taxation) only a second-best welfare level would be attainable. All this is well known to development economists familiar with recent developments in the theory and practice of project appraisal (see Little and Mirrlees [24] and Lal [19]). The latter provides the principles for deriving second-best shadow wage rates and hence implicitly the height and, in more complicated cases with multiple distortions and constraints on policy instruments, the structure of second-best wage subsidies. Elsewhere (OECD [27], pp. 59–60) I have suggested how the same principles can be applied to design manpower policies to take account of structural unemployment problems in industrial countries.

If a wage subsidy is not feasible, then a production subsidy to all industries facing the rigid real wage will be the next best policy. Such a production subsidy, the height of which will again depend upon the nature of the feasible taxes available to finance it, will not be as good as the wage subsidy. Though it will increase employment (as compared with a policy of *laissez-faire*) it will still not lead to the correct choice of factor proportions in different industries. Thus it will entail more distortion costs than a wage subsidy.

In comparison with the above policies protection would rank lowest (and might not even lead to any welfare improvement compared with *laissez-faire*). It would be equivalent to a production subsidy on import substitutes alone, financed by an implicit tax on their consumers. This would entail costs similar to costs of the distortionary taxation required to finance the subsidies to wages or production, and the additional cost of introducing a further bias against all non-import substituting industries (in both non-traded products and exports). If protection by a uniform tariff were combined with an equivalent export subsidy (which is tantamount to devaluation) the bias against export industries would be corrected, but not the one against non-traded goods industries. Hence, though better than a tariff alone, the latter combined with an export subsidy would still rank below a wage or production subsidy. Hence, once again we conclude that protection will be inferior to various other feasible domestic interventions as a policy for dealing with domestic distortions caused by real-wage rigidity.

Import Restrictions versus Devaluation

Professor Neild's discussion (as that of Godley and May [13]) of the relative effects of protection and devaluation on employment, output and real incomes is vitiated because they in effect *assume* without any demonstration that the relative effects of the two policies *will* be those summarised in Table 2.2. What Professor Neild terms Godley and May's rigorous exploration of their relative merits is really little more than juggling with national income identities on the basis of *assuming* the very relative effects that are at issue.

Examination of these effects in the light of modern balance of payments theory (as set out lucidly in Corden [10]) does not support the Cambridge assumptions. The first in Professor Neild's classification is the relative terms of trade effect. It is assumed that devaluation will necessarily worsen the terms of trade, while protection will involve no change if by quotas and an improvement if by tariffs. There is no general presumption that the terms of trade must (even in the short run) move in the way postulated. The assumption that a devaluation will necessarily worsen the terms of trade may go back to the old Cambridge tradition, stemming from Professor Joan Robinson's classic paper on the foreign exchanges [28], in which it was argued that for a devaluation to improve the balance of payments the terms of trade would necessarily have to worsen. As emphasised by subsequent theoretical and empirical investigations (surveyed by Clement *et al.* [8], for instance), for a devaluation to be effective there is no necessity for the terms of trade to deteriorate, nor any general presumption that they will. The earlier presumptions were based upon partial equilibrium models which ignored non-traded commodities, whereas the modern theory works with a general equilibrium model which distinguishes between non-traded and two classes of traded goods (importable and exportable). This makes it easy to show that, for a small country which for all practical purposes is a price-taker in world markets and faces given (though not necessarily unchanging) terms of trade, a devaluation, by raising the relative prices of both classes of tradeables to non-traded goods, will (in the absence of real-wage rigidity) lead to a switching of both domestic and foreign expenditure towards domestic output. Given appropriate policies for maintaining internal balance by varying overall domestic expenditure, the balance of payments will improve. Thus, whether the terms of trade change after a devaluation will depend upon whether the country concerned has monopoly or monopsony power in world markets. If it does, then without retaliation (as assumed by Professor Neild) it is always in the national interest to exploit this power by levying the optimal tariff whether or not the country has a temporary balance of payments or unemployment problem. The important question therefore is whether it is seriously contended for the United Kingdom that, even in the absence of these disequilibria and without retaliation, foreigners could be exploited by levying optimal tariffs and export taxes. I doubt whether many would accept this implication. In my view, for all practical purposes Britain is a small country which cannot in general affect the foreign prices at which it trades internationally, while presumably those exporters trading in relatively monopolistic world markets would in effect levy their own optimal export tax (or at least a large part of it) by equating their marginal revenue from exporting with their marginal costs. Thus the supposedly differential terms of trade effect of import restrictions and devaluation is the first highly questionable assumption in the Cambridge case.

The second such assumption is that, with autonomous public expenditure constant and the balance of payments to be maintained at its initial level, a devaluation must necessarily be accompanied by raising taxes, or in modern terminology reducing absorption through expenditure reduction, whereas the import tariff must necessarily mean increased absorption due to tax cuts. This is paradoxical, because one would expect that as both import tariffs and a devaluation are expenditure switching devices their effects on total incremental demand for domestic output would be similar and hence would lead to absorption or expenditure policies at least in the same direction. That this is not so in the Cambridge world is partly because it assumes that devaluation will worsen the terms of trade (hence entailing a cut in domestic expenditure) and also worsen the short-run balance of payments. But much of the J-curve effect relates to periods when countries altered exchange rates reluctantly and discretely. With floating rates and more continuous adjustments fairly common, a persistent J-curve effect would require imbecilic exporters who continued to set export prices in a weak home currency, thus eschewing potential profits from its depreciation. Thus the dangers of the J-curve effect seem likely to decline.

We have already cast doubt on the supposed deterioration in the terms of trade following a devaluation. With the elimination of the dubious J-curve effect, a devaluation (given domestic unemployment at a given *money* wage but not a rigid real wage) will through its expenditure switching effects both raise domestic employment and improve the balance of payments (until 'full' employment is reached) Hence, contrary to the Godley–May–Neild assumption, domesti expenditure will need to be expanded by a tax reduction (giver constant public expenditure) if the balance of payments is to be maintained at its initial level (as they also assume). In contrast, the required change in domestic expenditure (and hence in taxes) could be the exact opposite to that postulated in the case of protection. Professor Neild writes that with an across-the-board tariff: 'Since the propensity to import is reduced, tax cuts are necessary if the balance of payments is to be kept constant.' But with a tariff the export propensity is also reduced; hence the net effect on the balance of payments from reduced imports and reduced exports could go either way, as numerous developing countries following protectionist policies have found to their cost (see Little, Scitovsky and Scott [25], Bhagwati [4], and Krueger [18]). Professor Neild seems to ignore the well-known theorem due to Lerner [22] about symmetry of import and export taxes. In a general equilibrium system a tariff raises the price of importables not only relatively to that of non-tradeables, but more importantly relatively to that of exportables. This latter relative price change induces switches in consumption towards exportables, as well as shifts in resources from export industries and hence a shrinking of their output. For both reasons the propensity to export is reduced. This is the additional cost of a tariff as compared with a devaluation, which, by raising domestic prices of exportables in equal proportion to those of importables, prevents the above switches in domestic consumption and production of exportables from taking place.

Thus, contrary to the assertions made by Godley, May and Neild, with domestic unemployment and with the balance of payments to be maintained at its initial level, an effective devaluation (in an economy with money-wage but not real-wage rigidity) will require expenditure increases (and hence tax cuts), while an import tariff alone (because of its indirect deleterious effects on exports and hence on the balance of payments) could require expenditure reduction (and hence tax increases). If we reject accordingly the assumptions concerning the differential terms of trade and tax (expenditure) changes shown in Table 2.2, the implication in the bottom line that the real wage worsens with devaluation and improves with protection cannot be sustained either. This leaves the assumptions on the differential effects of the two instruments on the distribution of income.

In general a devaluation is likely to reduce the real wage, as it raises relative prices of tradeables (which will probably be more capital-intensive than non-tradeables) and hence raises the share of profits in national income. Though Professor Neild does not ascribe to protection any distributional shifts, his conclusion about a rise in the real wage with protection could (at least in principle) still be salvaged. In a world where importables are more labour-intensive than either exportables or non-traded commodities a straightforward application of the Stolper–Samuelson theorem [31] would yield a rise in the real wage at the expense of profits. But even if these assumptions about relative factor intensities are empirically valid the consequent rise in the real wage will not imply real national income (welfare) higher than with devaluation and the lowering of the real wage. This is because the tariff will involve the additional costs identified above.

If the *aim* is to shift the distribution of income from profits to wages because there is real-wage rigidity (and not merely money-wage rigidity, as we have assumed so far in line with Professor Neild's discussion), then of course his conclusions will hold as long as the only policy instruments available are devaluation or import restrictions and the relative factor intensities are as stated above. But with real-wage rigidity we are in the world analysed in the last section, where the tariff provides an indirect wage subsidy to the most labour-intensive sector (importables). If other domestic tax and subsidy policies are also feasible (as they certainly are for the United Kingdom), then we must again compare them with protection in dealing with the domestic divergence between private and social costs caused by rigid real wages and taking account of the additional objective of raising the share of wages in national income. As we have seen, the tariff will be superseded (in terms of real income–welfare effects) by a general production subsidy, which in turn will be dominated by a wage subsidy in dealing with the 'unemployment effects' of real-wage rigidity. Moreover, in this case the 'balance of payments effects' in the assessment of the relative effects of devaluation and import restrictions are a red herring. For with real-wage rigidity, if the aim is also to shift the distribution of income towards labour at the expense of profits, this can best be done by a domestic policy of taxing profits and subsidising labour, which for reasons given in the previous section will be better (in the welfare sense) than the trade intervention policies of devaluation or import restriction.

The Effects of Surplus Countries on those in Deficit

The whole of Professor Neild's discussion in his section on 'Protection, World Trade and Output' is vitiated by his implicit assumption of fixed exchange rates. Since the move to floating rates (albeit 'dirty'), the supposed balance of payments constraint on domestic expansionary policies no longer applies. Consider a world of countries with floating exchange rates, which do not have real-wage rigidity in their domestic labour markets (or in which its deleterious effects on domestic employment and output are offset to the optimal extent by appropriate domestic tax and subsidy policies). With a flexible exchange rate the balance of payments could be insulated (over a period) against the domestic expansion of aggregate demand (see Corden [11]). Clearly if there is any short-run Phillips curve type of relationship there might be increasing inflation, with costs to be set off against the benefits from reduced unemployment, but each country could to a large extent choose its own domestic employment (and inflation) levels. If some countries still chose to run trade surpluses, this should be looked on as a preference for building up foreign instead of domestic assets. These surpluses provide an opportunity for the rest of the world (with deficits) to absorb more current resources for domestic consumption or investment than are domestically produced. Given the terms on which the surpluses are lent (in relatively well-functioning international capital markets), if a positive net return is still obtainable in terms of current and future consumption (the latter through any domestic investment that the borrowing finances) the borrowing countries cannot suffer. If there is still some worry about the future cost of servicing the foreign borrowing, it must mean that this has financed consumption rather than investment to a socially undesirable extent. The fault lies not in other countries' surpluses (which present the opportunity for raising real incomes in the borrowing country), but in inefficient use of the borrowings from them (see Lal [20]).

Conclusions

I hope this casts some doubt on Professor Neild's arguments for protection or, as the title of his paper more euphemistically has it, managed trade. As he emphasises, the important assumption in his case is real-wage rigidity. Even if this assumption is accepted, it has been argued that the proper policy is not protection but various combinations of domestic taxes and subsidies. His arguments based on increasing returns are also shown to require (if anything) optimal intervention at home rather than in foreign trade, while the arguments based on the differential effects of devaluation and import tariffs on domestic output, employment and the balance of payments are shown to depend on highly dubious assumptions. Finally, his arguments for protection flowing from the supposed deleterious effects of the non-expansionary countries on domestic employment and output in deficit countries are based on thinking in terms of fixed exchange rates and are thus at odds with contemporary reality. No harmful effects (on deficit countries) can be adduced with floating exchange rates from what are in effect the differing portfolio choices of different countries, which require that some of them run trade surpluses, others trade deficits.

Finally, it should also be said that the major source of worry (the presumed real-wage rigidity) which seems to have prompted 'New Cambridge' to propound its protectionist case is probably peculiar to this country. The United Kingdom's real-wage rigidity is due to political factors and requires political solutions. In the absence of feasible lump-sum instruments of taxation, even with the second-best domestic tax and subsidy policy, clearly levels of domestic output and employment will be lower than in the absence of this real-wage rigidity. To pretend, on the basis of highly dubious assumptions and assertions, that protection provides a possibility of completely off-setting the real income and employment consequences of this rigidity is a snare and a delusion.

References

[1] Arrow, K. J. and Hahn, F. H., *General Competitive Analysis*, San Francisco, Holden Day, 1971.

[2] Bardhan, P. K., *Economic Growth, Development and Foreign Trade*, New York, Wiley, 1970.

[3] Bhagwati, J. N., *The Theory and Practice of Commercial Policy*, Special Papers no. 8, Princeton University International Finance Section, 1968.

[4] —, *Anatomy and Consequences of Exchange Control Regimes*, New York, Ballinger, 1978.

[5] Bhagwati, J. N. and Ramaswami, V. K., 'Domestic distortions, tariffs and the theory of optimum subsidy', *Journal of Political Economy*, February 1963.

[6] Brecher, R. A., 'Minimum wage rates and the prime theory of international trade', *Quarterly Journal of Economics*, February 1974.

[7] —, 'Optimum commercial policy for a minimum wage economy', *Journal of International Economics*, May 1974.

[8] Clement, M. O. *et al.*, *Theoretical Issues in International Economics*, New York, Houghton Miflin, 1967.

[9] Corden, W. M., *Trade Policy and Economic Welfare*, Oxford, Clarendon Press, 1974.

[10] —, *Inflation, Exchange Rates and the World Economy*, Oxford, Clarendon Press, 1977.

[11] —, 'Expansion of the world economy and the duties of surplus countries', *The World Economy*, January 1978.

[12] Ethier, W., 'Internationally decreasing costs and world trade', *Journal of International Economics*, February 1979.

[13] Godley, W. A. H. and May, R. M., 'The macro-economic implications of devaluation and import restrictions', *Economic Policy Review*, no. 3, 1977.

[14] Graham, F. D., 'Some aspects of protection further considered', *Quarterly Journal of Economics*, February 1923.

[15] Haberler, G., 'Some problems in the pure theory of international trade', *Economic Journal*, June 1950.

[16] Johnson, H. G., 'Optimal trade interventions in the presence of domestic distor-

tions' in R. E. Caves *et al.* (eds), *Trade, Growth and the Balance of Payments*, Amsterdam, North-Holland, 1965.

[17] Kemp, M. C. and Negishi, T., 'Variable returns to scale, commodity taxes, factor market distortions and their implications for trade gains', *Swedish Journal of Economics*, January 1970.

[18] Krueger, A. O., *Liberalization Attempts and Consequences*, New York, Ballinger, 1978.

[19] Lal, D., *Methods of Project Analysis: a review*, Baltimore, Johns Hopkins University Press, 1974.

[20] —, 'The wistful mercantilism of Mr Dell', *The World Economy*, June 1978; to which a reply was given by E. Dell, 'The wistful liberalism of Deepak Lal', *The World Economy*, May 1979.

[21] Lefeber, L., 'Trade and minimum wage rates' in J. N. Bhagwati *et al.* (eds), *Trade, Balance of Payments and Growth*, Amsterdam, North-Holland, 1971.

[22] Lerner, A. P., 'The symmetry between import and export taxes', *Economica*, August 1936.

[23] Little, I. M. D., 'Trade and public finance', *Indian Economic Review*, October 1971.

[24] Little, I. M. D. and Mirrlees, J. A., *Project Appraisal and Planning for Developing Countries*, London, Heinemann, 1974.

[25] Little, I. M. D., Scitovsky, T. and Scott, M. FG., *Industry and Trade in Some Developing Countries*, London, Oxford University Press, 1970.

[26] Meade, J. E., *The Theory of International Economic Policy*, vol. 2: *Trade and Welfare*, London, Oxford University Press, 1955.

[27] OECD, *Unemployment and Wage Inflation in Industrial Economies* by D. Lal, Paris, 1977.

[28] Robinson, J., *Essays in the Theory of Employment* (2nd edn.), Oxford, Blackwell, 1947.

[29] Samuelson, P. A., 'Social indifference curves', *Quarterly Journal of Economics*, February 1956.

[30] —, 'The gains from international trade once again', *Economic Journal*, December 1962.

[31] Stolper, W. F. and Samuelson, P. A., 'Protection and real wages', *Review of Economic Studies*, November 1941.

[32] Tinbergen, J., *International Economic Co-operation*, Amsterdam, Elsevien, 1945.

[33] Viner, J., *Studies in the Theory of International Trade*, New York, Harper, 1937.

3 The Management of North–South Trade: Experience and Prospects

by V. Cable

Introduction

Postwar liberalisation has affected mainly trade between industrial countries; few developing (or Communist) countries have participated – indeed direct controls over their imports have often been extended and they are seeking to regulate trade in all their major export commodities. As Sheila Page's paper shows, import controls applied by the industrial countries reflect their fears of competition from the newly industrialised countries and also apply mainly to North–South trade. The aim of this paper is to consider why this is significantly more regulated than trade between industrial countries and to assess the implications for both sets of partners. (For the purposes of the paper the 'developing countries' or the 'South' are as defined by the United Nations and make up a category which includes Cuba, Romania, Yugoslavia and some rich Arab oil states, but excludes the not-so-rich OECD countries of Portugal and Turkey; 'newly industrialised countries' (NICs) comprise some of these developing countries, plus Greece, Hungary, Poland, Portugal and Spain.)

The Concept of Trade Management

For an assessment of the growing role of the state as trader a useful starting point is provided by Zysman's distinction between governments' traditional function in 'simply promoting exports and determining the terms of entry to their own markets' and their new one in 'directly determining trade outcomes' by settling volumes and prices of exchange for particular goods (Zysman [26]). However, this distinction needs amplification.

The alternative to government regulation may be scarcely recognisable as a competitive market place. Centralised decisions of multi-national corporations lead to trade and factor flows which are not governed by market forces, and markets for many commodities are regulated by a few private firms. This could be said of oil, before OPEC managed it, several metals (including nickel, iron ore and aluminium) and even some foodstuffs. (Three firms account for about 70 per cent of international trade in bananas.) In the case of mining it is argued that the uncertainties of an unplanned market would militate against appropriate levels of investment and that the lumpiness of demand and long lead-times call for early signals of the need for deposits to be developed (Smith [17]).

Uncompetitive behaviour is not confined to commodity markets. Developing countries which import sophisticated capital goods are likely to be dealing with a very small number of firms and may be faced with colluson and price fixing. As exporters of manufactures they also run up against restrictive practices, such as private agreements which preclude or regulate exports to particular markets (UNCTAD [21]).

Greater control over output by governments of developing countries may, by breaking the vertically integrated international structure of production and marketing, increase 'free' arms-length trade, as Italian and French state companies did for oil when the world market was controlled by an oligopoly of private companies. State enterprises are substantially involved in export activities of NICs and increase competition in the markets concerned. Thus the dividing line between state–regulated and private–competitive international markets is blurred.

The allegedly traditional and new roles of the state also overlap. The main evidence of a 'new protectionism' (Balassa [2]) is the treatment of developing country textile exporters under the Multi-Fibre Agreement (MFA). But international management of the textile trade (between developing and developed countries) goes back in its present form to the early 1960s. A decisive commitment to protect the United Kingdom textile industry from developing country competition was made when labour was scarce; the history of protection in textiles is much longer. Indeed arguments used by the British Textile Confederation today differ little from those which Lancashire calico manufacturers successfully used against textile imports in the reign of Queen Anne. This continuity has led apologists for the 'new protectionism' to justify it in mercantilist terms (Lal [14], pp. 263–78).

Significantly, the whole postwar 'liberal' trading order has been characterised as 'new mercantilism' powered by economic nationalism and manifested in export subsidies, export credit competition, tied aid and protection of (mainly) high-technology national industries (Johnson [12]). Intervention by Western governments in exports to OPEC and Communist markets – by organisation of 'jumbo projects' and selection of 'chosen instruments' to represent the national export effort – stems naturally from 'new mercantilist' methods of competition.

The advocacy of state management of commodity trade as part of a 'new international economic order' has obscured the historical antecedents. OPEC apart, regulation of commodity markets has probably lessened in the 1970s despite efforts by developing countries to the contrary. The present desultory discussions of commodity agreements in the wake of failures to emulate OPEC are reminiscent of those which took place in the 1920s and 1930s in the aftermath of largely unsuccessful attempts at control by producers after the First World War. Taken as a whole, therefore, the role of the state in trade may have changed in emphasis but is not new.

Types of Regulated Trade

Appendix 1 seeks to analyse regulation of North–South trade within the limits imposed by the need to assign complex phenomena to simple categories. The borderline between explicitly trade measures and domestic measures with trade implications is, however, impossible to define and the distinction between 'complementary' and 'substitutive' trade is not absolute. Most 'complementary' products can be replaced at some cost in terms of resources misallocated; restriction of access to the EEC market for sugar and vegetable oils is an example. Protection of import-substituting manufacturing industry in developing countries illustrates the same process in reverse. Most economists would argue that a major source of complementarity in trade is the disparity between developing and industrial countries in factor-endowments: capital (human and physical) and labour. This argument is significant in explaining past patterns of North–South trade in manufactures in spite of rather than because of commercial policies in industrial countries, most of whose governments regard imports of labour-intensive manufactures as competitive rather than complementary. This is how such trade is treated. 'Complementary' trade essentially involves developing countries' exports of raw materials and imports of technology and capital goods including armaments.

Hybrid cases, with mixed motivation, include the attempts of developing countries to reform world shipping in a way that simultaneously benefits 'consuming' developing countries (by increasing competition) and 'producing' countries (by increasing uncompetitive regulation designed to guarantee them a larger market share). A similar mixture of objectives in developing countries has added grist to the mills of European sugar beet producers. Developing country sugar cane exporters, faced with the objectives of both raising world prices and obtaining greater market access, have pressed for the former: the higher guaranteed price which the Lomé sugar producers have been seeking from the EEC is linked to increases in EEC intervention prices, thereby ensuring greater EEC production (and ultimately depressed world market prices). Potentially the most important hybrid cases concern processing, where attempts to regulate 'complementary' primary commodity markets and market access for 'substitutive' processed products may be increasingly linked together. These examples may illustrate a general tendency for management to be concerned more and more with substitutive rather than complementary trade as developing and industrial countries acquire overlapping economic structures.

The other major distinction is between varying degrees of international organisation. The simplest case is unilateral action by individual governments. Most commodity agreements and cartels originated in attempts by one or two producers to manage trade and multilateral 'orderly marketing agreements', such as the textile MFA, originated in national import controls. The next state is agreement between exporting or importing countries having common interests. Thirdly there is bilateral barter trade. The most favourable conditions for traditional clearing barter do not exist in North–South trade. Industrial countries with convertible currencies have had no incentive for it, except temporarily when oil-consuming countries scrambled to secure supplies through bilateral arrangements (especially with the Shah's Iran). There has, however, been some interest in compensation trading and buy-back barter. The latter, which is common in East–West trade and may be developing in North–South, involves the provision of factories, or the technology to construct them, in return for some of their output. The eagerness of Western plant contractors for such business led to demands for regulation of the allegedly disruptive imports which resulted.

The most sophisticated form of trade management, the genuinely multilateral, is rare. Producer–consumer commodity agreements are one example, but few enjoy even a formal existence and none is functioning effectively. In manufacturing, the nearest approach is the textile MFA, where the continued adherence of the developing countries has been obtained only by threats of even more severe protection if they defect.

The progression from unilateral to multilateral trade management reflects differences not only of degree but also of motive. Unilateral action stems from attempts by governments to evade international market rules (Tumlir [20]). Multilateral action involves attempts to create sets of rules to replace those of the market which are still binding.

The Motivation Behind the Regulation of North–South Trade

Motives for trade management can best be studied at the level of particular products and industries. But there are some general factors influencing management of North–South trade.

The first is that developing countries hope by management of markets to rectify what they regard as inequitable treatment and to create a new international economic order reflecting their preference for *dirigiste* economic policies (Lal [13] and Donges [4]). One central objective is 'more equitable and remunerative' raw-material prices, to be achieved through inter-government negotiation and, failing that, cartel action amongst exporting governments. Greater price stability it is hoped will be achieved through international buffer stocks. Third world industrialisation is to be promoted by 'planned restructuring' of production to create a new division of labour. And developing countries have claimed that 'every state has a right to enjoy fully the benefits of world invisible trade and to engage in the expansion of such trade based on efficiency and mutual equitable benefit' (United Nations [23]). The rhetoric corresponds with reality only in a few limited areas, but it is influential in others.

A second, and related, point is that the state usually has a more active direct role in developing countries in production of internationally traded goods and services. The successful Far Eastern NICs are exceptions, and others appear to be moving in the direction of economic liberalisation. But the state generally plays a leading developmental role in mining, energy and the more capital-intensive manufacturing industries. Even in Brazil, which proclaims the need to avoid 'encroachment of state ownership', 17 of the 25 largest firms are government enterprises.

So much government intervention in developing countries gives international trade a more political flavour. Government enterprises often express a preference for dealing with other government enterprises; Britain now has 30 inter-government joint commissions with Communist and developing countries, and the latter often prefer such a framework even when they espouse private enterprise systems. But the most significant consequence of the enlarged role of the state in developing economies is in the field of natural resources, especially mining, where governments' control of production, exploration, investment and marketing decisions leads logically to global planning and market rationalisation by associations of mineral producers (Hager [7]).

Loss of control over markets by private companies has forced Western countries to look in turn for government-managed solutions to problems of commodity supply. Unilateral attempts by producers to manage energy and other raw-material markets have made Western governments perceive trade relations increasingly in terms of economic security. This was a powerful motive behind the setting up of the International Energy Agency to counter OPEC and the raw-material price boom in 1973–4 prompted an abortive attempt by the European Commission at a raw-materials policy to make Europe more self-sufficient where possible or to reach more secure arrangements for supply where Europe was highly dependent on 'unsafe' sources. Similar thinking inspires much of European policy on agriculture. Criticism of surpluses has not prevented greater acceptance of the implied objective of self-sufficiency even where (as with sugar) it would almost certainly be a more efficient use of resources to import more (Ministry of Agriculture [1]).

Lastly there are certain forms of North–South trade where political factors necessarily impinge substantially. One is trade in arms; trade in nuclear technology, plant and fuels to developing countries is also heavily constrained by non-market factors. Finally, bilaterally tied aid has mixed commercial, political and developmental objectives. The British programme is explicitly designed to direct aid to the 'poorest people in the poorest countries', but there are in practice many exceptions. French, Japanese and United States aid is more consciously manipulated.

**Experience of Commodity Market Management,
and Prospects**

While the main extension of trade management has taken place, paradoxically, in manufactures, where trade partners proclaim that trade
is, or should be, free, in the more traditionally regulated field of
commodities it is proving impossible or ineffectual except in the major
case of OPEC. No new agreements on commodities have been
effectively established since UNCTAD IV in 1974 and existing agreements, on tin and cocoa for example, are not operating their provisions for buffer stocks. A new International Sugar Agreement has
just been launched, inauspiciously, but attempts to establish producer
cartels for copper, phosphates and bananas have so far failed and only
the bauxite producers' association holds out promise. It would be
premature to write obituaries for the Common Fund before it is born,
but recent experience does not suggest that its existence will be easy,
and its funds are sufficient for only a modest role in support of buffer
stocks.

Appendix 2 summarises the main attempts apart from OPEC's
being made currently to manage commodity markets through supply
control and buffer stocking. Some minor products such as mercury
and paper are excluded, even though they have been subject to actual
or attempted trade management. Others, including lead and zinc,
olive oil, and jute and coir, are left out because they appear to
involve only joint consultation, research and generic market promotion. Some products for which UNCTAD has envisaged market
management also appear so far from any serious negotiation as to be
worth only a mention (cotton, meat, tropical timber, manganese,
tungsten and 'technical' vegetable oils). Two other forms of trade
management are not explicitly covered: first, attempts at control not
coordinated internationally but nevertheless exercised nationally (by
India, in its export controls and taxation on tea); secondly, as
mentioned above, some markets 'managed' other than by governments (for example, the iron ore producers' association launched to
'rationalise supply' in a market in which 40 per cent of world trade
is already from captive mines owned by steel enterprises and 30 per
cent is subject to commercial contracts for over one year).

Motives for commodity market management vary, but the following are the most important:

(a) Price raising: the demand of the Group of 77 for 'fair and renumerative' raw-material prices covers several distinct objectives. That of putting a floor to the market is particularly pressing in extractive industries, which are capital intensive and where sales in depressed markets at marginal cost may fail substantially to cover fixed costs. Producers' willingness to accept output cuts in the current sugar agreement also has its origin in depressed prices. Other agreements aim at high monopoly profits, following OPEC. Another factor is the sense that there is a fair price for commodities linked to the price of manufactures (bauxite to be related to aluminium, for example).

(b) Price stabilisation: this objective, central to the demand of developing countries for a Common Fund to finance buffer stocks, has been obscured by arguments over the relationship between price stabilisation and price raising, by doubts whether the former is being pursued as an end in itself or as a means of stabilising earnings (for which there may be better mechanisms) and by criticisms that price stabilisation may not be achieved even by buffer stocks (see also, Smith [19] and Henderson and Lal [9]).

(c) Processing and market access: improved access to markets in industrial countries is the chief rationale for some commodity organisations planned by UNCTAD (to cover vegetable oil and possibly rice, for example), and it is a subsidiary but potentially important aim in other cases (aluminium).

(d) Economic security: the use of oil as a political weapon has prompted governments to look for more secure supply arrangements. So far, however, apart from oil, the greatest concern in Europe has been over metals (except possibly manganese and tin) not high on the UNCTAD agenda mainly from Southern Africa. And preferred solutions (greater self-sufficiency, strategic stockpiling, control over client states such as Zaire, diversification to politically safer developed country sources) have not so far involved any major concession to the developing countries' ideas. Fears about economic insecurity extend to factors other than political disruption. The mining companies seem to have convinced the European Commission and several member state governments of the validity of their argument that loss of traditional 'captive' mines in developing countries is leading to under-investment in mining, and in turn to supply deficiencies in the 1980s (see Crowson [3] for a balanced presentation of the arguments). Another anxiety is that processing industries will be deprived of raw materials if developing countries try to do their own processing;

several already subject hides and timber to export bans or controls and the EEC has in turn instituted a ban on hides exports.

How far has recent commodity market management contributed to achievement of these aims? The limited experience of buffer stocking makes it difficult to be sure about price stabilisation. But the influence of the tin agreement seems to have been no more than marginal (Smith and Schink [18]), the coffee agreement and the introduction of controls on sugar exports were followed in each case by greatly increased annual price fluctuation, much the same is true of rubber, and cocoa prices have remained far above the maximum permitted in the 1970 agreement (USODC [24]), while greater stability for wheat and tea can be attributed to extraneous factors. Interpretations of the evidence may differ and control procedures could perhaps be improved, but experience is not encouraging.

Price fixing has achieved several short-run successes. Nothing else compares with OPEC's, but recent coffee agreements are estimated to have transferred $500–600 million annually from consumers to producers (Law [15]) and a bauxite levy $300 million per annum (Mingst [16]), while at national level export earnings have been substantially increased by harder bargaining, stiffer taxation and more effective government regulation (USODC [25], p. 17). There may however be long-term costs to producers within agreements through stimulation of output in other countries and of product-substitution (rubber producers seeking to raise prices by cartel action).

Price-raising arrangements operating through limitation of production of exports over more than a short period are likely to succeed only under highly restrictive conditions. The most important is that the import price elasticity of demand for the product in the consuming countries should be low and certainly below unity over a substantial period. In addition political conditions must be appropriate. A producer cartel covering tea, coffee and cocoa, for example, could be damaging to consumers, but the difficulties of organising all major actual and potential third world producers of tea and coffee even separately have so far proved insuperable. Unless Western demand revives strongly cartel action could probably be effective for only a small number of products (Edwards [5]), including bauxite, tin, natural rubber (but only for modest price increases since substitution is easy) and phosphates (given export restraint by Morocco, which has so far been unwilling to exercise it).

Unless there are serious threats of unilateral action by producers, Western countries are unlikely to see any advantage in the near future in management of commodity markets. There are however two considerations which might alter this attitude in the longer term. The first is worry about mineral supplies. Developing countries have partially disrupted the vertically integrated structure which previously guaranteed Western countries' raw-material security, without replacing it with alternative forms of global market management. Western countries have so far had little anxiety over the main metals, since stocks are generally high and demand slack, with substitute products and alternative sources of supply available. This may change for copper, bauxite or iron ore in the 1980s, though at first sight secure long-term bilateral contracts would seem more likely than multilateral commodity agreements. Secondly, developing countries may, in spite of practical difficulties, do more processing of primary materials, thus affecting their availability and competing directly with processors in industrial countries. Western countries could then come under pressure to accept direct market management, either to secure raw-material supplies or to control imports of processed products or to do both simultaneously.

Developing Country Manufactured Exports

Although some industrialised countries have also fared badly (for example, Japan in the EEC), developing countries have apparently borne much of the brunt of recent protectionist measures against manufactured imports. One obvious partial explanation of this selective treatment of developing countries and other NICs is that the share of NICs in OECD manufactured imports is rising – to 8.1 per cent in 1977 from 6.9 per cent in 1973 and 2.6 per cent in 1963 (5.8 per cent, 4.7 per cent and 1.5 per cent respectively if Southern Europe is excluded). But the strongest pressure for more intensive selective protection against low-cost NIC imports has come from Britain and France, and a recent official report confirmed that in the United Kingdom the NIC share of manufactured imports has been declining (9.9 per cent in 1977, 10.1 per cent in 1974, 11.3 per cent in 1963) (FCO [6]). There seems to be no inter-industry correlation in the United Kingdom or the United States between variations in the incidence of selective protection against NIC imports and the rate of increase of import penetration (but a high correlation with the *level*, suggesting a reaction against trade specialisation *per se* rather than rapid rates of change). Moreover the United Kingdom has a rising surplus on trade in manufactures with NICs.

One complaint against NIC imports is that they are more disruptive than equal values or volumes from OECD countries, being concentrated in a narrow range of labour-intensive products. NICs (including Southern Europe) accounted in 1977 for 45.6 per cent of United Kingdom imports of clothing (39.1 per cent for OECD imports), 25.1 per cent of imports of leather goods and footwear (31.3 per cent OECD) and 14.8 per cent of textile imports (12.1 per cent OECD). This picture is changing however with the diversification of the more advanced NICs into engineering exports. Concern over the effects of product concentration has focused on the effects on employment of NIC imports in these industries and the allegedly greater problems of labour adjustment which flow from a pattern of specialisation in which industrialised countries import labour-intensive goods. But there is evidence to suggest that, except in a handful of 'sensitive' industrial sub-sectors (men's shirts and knitted goods being the only cases found in over 100 in the United Kingdom), productivity improvements have so far displaced more labour than 'low cost' imports (UNIDO [22]), and that, even if trade diversion to non-NICs could be prevented, industry-specific trade protection would not in itself reverse more than a modest share of labour displacement in labour-intensive industries. There is evidence from cotton textiles and jute that protection may encourage capital-deepening investment and so accelerate the decline in employment.

The main category of labour adversely affected by imports from developing countries is unskilled women, who, though less geographically mobile than men (when the second breadwinner in a family), are probably more easily absorbed into the service sector. And, for the United Kingdom, there is no clear evidence that 'low-cost' imports disproportionately affect regions with above-average unemployment. It is not those parts of Lancashire with rates of unemployment significantly above the national average that are affected by textile imports (and indirectly by clothing imports), while the clothing and leather goods industries are widely dispersed. Nevertheless, there are of course adverse effects on employment and output in the short run.

Most analysis of the effects of NIC imports concentrates on employment and income distribution implications for British labour, but the role of capital may be more crucial. There is little doubt that the most powerful force behind the EEC (and United States) textile interests has been the man-made fibre lobby. Developing country textile and clothing imports have creamed off demand for man-made fibres at a time of considerable excess capacity. The chances of chemical companies selling fibres to developing country textile exporters have been reduced by Japanese competition and by newly emerging Korean and Taiwanese producers. These companies have therefore become a powerful force for protection against developing countries' exports. In other industries, such as transistor radios and calculators, capital has adjusted successfully to NIC competition by overseas investment and development of subcontracting arrangements or domestic diversification. But this form of adjustment has been achieved less easily in North–South trade than in trade among OECD countries, which is more heavily intra-industry and intra-firm (Helleiner [8]).

These partial explanations implicity assume that selective protection against NIC exports is rationally motivated, even if the reasons are not very good. In contrast, imports of manufactures from developing countries often produce an emotional reaction against being 'swamped' by goods produced by 'cheap labour' which bears little relation to the economic costs and benefits of trade or the modest size of trade flows. It could well be that economic logic is subsidiary and that NIC manufactured exports have become a scapegoat for problems which have other causes and other cures.

The Experience of Managed Trade in Manufactures
Most attempts to regulate imports of manufactures from developing to developed countries have so far been uncoordinated and individually small if cumulatively large. Others, including some of the most important such as those affecting steel, have also been recent, making *ex post* evaluation difficult. However one case of organisation at sectoral level stands out as of global significance, embracing a substantial volume of trade and a large number of partners, and having some historical experience. It is the 1974 textile MFA and its predecessor the Long-Term Agreement.

The criteria by which management of the textile trade can be judged are efficiency, stability and equity. These are incorporated as objectives in the text of the MFA. Detailed terms are however incorporated in bilateral agreements and it is the 1977 renegotiation of bilateral quotas by the EEC (the leading textile importer) rather than the MFA itself which has cast doubt on its proclaimed objectives.

Stability was to be achieved by fixed annual rates of import growth (6 per cent in real terms). Initially this failed to satisfy producers in developed countries, especially in Europe. This was partly because of delays in signing bilateral agreements, but also because those without a global quota permitted uncontrolled growth from new, unrestrained, low-cost sources. In addition, European producers complained that the fixed growth rate failed to reflect variations in demand and should be reduced in recession (though the corollary was never acknowledged). Finally they argued that 6 per cent import growth was too 'disruptive' in sub-sectors where import penetration was already high. In meeting most of these objections in 1977 by more restrictive bilateral agreements, the EEC eliminated much of the benefit of predictability which the MFA offered to suppliers. Developing countries which installed textile capacity to take advantage of apparently guaranteed access now face strict controls with little growth element and have been left with substantial excess capacity. The imposition of stricter quotas in a period of recession may have stabilised EEC markets, but it has de-stabilised demand for developing countries, which also face weak demand for their traditional exports. Under the revised arrangement, moreover, only a few categories have strict if predictable global ceilings. Most of the less sensitive items have been left to a mechanism which can be activated with minimum consultation at the request of developed country producers. The one advantage to developing countries, however, is that even the revised MFA provides some guarantee against unrestrained and unpredictable protection at national level.

The economic efficiency objectives of the MFA have been largely forgotten. Those sub-sectors in the clothing and textile industries enjoying greatest protection are those with least efficiency in terms of cost and the highest levels of import penetration. Also, contrary to the spirit of the MFA, provision for carry-overs between categories, countries and products has been reduced, while sub-categories subject to separate quantitative regulation have proliferated. Administrative complexity is further compounded by a set of EEC tariff quotas parallel to the quantity restriction, applying different ceilings and requiring a separate system of certification. In addition, the least efficient third world producers are protected; current arrangements may help to protect increasingly high-wage economies such as Hong

Kong, Korea and Singapore from competition from the Philippines and Thailand. Finally, and perhaps most important, protection has become permanent. Past protection may have been designed to ease the process of decline, but it also encouraged investment in industrial countries and led to further pressure for protection. Textile companies in industrial countries have consistently argued that temporary protection will not 'maintain confidence'; their case has now been accepted at least in the United Kingdom. The cost of these concessions in terms of economic inefficiency, borne jointly by frustrated developing country exporters and developed country exporters to them, as well as by all developed country consumers, cannot be accurately calculated, but preliminary evaluation of the effects of the MFA renegotiation on final shop prices suggests a significant impact (according to surveys by the Consumers' Association to be published shortly).

Developed country concepts of 'equity' stem from a belief that it is 'unfair' for textile exporters in developing countries to profit from wage differentials. 'Cheap' or 'low-cost' textile imports represent a 'burden' to be shared. It is scarcely conceivable that developing country exporters would share this view. There has been rather more agreement that it is 'fair' to help new entrants to the market, though quotas on very small suppliers make it unlikely that Bangladesh or Sri Lanka, for example, will ever be able to generate viable economies of scale. There has always been a presumption of discrimination in favour of poorer textile exporters, and the more developed Far Eastern exporters were penalised by being granted lower base quotas in 1978, pegging imports to 1975 or 1976 levels. It is doubtful however if in the long run very poor countries will benefit from a highly regulated rather than a more market-orientated textile regime. Korea, Singapore and Taiwan can adapt their production patterns to the quota arrangements in a way that less sophisticated producers cannot. They are also at a stage where, in any event, higher wage costs would have prompted an adjustment to more capital-intensive industries. As it is, quotas based on historic performance protect them from new sources of competition. Moreover some lines of labour-intensive production most suitable to the poorer developing countries are restricted particularly severely. Cotton shirts are an example.

Finally the MFA aspired to multilateral rules for trade management at least as effective as those governing 'free' trade. The impartiality of the Textile Surveillance Board which it accordingly created has been questioned and its findings have been ignored (most openly by the EEC, which objects to having its freedom to take unilateral action impeded by a multilateral body with judicial functions). None the less there remains an attachment to the letter if not the spirit of the 'rules'; the EEC was able to secure an amendment to legitimise retrospectively 'reasonable agreed departures' from the MFA (that is those departures which it had itself made).

If the MFA has not been conspicuously successful in achieving its declared objectives of stability, efficiency, equity and orderly rules, the alternative of protectionist anarchy has been avoided. And, at the end of the 1977 renegotiations, all the developing countries, however reluctantly, did sign up for another four years.

Prospects for Future Management of Developing Country Manufactured Exports

The commitment of the EEC to extend the area of control is implicit in the high priority given in the multilateral trade negotiations to more easily used and selective safeguard clauses against 'disruptive' imports. Since agreement has not been forthcoming, the Community's declared intention is to use GATT Article 19 selectively, contrary to the 'most favoured nation' principle of the GATT. Apologists for it argue that Japan is the main target rather than the developing countries, but how sparingly the new powers are used will depend on a variety of factors.

One is the growth rate of manufactured exports from developing countries. In 1965–76 this was, on one measure, 12.7 per cent per annum (15.2 per cent excluding non-ferrous metals) as compared with 9.1 per cent for developed countries (IBRD [11]). World Bank projections point to comparable growth in the period to 1985, lifting the total from $33 billion in 1975 to $94 billion in 1985 (in 1975 prices). More export-orientated policies in countries with supply deficiencies (notably in South Asia) could raise this figure substantially. If Western markets continue depressed it is highly improbable, however, that import growth of this order would be accommodated. Very preliminary data for 1978 suggest that for Korea, India and some other NICs export growth has been substantially reduced by difficulties in access to markets. These will, if sustained, reduce investment in manufactured exporting in developing countries and result in redirection of resources to import substitution, or, simply, in slower growth. The adjustment problem is then shifted from the Western countries' import-competing industries to their exporting industries. But the pressures to organise trade are less.

A second factor is whether or not affected countries can successfully react against protection otherwise than by spending less. There are signs of greater willingness among NICs to take coordinated re-taliatory action against selective targets (for example, by ASEAN against Australia). Scope for such action is limited, but one of the long-term dangers of the 'new protectionism' is that the area of conflict could conceivably be widened to supplies of raw materials, debt repayments and respect for rights of foreign investors. More positively, some NICs may seek to 'graduate' from developing country status, as in effect Greece, Portugal and Spain are doing through EEC accession. However, the experience of those NICs which accept free trading disciplines does not suggest that this will guarantee more favourable treatment for competing manufactured exports.

Thirdly, Western countries may be able to adjust to NIC competition in the long run. Even within the textile industry some firms would welcome freer trade with NICs because of their own success in diversifying into non-competing products or developing 'offshore' processing. Many German clothing firms have developed such trade with Mediterranean countries and there are pressures to extend it in France. Hence the proposal by the European Communities of a more flexible long-term policy for textiles (House of Lords [10]), which, however, is being vigorously opposed by the main European textile federations.

The form of any extension of market regulation depends largely upon the product-mix. It seems probable that the main growth of manufactured exports from developing countries will be in: (a) labour-intensive 'traditional' manufactures where protection does not fore-stall this; (b) processing of raw materials where cost advantages favour processing near the source of raw material or fuel feedstock in some cases; (c) non-traditional labour-intensive manufactures mainly within the engineering sector broadly defined, which has been the main area of recent NIC export growth and is likely to become increasingly so as items under (a) and (b) are already relatively heavily protected by tariff and non-tariff measures, whereas most engineering goods attract zero duty under the Generalised System of Preferences.

If protection is the developed countries' response, it could be either through global sectoral agreements or through piecemeal restrictions at sub-product level. Sectoral agreements have their advocates, not only amongst protectionists. There could in theory be efficiency gains from orderly expansion of capacity in some industries such as steel, but in practice sectoral trade diplomacy seems likely to lead to cartels designed to favour established (developed country) producers. Government negotiating performance is judged by what it does for the producers concerned. The textile MFA excluded both natural fibres (cotton and wool) and textile machines from its terms of reference, let alone the interests of consumers, suppliers of inputs to production, and other industries which might benefit from inter-industry special-isation. In any event, in the engineering sector, which is likely to see most conflict over trade policy with NICs in the future, a wider sectoral approach would have little relevance given the complexity of the industry and of the interests involved.

There might be advantages, in principle, from sectoral arrange-ments when there are simultaneous conflicts over raw-material supplies and market access for finished products. So far, however, the most serious problems over access concern items for which raw-material supplies are not sufficient of a problem to draw developed countries into serious negotiation.

Conclusions

If trade 'management' between developed and developing countries has any unifying characteristics they are selectivity and pragmatism. Policy has been dictated case-by-case by national or, more usually, sectional interests. In the commodities field such order as is provided by vertically integrated multinational enterprises remains in some areas, but is being eroded in others by developing country efforts to control production. In one major case only (OPEC) has a new form of order been created by producers' government organisation. In no case has a satisfactory and durable system of multilateral commodity management yet emerged involving governments of producers and consumers. Whereas trade within Western Europe and within OECD generally (except for Japan) still conforms in a rough and ready way with liberal trade rules, the attempt of a few developing countries to take advantage of liberal market access for their exports of manu-factures has produced a protectionist reaction. The one major attempt to create a new framework for 'managing' trade in manufactures between developed and developing countries, the MFA, has not realised its global objectives of equity, stability and efficiency, and

North–South trade is characterised by increasing disorder and dissension. These are one aspect of a wider lack of understanding over a whole set of interconnected issues: international demand management, international liquidity, external debt, management of balance of payments disequilibrium and concessional resource transfers. Unless there is an unexpected resolution of such 'macro' issues, arbitrary interventions in North–South trading relationships must be expected to increase at 'micro' level, with results no less unhelpful than they have been hitherto.

Appendix 1: A Classification Scheme for Managed North–South Trade

Complementary trade
(1)   Action by producers (exporting countries):
    (a)   by a single country – export licensing (e.g. armaments); export restrictions on raw materials (e.g. hides, timber); state export marketing boards (e.g. Canadian and Australian wheat); 'aid' with strings; export cartels and organisation (e.g. 'chosen instrument' policy);
    (b)   joint action – raw-material producer cartels (e.g. OPEC, bauxite in the IBA; regulation of sales (e.g. nuclear technology); generic marketing (e.g. tea).
(2)   Action by consumers (importing countries):
    (a)   by a single country – state purchasing (e.g. Indian State Trading Corporation); buffer stocking and strategic stockpiling;
    (b)   joint action – International Energy Agency.
(3)   Action by consumers and producers:
    (a)   bilateral – oil for arms or nuclear power (e.g. from Iran or Venezuela); planning of trade through joint commissions; long-term contracts for commodity supplies;
    (b)   multilateral – commodity agreements (e.g. tin, cocoa).

'Hybrid' cases
(1)   Action by producers (exporting countries):
    (a)   by a single country – export restrictions designed simultaneously to raise raw-material prices and to secure access for processed products (e.g. hides and leather);

(b) joint action – linking of producer cartels to attempts to increase processing in producing countries (possibly in the bauxite IBA).

(2) Action by consumers (importing countries):
   (a) by a single country – some state import activity (e.g. French and Italian on tobacco); some non-tariff barriers (e.g. government procurement or health and safety standards);
   (b) joint action – none.

(3) Action by consumers and producers:
   (a) bilateral – buy-back barter (mainly with Eastern Europe); deals involving raw materials and access for processed products (e.g. iron ore from Venezuela and steel, Arabian oil and petrochemicals);
   (b) multilateral – International Sugar Agreement; United Nations Liner Code for Shipping; agreements on beef, wheat and rice (if achieved).

Substitutive trade

(1) Action by producers (exporting countries):
   (a) by a single country – export controls to improve market access (e.g. Mediterranean countries' licensing of textiles exported for processing);
   (b) joint action – attempts to negotiate collectively or retaliate on problems of market access (e.g. India and Bangladesh on jute products and Australia on textiles).

(2) Action by consumers (importing countries):
   (a) by a single country – selective import controls; anti-dumping action; CAP levies; variable export refunds; other non-tariff barriers;
   (b) joint action – some proposed market-sharing arrangements (e.g. shipbuilding, steel); orderly marketing agreements.

(3) Action by consumers and producers:
   (a) bilateral – variable export refunds;
   (b) multilateral – orderly marketing agreements (e.g. textile MFA); air traffic regulation.

Appendix 2: The Current Status of Commodity Market Management

5th International Tin Agreement (1976–81)

Members include both producers and consumers. Major producers are Bolivia, Indonesia, Malaysia, Nigeria, Thailand and Zaire, with 70 per cent of world mine production. Brazil is a substantial non-member, also Taiwan. Major consumers are members, including the United States, which joined recently.

The objective is to fix prices in the range $3.61 – $4.5 per lb. The ceiling price is currently broken, but the floor price has only failed once (in 1958). The price range was raised in mid-1977.

The maximum buffer stock is now 40,000 tons (half voluntary); it was 20,000 tons in previous Agreements. The United States national stockpile is 200,000 tons.

Export quotas, used to support floor prices previously, have not been used since 1976.

International Bauxite Association (IBA) (1974–   )

Members are producers only: Australia, Dominican Republic, Ghana, Guinea, Guyana, Haiti, Indonesia, Jamaica, Sierra Leone, Surinam and Yugoslavia. They account for 85 per cent of world production and almost all exports. Brazil is an important non-member. Australia does not support 'cartel' activities.

The major objective is to raise returns through an export levy (imposed by the Dominican Republic, Haiti, Jamaica and Surinam). A minimum price was fixed in December 1977 linked to aluminium prices and below current market prices. Another objective is to raise the members' processing share in the output of aluminium.

There is no buffer stocking and no control on exports or production has yet been found necessary to support the price.

Copper Producers' Cartel (CIPEC) (1967–   )

This is currently ineffective.

Members are producers only: Chile, Peru, Zambia and Zaire, with 30 per cent of world production. Major producers, including Canada, did not join.

An attempt to fix prices in 1975 failed due to inadequate implementation of production cuts (Chile especially was a problem). While buffer stocking has been advocated no action has been taken.

Copper Consultative Group (1978–   )

This is still very embryonic. It is a producers' and consumers' group which has discussed buffer stocking under the Common Fund programme, but so far reached no agreement.

Association of Iron Ore Exporters (AIEC) (1975–   )

Also very embryonic, this covers producers only: Algeria, Australia, India, Liberia, Mauritania, Peru, Sierre Leone, Sweden and Venezuela, with 70 per cent of world (non-Communist) trade. Chile and Tunisia withdrew; Brazil and Canada never joined.

The objective is to fix prices ultimately, but not yet as some members would not support sharp price increases. Australia and India with Brazil are currently making a joint attempt outside the Association to get better prices from Japan. Meanwhile the objectives are to exchange information and rationalise supplies through coordinated investment.

Association of Natural Rubber Producing Countries (ANRPC) (1976–   )

Also embryonic, this covers producers only: Indonesia, Malaysia, Singapore, Sri Lanka and Thailand, with over 90 per cent of world exports.

Price stabilisation with both ceiling and floor prices is an objective. It is also the aim to 'rationalise commercial policies' and exchange information. A 100,000-ton buffer stock is envisaged but not yet implemented.

Negotiating Conference for an International Rubber Agreement

So far there is no result from this conference covering producers and consumers, which aims to set up a buffer stock with consumer support.

International Sugar Agreement (1978–82)

Members include all major consumers and producers except the EEC and Taiwan. The target price range is 11–21 cents per lb. Reserve stocks are 2.5 million tons (1.5 million tons in previous Agreements). Members have export quotas and EEC restraints have been promised but not guaranteed.

2nd International Cocoa Agreement (1975–9)

Members are all the major consumers and producers except the United States (until 1979). 45 members account for 95 per cent of world production.

The target price range is 65–81 cents per lb, which has been adjusted upwards several times, but the market price is consistently higher. Other objectives are the promotion of consumption and an extension of processing in less developed countries.

A buffer stock of 250,000 has been agreed, but never put into operation since the price is above the intervention range. Annual export quotas have also never been invoked.

International Tea Agreement

So far these are only tentative proposals by an FAO Inter-government Group. It is intended to cover producers and consumers, and price support with buffer stocks is envisaged, also generic marketing. National export quotas are proposed, but no agreement has been reached between producers.

International Coffee Agreement (1976–82)

This Agreement, the third in its present form, covers all major consumers and producers, but is mainly a standby arrangement at present as prices exceed the floor price level. There are no provisions for buffer stocks and although export quotas are envisaged they have never been invoked so far. Other objectives are consultation (over processing, etc.), promotion of consumption and the removal of high taxes and tariffs.

There are also various coffee producers' groups: Cafe Mundial (Angola, Brazil, Colombia, Ivory Coast), Otros Suaves (Costa Rica, El Salvador, Honduras, Mexico, Nicaragua), OMCAF (French-speaking producers).

Union of Banana Exporters (1974–   )

Members are Colombia, Costa Rica, Guatemala, Honduras and Panama, with about 40 per cent of world exports. Ecuador (the world's largest exporter), West Indies and African producers are not members.

The objective was to raise earnings through an export tax, but the attempt failed due to United States pressure.

Phosphates Cartel (1976–)
This is an informal arrangement. Members were Algeria, Jordan, Morocco, Senegal, Togo and Tunisia, with 55 per cent of world exports, but Algeria and Togo have withdrawn.

An attempt to establish a reference price failed because Morocco offered discounts when faced by excess capacity. There are no buffer stocks and no export controls are envisaged.

References
[1] Agriculture, Fisheries and Food, Ministry of, *Food from Our Own Resources*, Cmnd 6020, London, HMSO, 1975.
[2] Balassa, B., 'The new protectionism and the international economy', *Journal of World Trade Law*, October/November 1978.
[3] Crowson, P., *Non-fuel Minerals and Foreign Policy*, London, Chatham House, 1978.
[4] Donges, J. B., 'The Third World demand for a new international economic order', *Kyklos*, no. 2, 1977.
[5] Edwards, A., *The Potential for New Commodity Cartels*, London, Economist Intelligence Unit, 1975.
[6] Foreign and Commonwealth Office, 'The newly industrialised countries and the adjustment problem', (Government Economic Service working paper no. 18), 1979.
[7] Hager, W., *Europe's Economic Security*, Paris, Atlantic Institute, 1975.
[8] Helleiner, G. K., 'Transnational enterprises and the new political economy of U.S. trade policy', *Oxford Economic Papers*, March 1977.
[9] Henderson, D. and Lal, D., 'UNCTAD IV: the commodities problem and international economic reform', *ODI Review*, no. 2, 1976.
[10] House of Lords, *Select Committee on the European Communities (16th Report)*, London, HMSO, 1979.
[11] IBRD, *World Trade and Output of Manufactures: structural trends and developing countries' exports* by D. B. Keesing, Washington (DC), 1978.
[12] Johnson, H. G. (ed.), *The New Mercantilism: some problems in international trade, money and investment*, Oxford, Blackwell, 1974.
[13] Lal, D., *Poverty, Power and Prejudice*, London, Fabian Society, 1979.
[14] —, 'The wistful mercantilism of Mr Dell', *The World Economy*, June 1978 (see also Mr Dell's reply in *The World Economy*, May 1979).
[15] Law, A. D., *International Commodity Agreements: setting, performance and prospects*, Lexington (Mass.), D. C. Heath, 1975.
[16] Mingst, K., 'Economic determinants of international commodity regulation', *Journal of World Trade Law*, March/April 1979.
[17] Smith, B., 'Security and stability in mineral markets: the role of long-term contracts', *The World Economy*, January 1979.
[18] Smith, G. W. and Schink, G. R., 'The international tin agreement: a reassessment', *Economic Journal*, December 1976.

[19] Smith, W., *Commodity Instability: new order or old hat in challenges to liberal international order?*, Washington (DC), American Enterprise Institute, 1978.

[20] Tumlir, J., *National Interest and International Order*, London, Trade Policy Research Centre, 1978.

[21] UNCTAD, *Restrictive Business Practices: review of major developments*, Geneva, 1975.

[22] UNIDO, *The Impact of Trade with Developing Countries on Employment in Developed Countries*, New York, 1978.

[23] United Nations, *Declaration on the Rights and Economic Duties of States*, Article 27.

[24] United States Office of Domestic Commerce, *International Commodity Agreements* by J. Behrman, Washington (DC), USGPO, 1977.

[25] —, *World Market Imperfections and the Developing Countries* by G. K. Helleiner, Washington (DC), USGPO, 1978.

[26] Zysman, J., 'The state as trader', *International Affairs*, April 1978.

Comment

by L. Turner

If Cable's paper makes one point, it is that we mangle the English language if we argue that North–South trade is currently 'managed'. What we have is a hodge-podge of proposals, negotiations and (a few) agreements designed to improve the workings of certain sectors of the world's trading system. In the commodity field it is generally the third world countries which are trying to take the initiative. In the case of manufactured trade it is the industrialised world which is engaged in a steadily widening series of damage-limitation exercises. Cable leaves the impression, however, that there is slowly growing interest among industrial countries in getting involved in a few more commodity agreements primarily for the sake of economic security. In fact there are other motives. Increasingly concern about inflation has interested Northern governments in ironing out upward fluctuations in commodity prices (particularly since experience with oil suggests a ratchet effect, whereby prices do not come down in troughs). Secondly, industrial countries have increasingly accepted the principle of stabilising third world export earnings (mainly through the European Communities' STABEX scheme and the IMF's Compensatory Financing Facility) and to accept that buffer stocks can help to stabilise the export earnings of certain producers is a relatively small further intellectual step. My guess is that, whatever the precise future of UNCTAD's Common Fund, a slowly but steadily increasing proportion of trade in non-oil commodities will be marginally affected by North–South cooperative management pacts.

Of course, what happens to oil will have a disproportionate impact on the North–South trading environment. Oil is perhaps the one industry affecting North–South relations in which one can see a relatively effective third world cartel continuing to exist well into the next century. If OPEC's effectiveness is to be broken, it will have to be over the coming decade. However, lack of a coherent American energy policy, growing doubts about nuclear energy and Saudi Arabia's apparent determination to limit production all suggest that OPEC will retain a central place in world energy trade. The extent to which it will become an effective central decision-making forum on issues such as gas pricing, oil allocation, or coordination of downstream processing industries such as petrochemicals still has to be seen, but it seems unlikely that its members will make long-term deals with Northern governments. Any 'management' of the oil sector will be through the OPEC nations acting as a loose cartel, with the IEA (International Energy Agency) gradually extending its role in coordinating the industrial world's reactions in the overall field of energy. Any OPEC–IEA deal on oil prices or specific production levels seems extremely unlikely.

In regard to manufactures, Cable is right to point to inconsistencies in industrial countries' protectionism. However, whatever the motives, it has increased rapidly – in the early 1970s the European Communities were taking about four actions a year which could be classed as protectionist; these climbed to 41 in 1977 and 94 in the 18 months to December 1978 (Franko [2]).

As Cable points out, much work is still needed on the dynamics of protectionism. He is right about the role that capital, as well as labour, plays in stoking protectionist fires, but his analysis probably needs to be a bit more subtle. For instance, the man-made fibres producers, whom he correctly identifies as prime forces behind the industrial world's textile restrictions, are a peculiar lot. Certainly, they led the campaign against the leading textile producers in developing countries, even though the net trade balance of the European Communities in textiles (not clothing) was little less healthily positive in 1977 than in 1973 (Cable [1]). In the European Communities they almost persuaded the Commission to set up a cartel which would have controlled both capacity rationalisation and future market shares. This, however, was after they had managed to over-invest on a remarkable scale. Cable points out the contrast with radio and calculator manufacturers, who seem to have accepted relocation of their industries without much fuss (though United States and Japanese companies have had surprising success in keeping control of calculator technology through product innovation and automation of assembly lines).

What then determines whether companies or industries go protectionist or remain liberal? Clearly, an important factor is whether they are diversified by geography or by product. Conglomerate multinationals may not be particularly enthusiastic about third world competition but often adjust to it without protection. The problems are more with the single-product, single-country company, which governments often see as some form of 'national champion'. In general, the synthetic fibres producers fit this category, with companies like Montefibre and SIR seen as national (or regional) champions within Italy. The steel companies fit this pattern too. Again, it was not the European branches of the oil majors, but firms like CFP, Elf-Aquitaine, Petrofina, ENI and Veba which wanted the Commission of the European Communities to create a kind of recession cartel for refining.

It may be unwise to dogmatise about the motives of companies still on the side of liberal trade, as few industries have been tested as much as textiles and clothing. In electronics, which competition from the leading third world countries particularly affects, a number of major companies have decided to start operating there rather than call for protection, but in the United States television sector the established American companies proved less tolerant when, without the protection that the network of patents round the PAL system has hitherto given to producers in Western Europe, they came close to being swamped by exports from Japan. In the last couple of years an orderly marketing agreement was imposed on the Japanese industry and when Taiwan and Korea moved in to take up the running both were similarly reined in.

What makes United States colour television different from radios and calculators? Is it size and 'visibility' (no pun intended)? Was it the difficult time at which the product came under competition? Or was it that American television manufacturers do not innovate (note their failure to develop their own video-recorder systems), whereas the calculator manufacturers (coming primarily from the micro-electronic sector) know that without constant innovation they cannot survive? It bodes ill for any developing country which chooses to export cars outside the aegis of the Detroit majors that, though geographically diversified, they have forced their Japanese competitors to restrict exports to the United States. Does the relatively informal protectionism of the motor industry there and elsewhere indicate that long lead-times and capital-intensive investment within an industry may effect the likelihood of attempts to control competitive imports? Whatever the answer, much work needs to be done on why some companies have adjusted to third world competition and others have not (in particular, on why the big importing companies are relatively ineffective lobbyists for liberal trade).

There is a very real possibility that the MFA and the increasing number of more-or-less forcibly imposed trade restrictions on developing countries in industries such as shoes, steel or electronics may coalesce into a general environment for North–South trade which is designed to create a kind of two-tier trading world. The MFA itself sprang from very narrow trading concerns, which primarily involved Japan and then Hong Kong, in the cotton sector. As new textile producers emerged and diversified into new fibres, the new elements were integrated into an ever-expanding web of bilateral agreements. A similar process may be emerging in consumer electronics, so far involving limited numbers of producing nations and products. Doubtless, though, it will not be long before countries like Malaysia and China will be producing television sets; and how long before Taiwan and Korea get into video-recorders or semi-conductors (where Korea already has production capabilities) or massively into hi-fi equipment? And after electronics, what about base petrochemicals (the oil producers), process plant (the NICs) or components for motor cars? How many of these new export sectors will be caught within a web of controls designed to slow the third world entry into fields which were once the preserve of the industrial countries?

The world economy evolves ponderously and our relatively recent, thoroughly restrictionist textile regime covers an industry whose trade tensions go back into the last century. On the other hand, any paper which discusses (as Cable's does) the extent to which measures such as the MFA are providing equity, stability and efficiency must take into account whether we are in the early stages of a long-term irreversible shift towards the developing countries of comparative advantages in manufacturing. I would argue, from experience with Saudi Arabia, Hong Kong and Korea (also Iran and India), that things are swinging their way because of the rapid improvement in communications (air freight, containerisation, telex, passenger jets, long-distance computer interaction) and rapid development throughout leading third world societies of educational levels and managerial capabilities in the widest sense of the word. In a city like Hong Kong you cannot fail to be aware of systematic discussion by entrepreneurs and government officials of the comparative advantages of investment in countries as developmentally and geographically diverse as Mauritius, the Philippines, China, Japan, Malaysia and Thailand. Recent statistics may show that only a handful of third world countries are currently important in the global trade in manufactures. But these countries are themselves only too aware of the growing competition from economies with yet cheaper labour.

My belief is that, within the manufacturing sector, the pendulum will continue to swing towards the developing countries, though whether and when different industries will migrate from North to South will be influenced by transport costs, raw-material availability and relative research ingenuity. This obviously affects the extent to which trade relations will grow increasingly restricted or liberal. I would suggest that OECD growth will have to accelerate quite sharply before trade restrictions are reduced. In relatively mature, capital-intensive industries, such as steel, shipbuilding or cars, bodies like the OECD's Steel and Shipbuilding Committees may gradually be extended to include leading third world newcomers. It is not clear what the latter would gain, but one would expect consistent pressure from the industrial countries for some form of investment coordination to avoid continued excess capacity. We would also expect a slow spread of formal and informal quotas, as other third world exporters emerge or existing ones diversify.

Growing diversity of trading relationships may, however, make trade restrictions ever harder to enforce. I was struck, for instance, recently how Korea's colour television trade had run into restrictions which Hong Kong entrepreneurs in electronics seem to have avoided by their much more diverse and low-key approach. As North–South trade increasingly becomes intra-trade rather than inter-trade, the loopholes in any protectionist ramparts should widen significantly, though when the United States–Philippines textile agreement even puts restraints on 'other products' (*Textile Asia* [3]), one should obviously never underestimate the subtlety of commercial diplomats. However, even if the complexity of future North–South trading patterns does make 'management' of this trade extremely difficult, there is very little sign that less of it will be attempted in the years ahead.

References

[1] Cable, V., *World Textile Trade and Production*, London, Economist Intelligence Unit, 1979, p. 48.
[2] Franko, L. G., 'Problems of structural adjustment for the industrialised countries', comments to Atlantic Institute Conference, Paris, 19 March 1979.
[3] *Textile Asia*, March 1979, p. 18.

4　The United Kingdom and the European Monetary System

by M. Emerson*

The European Monetary System (EMS) came into operation on 13 March 1979, one year after the idea had been proposed by Chancellor Schmidt in the European Council, and eighteen months after the President of the Commission, Roy Jenkins, had relaunched serious debate on European monetary integration with his Florence Lecture (Jenkins [4]).

Although the United Kingdom is not participating in the exchange-rate intervention obligation of the EMS, it has signed the agreements adopting its mechanisms and is party to the joint proceedings of EMS central banks. In addition, the government of the day declared when the EMS was introduced that so far as possible intervention policy would be conducted as if the pound was a fully participating currency.

The British authorities and the rest of the Community basically agreed on two strategic points: (a) that more stable exchange rates were desirable; (b) that there should be a system which should be neither a narrow, special-purpose club like the 'snake' became, nor an inward-looking mechanism, but should contribute towards improving wider international monetary cooperation. The new prime minister has indicated that the government will take a position on the EMS in September, which coincides with the review of the system that is due after six months' operation.

Mechanics of the EMS

The central feature of the intervention system is the obligation to keep

* Unless otherwise indicated views expressed in this paper are attributable only to the author.

exchange rates within $\pm 2\frac{1}{4}$ per cent of a specified set of central rates for each currency against each other currency, although member states so wishing can temporarily claim wider ± 6 per cent margins. Thus the obligatory intervention points are correctly expressed as a grid or matrix.

The grid of bilateral margins is derived from a set of central rates expressed in terms of the ECU (European Currency Unit) and adjustable in relation to the ECU only with the agreement of all participants. The ECU has the same definition as the European Unit of Account, a basket of all nine member states' currencies in which the quantity of each currency is fixed. The effective weights therefore normally change with exchange rates, but they may be revised within six months of the system coming into force, or after five years, or on request if the weight of any currency has changed by 25 per cent.

In principle intervention is made in the currencies at their bilateral limits, but provision is also made for 'diversified intervention' in currencies not at intervention limits. This can include either other Community currencies or the dollar.

Implementation of the central mechanism is conditioned by the 'divergence indicator', which is seen as contributing to a code of conduct for adjustments to domestic economic policy or to central rates in the event of pressures on an exchange rate. This is based on the monitoring of exchange-rate movements in relation to $\pm 2\frac{1}{4}$ per cent or ± 6 per cent margins directly on either side of the ECU central rate, as opposed to movements against each participating currency. As the ECU represents the weighted average of all currencies, the intention is that this will help identify currencies which are out of line. The indicator is deliberately 'symmetrical' as between strong and weak currencies. Whereas under the obligatory bilateral margins two countries at least, one at the top and one at the bottom, have to be at their limits together, a single currency may pass its 'threshold of divergence' alone. Four further technical features used in the calculation of the 'threshold of divergence' should be noted:

(i)   the margins are 75 per cent of $2\frac{1}{4}$ per cent or 6 per cent so as to permit the indicator to give its signal before obligatory margins are reached;

(ii)   none the less the bilateral margins may be reached first because they are based on the maximum bilateral movements between currencies, rather than against the average as represented by the ECU;

(iii)   the margins of the divergence indicator are further adjusted as a function of each currency's weight in the basket so as to avoid bias in the system in favour of weightier currencies which carry the basket in greater degree with their own movement;

(iv)   certain other technical adjustments are also made, for example to exclude the effects of excessive movements in currencies which are in the ECU basket but not in the $\pm 2\frac{1}{4}$ per cent margin system (sterling and the lira at present).

Experience in the first weeks provided an illustration of how these arrangements work. In April Denmark and Belgium found their currencies hitting respectively their top and bottom margins, but neither currency initially passed its 'threshold of divergence'. This was because the main EMS currencies were bunched in the middle of their margins and so neither of the two smaller currencies diverged much against the ECU. In early May, however, the Belgian franc passed its 'threshold of divergence' and in response monetary policy adjustments were made.

Credit is available in support of the obligatory margins. Very short-run credit is an unlimited automatic facility. Repayment takes place 45 days after the end of the month in which the debt is contracted, with the possibility of one renewal for three months. Short-term credit is available virtually automatically in amounts defined in terms of quotas placed on each central bank as a debtor and a creditor. The total of debtor quotas is 7.9 billion ECU, plus a further 8.8 billion ECU known as the 'rallonge', thus totalling 16.7 billion ECU. Short-term credits are available for a period of three months, with the possibility of two renewals, making a nine-months maximum (see Table 4.1). Medium-term credits, in principle of two to five years maturity, are available subject to a total of 14.1 billion ECU of creditor quotas.

In total the short-term and medium-term credit facilities amount to 25 billion ECU effectively available, so fixed as to be equivalent to about 20 per cent of the gross external reserves of member states. This is somewhat less than the sum of the quotas, since not all countries could draw at the same time. There is a further credit facility whereby the Commission borrows from capital markets for medium-term lending to member states. The short-term and very short-term facilities function purely as agreements between central banks without economic policy conditions. The medium-term facilities are between

Table 4.1   Composition of the ECU and credit mechanisms of the EMS

	Central rate in ECU (national currency)	Weight in ECU (%)	Short-term quotas[a]		Medium-term ceilings (ECU b.)
			Debtor	Creditor	
			(ECU billion)		
Belgium–					
Luxembourg	39.4582	9.63	0.58	1.16	1.035
Denmark	7.08592	3.06	0.26	0.52	0.465
France	5.79831	19.83	1.74	3.48	3.105
Germany	2.51064	32.98	1.74	3.48	3.105
Ireland	0.66264	1.15	0.10	0.20	0.180
Italy	1148.15	9.50	1.16	2.32	2.070
Netherlands	2.72077	10.51	0.58	1.16	1.035
United Kingdom	0.66342[b]	13.34	1.74	3.48	3.105

Source: Commission of the European Communities.
[a]Excluding 'rallonges' of 8.8 billion ECUs in both debtor and creditor totals.
[b]Market rate on 12 March 1979.

member states and the Community and are subject to economic policy conditions.

Borrowing and lending in the system is denominated in ECUs and the exchange risk is thus spread in terms of the basket of currencies. Debtors have the right to settle half of their debts in ECUs; the other half depends on the agreement of the creditor central banks, failing which settlement is in other reserve assets.

The supply of ECUs is created by central banks depositing 20 per cent of their gold and dollar reserves in the European Monetary Cooperation Fund in exchange for credits in ECUs. This system will be renewed three-monthly in relation to the level of reserves; its form is at present an automatically renewable three-month swap.

Later developments, to be worked out within two years, include consolidation of the European Monetary Cooperation Fund into a European Monetary Fund and the creation of further ECUs, also amounting to 20 per cent of foreign exchange reserves, against deposits of national currencies. This will mark a further stage in the transformation of the ECU from a unit of account into an international reserve asset and from a credit facility into money.

The United Kingdom's original decision not to join the exchange-rate intervention mechanism but none the less to join the system as fully as might otherwise be possible means in practice an option to deposit 20 per cent of reserves against ECUs, access to the short-term and medium-term credit facilities, maintenance of sterling in the ECU basket and membership of the bodies governing the system. The present government subsequently announced that the deposit option would be taken up.

It was also agreed to extend special financial assistance to 'less prosperous' member states. Among countries fully participating in the EMS these were recognised to be Ireland and Italy. The assistance – shared by Ireland and Italy – consists for each of five years of 200 million ECU grants from the Community budget in the form of interest-rate subsidies on loans for infrastructural investment; the loan finance is also to come from Community sources in an amount of 1 billion ECUs for each of five years.

Interdependence and Exchange-rate Policy

Exchange-rate instability becomes increasingly costly as interdependence increases. Businesses are hit by disturbances to their profitability and competitiveness; uncertainty hampers planning and deters investment. The theory of optimal currency areas argues that the cost–benefit ratio of monetary integration becomes progressively more favourable with the free movement of trade, labour and capital – and with the *de facto* degree of openness and interdependence achieved under these headings – as well as certain other aspects such as parity bargaining over wages and demonstration effects over other conditions of employment. For governments, national economic policy becomes less able to bite on the determinants of economic behaviour to offset influences from abroad. The exchange rate becomes a less effective policy variable, being less able to influence the real side of the economy.

Trade remains the most easily measured aspect of interdependence. When the Community began in 1958 its (present nine) member states sold 34 per cent of their total exports to other member states. That ratio rose to 52 per cent by 1976. If one includes other European countries of the OECD area (which are all applicants to join the Community, or linked to it by special agreements) the Community's total intra-European exports have risen to 67 per cent of total exports or 19 per cent of GDP.

The United Kingdom's sales to the Community have risen from 4.7 per cent of GDP in 1972, the last year before joining, to 8.6 per cent of GDP in 1978. In that year 38 per cent of British exports went to the Community of nine and 54 per cent to OECD Europe as a whole; this latter figure, representing 16 per cent of GDP, is not so distant from the Community average and is still moving closer to it.

Historically, of course, the situation has been very different. It has been estimated that intra-continental exports accounted for close to two thirds of total European exports most of the time from 1830 to the present day barring periods of war (Bairoch [1]); in the same source it is estimated that 35 per cent of British exports went to Europe for most of the period 1860–1970, that is the United Kingdom's dependence on European trade was about half that of the Continent. Thus it may now have moved nearly two thirds of the way from its historical degree of interdependence to the average European position and it is continuing to converge on that average.

Exchange-rate Policy and Economic Performance

The EMS's primary objective is to promote better internal and external monetary stability and improve the level of economic activity compatible with reasonable price stability.

International monetary instability has contributed significantly to Europe's 'stagflation' during much of this decade. The broad correlation between the end of the Bretton Woods system and a poorer European economic performance is evident enough. The Community's annual growth in GDP averaged 4.6 per cent from 1958 to 1971, but 2.8 per cent from 1972 to 1978. The United Kingdom's annual growth in the same periods was 2.8 and 1.9 per cent.

The acceleration of inflation occurred in two waves. The first and lesser wave occurred in 1970–2, when the Community's annual average consumer price rise was 5.8 per cent compared to 3.4 per cent in 1958–69. The second wave followed the oil crisis of 1973, bringing double-digit inflation into almost every European country by 1975, when the Community average price rise reached 13.4 per cent; by 1978 this average had declined to 7 per cent.

The overall causes of the deteriorating price and growth performance are still a matter of controversy. Other important factors were undoubtedly economic disruption caused by the oil crisis itself, the effect of income distribution trends on investment, the growth of politically induced labour-market rigidities and the effect of tax and social security systems on employment incentives – although there are great differences between countries on most of these accounts. In this setting exchange-rate instability seems to have amplified the divergence between countries with stronger and weaker performance, to have redistributed inflation from revaluing to devaluing countries and to have intensified tendencies towards vicious and virtuous circles of economic performance. The mix and interaction of these factors would seem entirely consistent with the general deterioration of inflation and growth performance together – a creeping tendency towards accelerating inflation at the beginning of the decade, boosted by the 1973 oil crisis and further boosted to 20 per cent or more in devaluing countries as the exchange-rate depreciation interacted with domestic cost inflation.

Disillusion with floating has become such that, according to Williamson [7], hardly a currency in the world still floats freely. The main questions at issue have in effect become the optimal reference point or *numéraire* of exchange-rate policy and the optimal degree of fixity and formality given to intervention policy. The gross volume of exchange interventions has been constantly growing, as shown in Table 4.2.

Table 4.2   Gross exchange-market intervention by Western central banks, 1973–9 (US$ billion)

March 1973–February 1974	36
March 1974–January 1975	22
February 1975–January 1976	40
February 1976–January 1977	73
February 1977–January 1978	101
February 1978–January 1979	118

Source: Lamfalussy in Williamson *et al.* [7].

How more precisely can we make the case for trying a more structured exchange-rate system to help improve economic performance in Western Europe as a whole and in the United Kingdom in particular?

There are three main points. First, it should be possible in a more structured system to make balance of payments and exchange-rate adjustments with lower average inflation and less divergence of national inflation rates than over the last five years. In this respect floating exchange rates have been bad for both the United Kingdom and the Community as a whole. Britain's effective exchange rate based on 100 in 1972 (first quarter) declined to 62.7 for the year 1978. Adjusted for changes in relative wholesale prices (of manufactured goods excluding food, drink and tobacco), this gives an index of competitiveness that declined from 100 to 94.4 in 1978. The ratio of the real gain in competitiveness to the nominal depreciation of sterling was 1 to 6.7. In the first quarter of 1979 the real gain was further eroded. Floating rates seem to have made the securing of real devaluation more uncertain and much more expensive in terms of the extra inflation involved.

Secondly, exchange-rate instability appears to have impeded demand management in both devaluation-prone and revaluation-prone countries quite apart from the influence of other factors reducing growth. By 1978 all the devaluation-prone countries had observed the severity with which exchange markets regarded expansion of demand when used in an inflationary environment. But the international economy has suffered in a second respect. The revaluation-prone countries became sceptical of the likely effectiveness of demand management in highly export-oriented sectors, notably because the international environment was felt to be the principal influence on investment. When market growth abroad in devaluing countries looked doubtful and revaluation at home could well continue, the impact of demand management looked highly uncertain. The proposition that public sector deficits should be increased to uncomfortably high levels without any great probability of rapid cyclical recovery was politically unattractive. This is the combination of predicaments of devaluation-prone and revaluation-prone countries together, in which exchange-rate volatility seems to have been at least partly responsible for leading the European economy as a whole into sub-potential economic performance. This is a difficult argument to prove but vitally important. It certainly seems to be the overall perception of the leading sponsors of the EMS, who between them have quite a few years' experience as ministers of finance. In any case it is plausible that a long period of sub-potential growth will tend to become self-sustaining, as economic and social behaviour adjust to lower productivity growth with increasing resistance to change in economic structures, which means that need for a policy change is urgent.

The argument is closely linked to the case for policy coordination. This link seems recently to have been a positive one. German readiness to play a major part in the concerted demand management adjustments agreed in July 1978 was of course not unrelated to the efforts of the German authorities to get agreement on the EMS, which is stimulating the Community's system of economic policy coordination. The legitimacy of member states' concern for each other's policy is increased and new criteria of symmetry in adjustment responsibilities have been introduced (as mentioned). Resource transfers are also being treated for the first time in the context of Community macroeconomic policy, rather than exclusively in the context of sectoral policies.

This in turn is related to some well-known issues of controversy between the United Kingdom and the Community on agricultural and budget financing, on which I do not intend to dwell, except in passing to note what MacDougall said recently [5], when presenting the report of his Group (Commission of the European Communities [3]) on the role of public finance in European economic integration:

> The transfer of resources being discussed in this context [EMS] is minuscule compared with what we believe to be necessary to support a full monetary union. But this is perfectly in order. Quite different issues are involved in the current discussion. EMS is quite different from a full monetary union; and the argument is the quite understandable one about how far countries that may be less keen than others to join an adjustable peg system on a European basis can bargain to get a better deal for themselves regarding contributions, the CAP, help from the Regional Fund, and so on. I certainly would not want to argue that a large transfer of resources or a much larger Community budget is necessary to support an adjustable peg system in Europe if countries want one.

Thirdly, real, inflation-adjusted exchange-rate changes in the 1970s have been so erratic and successively contradictory as to have served little consistent objective bar that of absorbing the ebb and flow of political and economic events, which is in itself not negligible. Exchange-rate change – after discounting adjustments for inflation differentials – can, albeit with difficulty, be a powerful instrument, on the down side to boost competitiveness, or on the up side to dampen inflation. But either of these objectives requires steady implementation over a period of years; 'switchback' exchange rates, pushed by market sentiment from a year or two of overvaluation to a year or two of undervaluation, are hardly likely to achieve either objective. On the contrary they are likely to weaken economic performance on precisely the double objective of high stability and employment. Exchange-rate fluctuations encourage expectations of monetary instability, while on the real side industry is given no chance to establish a long-term investment strategy based on new assumptions of competitiveness. But a 'switchback' is what we have seen since 1971. The index of trade-weighted, exchange-rate adjusted, relative wholesale prices for manufactured goods for the United Kingdom, based at 100 in early 1972, fell to 82 by late 1973, recovered to nearly 92 by early 1975, fell to 79 by late 1976, and recovered to 97 by early 1979 (Table 4.3).

Table 4.3   United Kingdom index of relative wholesale prices for manufactured goods adjusted for changes in effective exchange rates, 1971–9

Year	QI	QII	QIII	QIV
1971	98.5	97.5	98.1	99.1	99.3
1972	97.0	100.0	100.2	94.9	93.0
1973	85.8	89.5	88.6	83.0	82.3
1974	85.9	82.8	85.8	87.0	88.0
1975	90.7	90.8	91.6	90.6	89.7
1976	84.1	90.5	83.7	83.3	79.3
1977	88.8	85.5	87.3	89.5	93.0
1978	94.4	97.1	92.3	93.8	94.5
1979	..	97.0	..	..	..

Source: Commission of the European Communities.

Notes: (i) Countries entering into the comparison of wholesale prices are Community members, Australia, Austria, Canada, Finland, Japan, Norway, Spain, Sweden, Switzerland and the United States.
(ii) Manufactured goods exclude food, drink and tobacco.
(iii) Effective exchange rates are export weighted.

The EMS is an attempt to provide a framework for doing better on these accounts. It is not possible to prove *ex ante* that it will succeed, but it is possible to rebut some of the main criticisms levied against it.

A first argument is that, while desirable, greater exchange-rate stability is not achievable. If Bretton Woods broke down and the 'snake' lost so many members, why should the EMS do better? A second argument is that it might improve monetary stability, but only through imposing lower real growth and employment on its weaker economies.

On the first argument, sceptics have to argue that exchange-rate movements would not have been significantly greater than they have been without the increasing volume of official intervention. It is of course true that internationally mobile capital has increased even more than official intervention, which is one reason why exchange rates have been highly unstable and why the resources behind official intervention have much increased through the EMS and internationally. More fundamentally, however, the Bretton Woods system broke down because of the excessive fixity of its parities, and the inadequacy of gold and the dollar as its *numéraire* and main reserve assets. The EMS is different in both respects. It allows greater flexibility in adjusting central rates, its *numéraire* is the ECU, which is closer to member states' predominant trading interests, and it is the beginning of a significant strengthening to the reserve assets of the international monetary system.

The second argument, that the EMS risks imposing a deflationary bias, also focuses attention on the rules for making exchange-rate changes. Here there are four points:

(a)   the wider margin option ± 6 per cent exists for countries which feel they need it;

(b)   to counter concern that the accusing finger is always pointed at the weak currency the divergence indicator helps to provide an objective, unbiased signal when a country is getting out of line;

(c)   action presumed to follow such a signal includes central rate changes no less than intervention policy and monetary and other economic policy measures;

(d)   experience of negotiating central rate changes carried over from the 'snake' includes a style of fairly frequent pre-emptive multilateral realignments. The experience of the latter days of the 'snake', as recently analysed by Thygesen [7], is a good deal more positive than is often supposed. Thygesen finds no evidence of a deflationary bias in its impact on the smaller countries, including his own Denmark, which has had persistent problems of high inflation and balance of payments deficits. Although it is difficult to generalise from the special case of small economies linked to a single larger one, it is also important not to judge the EMS on the basis of a superficial misinterpretation of the 'snake'.

The other equally fundamental rebuttal of fear of deflationary bias hangs on one's view of the kind of trade-off between inflation and employment, if any, actually on offer nowadays. There was a time in the 1960s perhaps when economists seriously contemplated international constellations of Phillips curves – fixed inflation–unemployment trade-offs for each country. According to this broad approach, the trade-offs differed between countries, thus carrying the threat that the strong countries impose their preference on the weak. But this system of models is now hardly more than a skeleton in the cupboard. I see no evidence whatsoever that continental European governments are in any sense less concerned about unemployment than British governments. Two of the countries with least unemployment – Germany and Switzerland – have the least inflationary economies in Europe, and this is no short-run fluke. Over the years of the present decade inflation and unemployment have shown no systematic or simple relationship, but the trend has been going if anything towards a positive rather than an inverse correlation. Reasonable price stability seems now generally recognised to be a necessary though not a sufficient condition for sustained growth. Other major conditions for improving growth and employment for a sustained period include income distribution and resource allocation issues of massive importance. In short, supply management policies and monetary stability must at present in Europe be major ingredients in growth and employment policies.

This is not to say that demand management policy is obsolete. On the contrary a better exchange-rate system is required to help demand management work better. Thygesen makes the point that for the weaker (or at least smaller) 'snake' countries this exchange-rate relationship has if anything given a somewhat greater margin of manoeuvre for demand management aimed at sustaining high employment. The argument here is that confidence in the exchange rate has allowed demand management adjustments to be made without immediate consequences for the exchange rate or expectations of exchange-rate changes. This point is crucial to the issue of what mix of real and price effects can be expected from demand management adjustments at the margin. If the exchange rate is likely to react very quickly (on the down side) this is one of the best prescriptions for assuring an unfavourable mix of price and real effects. Of course, the other side to this argument is the 'investment' required to create confidence in the exchange rate, which once created is a capital asset of value to demand management instruments. The political and technical act of setting up the EMS is such an 'investment'; it requires at least a convincing political commitment and a certain evidence of convergence of economic policy thinking. There is no indication whatsoever that the full EMS participants envisage slower growth and higher unemployment as a result; on the contrary the aim is to establish one precondition for stronger performance – monetary stability. It is a spur too to working harder at supply policies, which are another condition.

International Monetary Relations and Sovereignty

It would seem a little bizarre to argue that an EMS in 1979, which is less constraining than the Bretton Woods rules of 1944, could be seen as jeopardising effective national power over economic policy. As already pointed out, the latter days of the 'snake' saw relatively infrequent pre-emptive multilateral parity adjustments, miles away from the Bretton Woods style of hanging on until a fundamental disequilibrium of the balance of payments could be undeniably established.

As regards political control over conditional credit, it is not plausible to argue that the Community is a greater threat to United Kingdom sovereignty than the IMF. The United Kingdom vote has more weight in the Council of Ministers than on the Board of the IMF; the Commission and, increasingly in the future, the European Parliament are political institutions close to the realities of British politics – as of other member states. This leads sometimes to the reverse argument, that the Community would be softer in its conditions than the IMF in policy towards clients who are at the limit of creditworthiness. There is no evidence for these speculations either way in the macroeconomic policy conditions attached to Community loans extended in recent years to Italy (in a back-to-back operation with the IMF) or Ireland (the Community alone). Aside from specific loan conditions, the Community has a more diversified range of budgetary and investment financing instruments for helping the weaker economies of member states. The analogue at the global level is the World Bank, but the weaker Community economies can hardly expect special favours there.

As regards control over the world's reserve assets, the United Kingdom has plainly had no control over the dollar. London has been a major host to the vastly expanding Euro-dollar market, but this has not meant control. Indeed, the United Kingdom has been among the most reserved countries in response to ideas mooted from time to time for controlling the Euro-dollar market, because partial controls risk being diversionary rather than effective – to the benefit only of the Cayman Islands and Luxembourg, for example.

The United Kingdom has a say in the creation of SDRs (Special Drawing Rights) and is free to cast its vote in IMF negotiations as it wishes. In practice, in recent years the Community countries have found it worthwhile to prepare a joint position in these negotiations, also on questions of IMF quotas. There are no signs whatever, if anything the contrary, that the EMS will induce participating countries to be less constructive members of the IMF. However there are constraints on the speed and extent of the SDR's development as a world reserve asset; these are largely outside European control; they concern the role of the United States and the dollar on the one hand and the global membership of the IMF on the other.

United States international monetary policy has made important and positive changes in recent months – notably in November 1978 when it agreed on a more interventionist exchange-rate policy and on a more equitable distribution of the exchange risks entailed in the issue of foreign-currency denominated bonds. These moves were welcomed by the British authorities and the rest of the Community. The same economic needs for more organised and stronger exchange-rate intervention were being perceived on both sides of the Atlantic at the same time. Moreover, the prospect of a more organised European monetary bloc may have begun to remove a credibility gap that had earlier existed over whether there was in fact any conceivable alternative to a uniquely dollar-based system in which the dollar was largely exempted from active adjustment responsibilities by virtue of being pivot of the system (see Triffin [6]).

The reserve base to the international monetary system has been changing in other ways. In spite of the reluctance of the German authorities, the Deutschemark has become more used as an international reserve asset, held quite extensively by central banks outside the Group of Ten. On the European side the EMS and the ECU are moves in the direction of a more balanced system. The United Kingdom's say in the creation of ECUs as an international reserve asset could be substantial; it already does have a say, because the negotiations now beginning on the creation of the European Monetary Fund are conducted in the full Community institutions, but its weight in these negotiations would be enhanced if it was a full member.

Paradoxically, another particular concern in some quarters of British opinion is just the reverse of the sovereignty argument. This is that the EMS might be dangerous because it might be construed by the United States as an anti-dollar or anti-American initiative. Roy Jenkins has always argued straightforwardly that the EMS is neither pro- nor anti-American; it is an entirely legitimate European activity. Whatever apprehensions might have been held at earlier stages when the nature of the EMS was perhaps less clear, it is a matter of fact that the United States authorities have come to adopt a sympathetic attitude to the EMS. A recent poll of United States leaders (374 members of the Congress and administration) conducted by the Chicago Council for Foreign Relations [2] showed that 60 per cent considered the EMS to be a favourable development, as against 5 per cent who considered it to be unfavourable. Of course many questions of EMS policy lead quickly to questions of dollar policy – be it on short-run exchange-rate policy or on long-run reserve asset policy – and there will no doubt at times be matters of controversy and differences of interest to resolve. But this can be no more of an objection to the EMS *ex ante* than the mere existence of a Community negotiating position in the GATT (General Agreement on Tariffs and Trade) can be an objection to the Community's trade policy. Dr Brzezinski put it very clearly in an interview on 30 April 1979: 'If the choice is between a passive and pliant Europe, or an allied, active but occasionally contesting Europe, it is the latter which is more in keeping with our image of a stable international system.' The evolution of a Community dollar policy, and for that matter a yen policy, is a crucial area of potential EMS activity that could develop in the period ahead. The United Kingdom submits itself to certain risks by not being fully in the EMS.

Conclusions

After a few years' disappointing experience with floating exchange rates there is a general move back towards exchange-rate policies which give a stronger weight to stability. While in part reflecting this global change of inclination, the EMS is particular in being regional, in offering a choice of intervention obligations and in being part of an integrationist political structure rather than just an international one.

The United Kingdom's economic interest in participating fully in the EMS is:

(i)   to have more predictable exchange-rate relations with its main trading partners and competitors for third markets;

(ii)   to use the Community and the EMS as the most plausible means of developing an effective policy towards the dollar, the yen and the IMF;

(iii)   to have a full say in the wider implications of the Community's monetary system, linked as it is to the economic policy of other member states, and the development of Community policies and mechanisms aimed at convergence of economic performance in Europe;

(iv)   to be in a position to influence the evolution of a monetary system which is still at a formative stage and which stands to develop in the next two years with the establishment of a European Monetary Fund, as well as in the longer run with further moves towards economic and monetary union.

The EMS is not an alternative to national measures to tackle the United Kingdom's obdurate economic problems that have persisted through a variety of exchange-rate regimes in the postwar period – problems of industrial productivity, qualitative aspects of competitiveness, etc. – but it could help create a more favourable climate for tackling these problems. Exchange-rate movements over the past six years have been important to the British economy, swinging to and fro from large gains in price competitiveness at one extreme to large gains in terms of imported stabilisation at the other, and vice versa in terms of disadvantages. The EMS would imply a greater steadiness in the trade-off between the two. But it is not just a matter of trade-offs. It is also a matter of trying to organise economic and monetary policy to achieve a better combination of results in terms of stability and employment. The judgement behind the EMS is that both re-valuation-prone and devaluation-prone countries have experienced sub-potential economic performance in recent years in part because of monetary disorder and that the highly interdependent members of the European economy could do much better together with a stronger monetary system.

References
[1]   Bairoch, P., 'Geographical structure and trade balance of European foreign trade from 1800 to 1970', *Journal of European Economic History*, Winter 1974.

[2] Chicago Council on Foreign Relations, *American Public Opinion and US Foreign Policy 1979*, Chicago, 1979.

[3] Commission of the European Communities, *The Role of Public Finance in European Integration* by Sir Donald MacDougall *et al.*, Brussels, 1977.

[4] Jenkins, R., 'Europe's present challenge and future opportunity' (first Jean Monnet lecture, European University Institute, Florence, October 1977).

[5] MacDougall, Sir Donald, 'European Community budget and transfer of resources' (address to Royal Institute of International Affairs, London, January 1979).

[6] Triffin, R., 'The international role and the fate of the dollar', *Foreign Affairs*, Winter 1978–9.

[7] Williamson, J., Lamfalussy, A., Thygesen, N. *et al.* in 'EMS – the emerging European Monetary System' (ed. R. Triffin), *Bulletin of the National Bank of Belgium*, April 1979.

Comment

by C. Allsopp

Any move towards fixed exchange rates – such as the EMS – is surprising while the world economy remains in disequilibrium. Most economists think that fixity is possible only when underlying conditions are appropriate and that to seek convergence through a system which would work only if convergence occurred is to get the order of events dangerously wrong.

Michael Emerson presents clearly the considerations behind the initiative and the decision by all Community countries except Britain to join the initial phases. He also rightly observes that British policy has moved a long way towards consistency with at least the spirit of the proposals. In the event, the decision not to join but to hold the options open appears to have turned on technical difficulties. Had it not, the more fundamental issues involved in United Kingdom exchange-rate policy would, no doubt, have been more openly debated (House of Commons [1]).

One reason for the adoption of the scheme, and for the relatively favourable reception in the United Kingdom, is, no doubt, political. Relative fixity within the Community can be seen as part of the 'European ideal' and the first step towards more comprehensive Economic and Monetary Union (see Jenkins [2], for a recent revival of the case). Moreover, there has always been agreement on some of the aims of the arrangement – based partly on rhetoric in favour of greater exchange-rate stability, but also on the desirability of convergence in performance.

As is clear, however, from Michael Emerson's paper, the main reason for the political success of the EMS initiative is disillusion among officials and politicians with the experience of floating in the 1970s. Optimism that floating would be a panacea which would allow national governments to pursue domestic objectives – a major gain to national economic sovereignty – has evaporated. It is recognised that floating rates may overshoot and be destabilising, so that they actually exacerbate the external constraint on domestic action, especially if a falling rate feeds through quickly into domestic inflation. On the Continent of Europe, moreover, exchange-rate instability is blamed in some quarters for low investment in the 1970s, or even for ineffectiveness of demand management.

Disillusion with floating is reinforced by recognition of the limitations of management of exchange rates against market forces – other than by change in overall demand management policy. To some it seems only a small step further to give up exchange-rate variation altogether as a policy instrument. Others such as Michael Emerson suggest that return to the adjustable peg system – even for a region such as Europe – may actually increase the freedom of action of the authorities to change real exchange rates or manage demand.

Politically appealing as many of these arguments are, there are three obvious difficulties with them. (a) Many of them assume the favourable effects on stability and on convergence that sceptics regard as the main points at issue. (b) The EMS is often presented as if it were a necessary condition for other desirable policies – such as better demand management, or increased regional transfers, or even reform of the CAP – whereas it can be argued that all these could be introduced without it. (c) The kind of policies for Europe or for individual countries that the EMS is supposed to promote are left unspecified. Yet one of the weaknesses of the Community in recent years is that economic policy-makers disagree on what sort of lead is needed from the centre. There are important differences in diagnosis and prescription, for example on whether there should be coordinated moves on expansion or on a desirable pattern of real exchange rates. These differences impinge on the case for or against the EMS if it is seen as favouring some countries or some schools of thought against others.

This last point is particularly important in understanding the United Kingdom debate over the EMS. The apparent conversion of the last government to a high exchange-rate, or even 'monetarist', economic policy is open to several interpretations (see, for example, Treasury [3]). It is probably best, however, to regard it less as a full-blown conversion than as a commitment to external stability and a compromise, in default of any clear short-run alternative, between those who would prefer a higher and those who would prefer a lower exchange rate. Thus, controversy over the EMS has to be seen against the background of more important arguments over strategy for the United Kingdom and different views about what has gone wrong with the world economy in the 1970s. (Controversy is, moreover, likely to increase if the recent rise in sterling is maintained, or the new government decides to accept the intervention obligations of the EMS.)

Thus it is particularly difficult in the case of the United Kingdom to give the case for or against the EMS a narrow focus. But most of the economic issues can be covered under two broad headings – stability and competitiveness. The well-known problems relating to 'convergence' can be covered under the latter. If inflation does not 'converge', competitiveness will suffer (as well as employment). And if competitiveness is adversely affected, there is likely to be divergence on the real side.

Stability

No one favours unstable exchange rates. There is, however, a real question as to how damaging exchange-rate fluctuations have been in the 1970s. Much of Emerson's case rests on the proposition that they have been very deleterious – that they have redistributed inflation from revaluing to devaluing countries, that they have intensified virtuous and vicious circles, and that they are at least part of the reason for the reluctance of revaluation-prone countries, such as Germany, to take expansionary action. But even granted that the authorities in these countries have blamed exchange instability for inability to reflate, there remains the question of whether they are right to do so. The opposite view is well known and at least equally plausible. Floating exchange rates can be seen as the only feasible regime in a period of widespread disequilibrium. Movements have principally served to offset differences in inflation and in productivity performance, although they have also responded to policy differences. Actual movements in real competitiveness appear to have worked in the right direction for international adjustment. And if investment has suffered in Germany or Holland, the obvious explanation is not instability, but a rising real exchange rate combined with low demand.

The interesting questions involved here bear only marginally on the case for or against the EMS. The issue is not free floating against an adjustable peg, but managed floating as compared with the EMS. Increased stability may be an objective under either, and it is not at all clear that the EMS would have the advantage.

The objections to the adjustable peg are well known. It is worth noting, however, that it is likely to be viewed more sceptically in Britain, with a record of exchange crises, than in many continental European countries. Moreover, the Bretton Woods system coincided with relative economic decline in Britain, whereas in many countries fixed exchange rates get credit for economic success in the 1950s and 1960s. In the case of Britain, any attempt to hold to EMS limits could, in adverse circumstances, simply fail. And with an adjustable peg, such failures would, on past experience, be both expensive and destabilising.

The risk of failure is heightened by the obscurities that surround the EMS. Most important, policy *vis-à-vis* the dollar is undetermined. The European Monetary Fund is still in the future. And the mechanisms for parity change by agreement – crucial in assessing potential strains – are completely untested. As now set up the EMS looks too rigid and not comprehensive enough. In particular, if the intervention and credit mechanisms are too small, then stabilising exchange rates could be too costly in terms of destabilising domestic policy.

But it is the question of what should be stabilised that appears crucial in understanding British scepticism. (In Emerson's terms, what should be the *numéraire* of exchange-rate policy?) In 1977 and 1978 when the dollar and the Deutschemark were diverging widely the effective rate for sterling was highly stable and an EMS-type system would have been destabilising for the United Kingdom (though proponents of the system would maintain that the Deutschemark fluctuations would have been attenuated). If the intervention mechanism had been powerful enough the effective rate for sterling would have risen. Alternatively, unsuccessful attempts to maintain Deutschemark–sterling parity would have led to loss of reserves and sudden changes in either the rate or domestic policy.

This is one reason for opposition in the United Kingdom (and some other countries) to the parity grid system taken over from the 'snake'. Under the grid system, speculative forces applying to some country such as Germany would require others to intervene. As this is the essence of the arrangement, objections to it are not trivial. If the cause of the pressure were simply a random shock or speculation, there is much to be said for cooperative action against it. On the other hand, if the upward pressure were due, or thought to be due, to an inappropriate German domestic policy or exchange rate, then it should be the Germans who should adjust.

Under the parity grid system two currencies always 'reach their intervention limits simultaneously. The important point, however, is that the effects of gains and losses in reserves are not symmetrical – the pressure on the weaker economy to adjust being much the stronger. Thus opposition to the parity grid principle signifies deeper worries, implying perhaps that existing or prospective European exchange rates are undesirable or domestic policies in need of change. It then matters greatly which rates and policies are in fact changed. Of course, if countries agreed on what pattern of exchange rates and what policy for particular countries would be appropriate, then the parity grid would not lead to strains. Presumably consultation on policy and parity changes by agreement would then be amicable and effective. In reality, however, conflicts are inevitable. The compromise of using a divergence indicator to show which country is out of line, with a 'presumption' that the divergent country should change policy or its central rate, may not help much in resolving conflicts of interest, or of diagnosis, that are bound to arise.

The underlying disagreements are most obvious in relation to the dollar. It is probably not over-simplifying to characterise the German position as being that most of the recent dollar problem has been due to inappropriate United States policy. In that case it would be quite reasonable for all other countries to be simultaneously affected by a weak or strong dollar and for Europe to float as a group, much as was intended with the 'snake' agreement of 1972. The British position has been more sympathetic to the Americans. The problem has been compounded by German reluctance either to take expansionary action or to accept the consequences in terms of a rising real exchange rate. These fears were expressed by the Labour government insisting that the EMS 'should provide a basis for improved economic growth and higher employment in the Community, rather than impose *further* constraints on growth and employment' (Treasury [3]). Such worries go far beyond the narrower question of the exchange-rate regime.

From the time of the EMS initiative until the decision not to join, the crucial difficulty from the point of view of stability appeared to be the question of what should be stabilised. The effective rate seemed preferable to the rate against European currencies, being more in line with market forces, and its stabilisation did not appear to conflict too sharply with existing domestic policy. Clearly, however, the difference between stabilising the effective rate and obligations under the EMS would be small if European currencies and the dollar ceased to diverge. Does this mean that entry into the EMS would become appropriate in the absence of a 'dollar storm'? I do not think it does – for a number of reasons:

(a)   the difficulties that arise from adjustable pegs would still be present;

(b)   shocks, such as the Iranian crisis, are likely to occur, and it may be better to take them on the rate of exchange rather than by sharp changes in domestic policy;

(c)   most important, the effective rate of exchange may not be the appropriate target for intervention policy. One obvious alternative would be constant competitiveness. Another would be to manage the exchange rate so as to achieve, over the medium term, a balance of payments target (given a target for domestic activity). There are many who argue that the appropriate target for stabilisation is the domestic economy, not the exchange rate. Beyond a certain point the two are in conflict.

Although recently policy has looked consistent with entry into the EMS and sterling too strong rather than too weak, almost any medium-term assessment of the British economy suggests that the effective exchange rate will have to fall in the future – substantially on most analyses. The implication is that the exchange rate would have to be adjusted within the EMS – with the risk of instability if such moves were delayed – or domestic growth would have to be very low or even negative. The only alternative would be that inflation would adjust, or be adjusted, to produce convergence and consistency between internal and external policy. Desirable as they would be, is it realistic or feasible and what are the costs of failure?

It has become fashionable to suggest, as Emerson does, that the United Kingdom has no option, that no trade-off is involved and that control of inflation is a necessary condition for all else. It would however be foolish to discount the risk of failure. And in the short term there is a crucial set of questions about the order of events. Would the EMS promote convergence – of inflation and of growth? Or would it hinder the process? This raises the second set of questions relating to the effects of the EMS on the competitiveness of the United Kingdom and the consequences of any changes that might result.

Competitiveness

The effect on competitiveness of any given exchange-rate policy is a matter of controversy and empirical uncertainty. There is much to be said for posing the problem conditionally in terms of the risk of certain outcomes and the probable costs involved if undesirable outcomes eventuate. If there is a strong probability that adoption of the EMS intervention obligations would have unfavourable effects on competitiveness, and if the costs of such a result are high, then the combined weight is heavily against adoption of the policy.

Arguments in favour of the EMS usually contain some mixture of the following elements: (a) that the benefits dominate any costs envisaged; (b) that effects on competitiveness would be small, short-lived, or even favourable; (c) that even if competitiveness were adversely affected, the costs would not be great, or even – on an extreme view – that the result would be favourable to productivity. I want to concentrate on (b) and (c). I shall argue that competitiveness is likely to be adversely affected, and that the consequences could be very unfavourable.

One thing must be made clear at the start. There are other ways of decreasing competitiveness than by joining the EMS and they include the high exchange-rate policy. Most would agree that the EMS would tend to lead to a higher nominal rate for a high-inflation country. To avoid such a result rather frequent changes in the rate would probably be needed – which would raise the other difficulties of instability under the adjustable peg system. For clarity, therefore, I shall consider a fixed nominal exchange rate as compared to one that is free to depreciate – or be depreciated. The question of whether the EMS would operate in this way is taken up at the end. The costs then appear as the costs of giving up the option of exchange-rate depreciation.

There are two important cases where the costs of giving up this option appear small because competitiveness is unaffected (at least in terms of efficiency wages measured against foreign currency). First, a region or country may be already so closely integrated with another that depreciation cannot affect relative real wages and competitiveness. The most obvious case would be if there was parity in pay bargaining between areas (so that relative *real* wages were fixed). Secondly, real wages and competitiveness may be completely determinate and determined *domestically*, so that they are independent of the exchange rate. In both cases devaluation is ineffective (for example, in dealing with unemployment). The models rest, however, on diametrically opposed assumptions about wage determination.

Fixity of real wages between regions is an assumption commonly made in analysing the regional problem. If wages cannot adjust, a low-productivity region will be uncompetitive and will usually end up with a fall in employment. The loss from joining a common currency area or otherwise giving up the possibility of devaluation would be small and the potential gain from integration – for example, through regional policies – could be substantial. The other case assumes that the regional problem – due to relative fixity of (real) wages – cannot exist. There is no problem of parity in pay bargaining. Real wages are completely determined by domestic conditions *and* are independent of the money supply or the exchange rate. They move, broadly, with productivity and real competitiveness is unaffected by the exchange rate. Such a model would have the best chance of realism at a low degree of integration with completely separate national labour markets.

Both models enter the debate on the EMS. Emerson cites the increasing integration of the United Kingdom with other European countries as an argument in favour. The other approach is familiar from the writings of monetarist or international monetarist economists (though they are usually against fixed exchange rates or the EMS for other reasons). A case could be made on either ground, but not on both simultaneously. And there is an important practical implication. It is when real wages are neither fully determined by comparability criteria nor fully flexible and nationally determined that giving up the exchange-rate option may be most costly. (The reason is, of course. that the plausible application of incompatible equilibrium conditions is an indication of disequilibrium. And with disequilibrium there is a kind of economic indeterminacy in the real-wage.)

Measured in a common currency, there have been vast movements over the last decade in relative real wages between countries and particularly between the United Kingdom and Northern Europe. The latest data from the Swedish Employers' Federation suggest that by 1977, for manufacturing, total labour costs (including social charges) in Germany, Belgium and the Netherlands and Scandinavia exceeded United States levels, while in the United Kingdom they were less than half those in North America or Northern Europe. Thus the regional model based on comparability of wages does not appear to apply (except briefly to those countries in the Deutschemark zone which operated the previous 'snake' system). It may of course apply more in the future if integration proceeds and wage bargaining becomes international. But that is not a prospect to be welcomed. And it does not add up to a case for giving up exchange-rate flexibility on the way – quite the contrary.

In the United Kingdom the political attraction of the EMS appears to be associated with the swing in fashion towards monetarist and international monetarist modes of thought and the idea that a high exchange rate can help in bringing down inflation with little cost in terms of competitiveness. Thus appeal is being made to the second of the two cases above, in which the exchange rate does not affect real wages or competitiveness but only nominal wages and prices. This is not the place to rehearse the objections to the assumptions on which such models depend. The important relationship is the interaction between the exchange rate and inflation. Such an interaction is extremely plausible and there is nothing specifically monetarist about it. For an individual small country such a mechanism could equally well be combined with international Keynesian views of global problems in the world economy. It can also be tested empirically.

In practice, no one believes that competitiveness is unaffected by exchange-rate changes in the short term. The empirical question then centres on the speed of the pass-through to prices and wages and on the eventual effects. In the National Institute model, exchange-rate depreciation improves competitiveness even in the long run. In both the Treasury and the London Business School models, the *assumption* is made that, *ceteris paribus*, there will be in the long run a complete pass-through from exchange-rate changes to money wages. In the Treasury model the lag is substantial so that there is a useful improvement of competitiveness for a number of years. In the London Business School model the lag is shorter, but still amounts to years rather than months.

Such empirical results need to be interpreted with great care – especially as the accent in macroeconomic models is usually on short-term simulation. There are a number of difficulties. First, the period of floating is short and substantially disturbed, so that any empirical estimates of the extent and speed of pass-through are bound to be difficult. Secondly, in those models that have complete pass-through, the long-term property is frequently imposed *a priori*. (Although it may be consistent with the data it is not really tested.) Thirdly, given that there are substantial short-term effects on important economic variables such as competitiveness and profitability, the *ceteris paribus* clause is important. During adjustment investment, output and productivity could all be affected and in turn affect competitiveness.

The second difficulty is the key one. In considering determination of money wages it is rather natural to impose proportionality with prices in the 'long run' whatever the underlying view of the economy. This is because for large enough changes in prices one would presumably want the property that there would be similarly large changes in money wages – otherwise the real wage would, implicitly, be variable over an implausibly large range. But the empirical question at issue here is precisely whether relative prices and real wages can change – perhaps within some relatively narrow band of feasible values. In the short run all the evidence suggests they can and do. The longer-term property assumed by Treasury and the London Business School alike has little bearing on the real empirical issues at stake.

Competitiveness does change, substantially and for quite long periods. In the United Kingdom there is evidence of an erosion of competitiveness before devaluation in 1967. And in recent years the United States has become more competitive, Germany and Japan less so. The question is whether these changes owed anything to exchange-rate policy. The view that in the longer term competitiveness is unaffected by exchange-rate policy is very largely an *a priori* position and it is difficult to see how it could be either supported or refuted by the data. In practice, however, the issue is confused by the accepted empirical observation that recent changes in competitiveness have been much smaller than changes in nominal exchange rates. Though such an observation in a period of high inflation is consistent with almost any view of the mechanisms involved, it may none the less appear in political terms to support those who believe that in the long term exchange-rate changes have no real effects.

Though it can be argued that the crucial issue in looking at the

EMS is the extent to which competitiveness would be affected, disagreements do exist on the consequences of any deterioration. Most simulations, however, suggest substantial effects. Those obtained from the Cambridge Economic Policy Group's model and provided to the Expenditure Committee by their specialist adviser, Terry Ward, traced the effects of a fixed exchange rate as compared with constant competitiveness, with various assumptions about the development of money wages – treated as autonomous. At a 10 per cent annual growth in earnings the effect on GDP was estimated at 5.1 per cent by 1981. Adverse effects would also be suggested by the Treasury or the London Business School models. The significance of changes in competitiveness in this context is, however, sometimes denied. It is suggested, for example, that British trade performance is affected more by non-price elements than by prices or wages. Or that the British problem is low productivity rather than high wages and that the 'soft option' of exchange-rate depreciation is no solution to longer-term difficulties. On an extreme view, a high exchange rate with deteriorating competitiveness is regarded as beneficial both to price stability and to productivity. There are elements of this in the Green Paper of the Labour government, where it is stated: 'Once a virtuous circle of exchange rate stability, lower costs, and greater stimulus to efficiency has been established, the effects of the initial loss of price competitiveness may be removed.' Presumably the idea is that if inflation rates do not converge sufficiently, then productivity performance will (Treasury [3]). This seems to carry the curious implication that Britain's poor productivity performance could be remedied by greater wage pressure so long as inflation was controlled.

In fact the main danger in a reduction in competitiveness is more or less the opposite of the virtuous circle appealed to here. If competitiveness deteriorated, then unit labour costs measured in a common currency would tend to rise in relation to international prices. There would be risk of a squeeze on industrial profitability which might mean even greater import penetration and lower investment. Productivity in the short and long run would be adversely affected. In such circumstances, deflationary policies to protect the balance of payments would lead to even lower growth, greater problems for firms and further de-industrialisation. For those who believe that such an outcome is possible the importance of competitiveness is very great. What is at stake is not internal versus external balance in the short run, but longer-run growth or decline.

But why, it may be objected, should the EMS affect competitiveness like this? If the problem arises because of the relationship of real wages to productivity, should it not be as easy or as difficult to improve the situation with or without the EMS? There is a standard argument. In a world of imperfect information and uncertainty, with realistic wage bargaining mechanisms, it may be easier to achieve a given result on wages (measured internationally) by the exchange rate than through domestic adjustments. The principal reason is that there is a kind of 'public good' problem in changing wages which would exist even in the absence of real-wage resistance. Exchange-rate depreciation, which appears neutral distributionally (though it may not be), offers a mechanism for changing wages without interfering in the bargaining process and without achieving consensus.

This is not to say that the exchange rate can easily be used as an instrument to improve competitiveness. In the presence of real-wage resistance or of 'target wage' behaviour it may be impossible without an unacceptable cost in terms of inflation. But the converse does not follow, owing to the obvious asymmetry. An inappropriate exchange-rate policy can worsen competitiveness with the greatest of ease. And, as many countries have found, it may be necessary to devalue to offset the effects on industry of failures to cure inflation.

Fundamentally, the problem with the 'high' exchange-rate policy, and with the EMS if it raises the rate, is that it may not have the desired effects on wage inflation. It appears altogether too weak an instrument. The accent needs to be on domestic policies to reduce inflation and improve performance. If these succeed then, and only then, would a relatively fixed exchange rate become appropriate. Without 'convergence' the consequence would be either instability due to frequent changes of parity within the EMS, or a deterioration in competitiveness with at least the risk of serious longer-term effects on British industry.

Concluding Remarks

Michael Emerson points to the continuing economic problems in the world, in Europe and in the United Kingdom, and suggests on a number of counts that the EMS could help. He rightly notes concern about the way in which floating rates have operated and about instability. He believes that European integration can pay economic dividends. This appears to be based in part on the desirability of better

policy coordination within Europe and in part on the view that scope
for domestic action could be increased (in demand management, for
example) and the mix between price and real effects from expansionary policy improved.

Many of the possible effects he points to would be generally regarded
as desirable. The real question at issue, however, is whether the EMS
as currently conceived would operate in this way. Would it, in particular, foster desirable policies within Europe, and would it increase
rather than diminish economic sovereignty for the United Kingdom?

It is easy to suggest desirable policies for Europe – everyone no
doubt has views on what they should be. The hard thing is to get
agreement. The convergence in policy positions that Emerson notes is
good or bad depending on whether the policies are regarded as good
or bad. Within the United Kingdom present policy is highly contro-
versial. And controversy over domestic policy colours almost every
aspect of the debate over the EMS. The point of agreement is that the
EMS obligations would impose an additional constraint on policy.
This would not matter if domestic policy were in any case consistent
with the EMS, but all economists can point to possible sources of conflict.

The possibility of conflict between domestic policy and the
exchange-rate regime means that the EMS looks more desirable the
less rigid it is. When first suggested it might have been anything,
ranging from a kind of recycling scheme within Europe with long-term
balance of payments finance for deficit countries wishing to expand
without the fear of exchange-market reactions to a rigid Bretton
Woods system with a possible bias towards devaluation or deflation
and loss of competitiveness for weaker countries. It actually looks
remarkably like the 'snake', although it is still most uncertain how it
will in fact operate, or even whether it is feasible if exchange-market
instability increases again.

To be against the EMS is not to be against moves to mitigate
instability in exchange markets. But there is a real question as to what
should be stabilised. Would business confidence really be increased by
stability in Europe of nominal exchange rates? Or would a policy of
maintaining constant competitiveness be more favourable? And is the
adjustable peg preferable to managed floating? These questions are the
more important the less likely it is that convergence will occur easily
and rapidly.

Finally, if the EMS can work at all it is implied that exchange rates can be managed. At minimum this involves stabilisation. But if the authorities succeed in managing rates the difficult question must arise as to what the pattern of real rates within Europe (and for Europe relative to other areas) *ought* to be. And that question cannot even be discussed without some view as to what domestic policies ought to be. Given conflicting interests between countries and the well-known ideological differences, agreement or compromise may be hard to achieve. Paradoxically, the more successful the EMS became in controlling exchange rates the greater the potential tensions would become. They are muted now only because floating rates are impersonal and the authorities impotent in the face of market forces.

References

[1] House of Commons, *First Report of the Expenditure Committee Session 1977–78. The European Monetary System*, London, HMSO, 1978.

[2] Jenkins, R., 'Europe's present challenge and future opportunity' (first Jean Monnet lecture, European University Institute, Florence, October 1977).

[3] Treasury, *The European Monetary System*, Cmnd 7405, London, HMSO, 1978.

5 Exchange-rate Objectives and Macroeconomic Adjustment in the United Kingdom

by M. Beenstock and T. Burns*

Introduction

Fixing the exchange rate essentially replaces a price-adjustment mechanism (of exchange-rate variability) by a quantity-adjustment mechanism (of balance of payments variability). This paper focuses upon the issues in positive economics that are raised by reversion to a fixed exchange rate for sterling. Two main questions are considered:

(a) How is the United Kingdom likely to respond to a discrete change in the exchange rate? In particular, is it the case that exchange-rate changes by the United Kingdom have no long-term balance of payments benefit, and if so why?

(b) If the United Kingdom joins the EMS the sterling rate will be fixed to some extent. What effects are likely, especially in terms of inflation, economic activity and the balance of payments? In addition, what fiscal and monetary policies will be required if the United Kingdom remains a member?

These empirical issues are considered later, while in the next section we set out the theoretical premises upon which the analysis is based.

* We are indebted to Anne Aves, Tony Gosling, Heather Morley and Peter War-burton, who undertook the estimation and computational work involved in this paper. The study reported here has been supported by the Social Science Research Council, to whom we are extremely grateful.

The empirical relevance of these premises for the United Kingdom is discussed in the following section; our conclusions are in the final section.

Theory

Our basic theoretical premises are essentially neoclassical and restate the monetary theory of the balance of payments in a disequilibrium setting. We take the view that the balance of payments, output and the price level must be compatible with portfolio balance in the long run, although not necessarily in the short run. This implies that the model will have the following long-term properties (*ceteris paribus*) when the exchange rate is fixed but adjustable:

(a)   A rise in the exchange rate will cause the money supply to fall by a proportionate amount in equilibrium. Balance of payments deficits generated during the adjustment will die out as the new equilibrium is reached. The exchange rate therefore has no lasting balance of payments effect.

(b)   The domestic money stock varies proportionately with the quantity of money abroad, measured in a common currency. Therefore the balance of payments will depend on the rate of growth of the quantity of money abroad as well as the rate of growth of the exchange rate.

(c)   The balance of payments varies adversely and in line with the rate of domestic credit expansion (DCE).

(d)   The domestic price level varies proportionately with the world money supply and inversely with the exchange rate.

(e)   Output tends towards a 'natural' level, so that booms and slumps are self-correcting.

These properties must obviously be distinguished from those of 'Keynesian' models, where the balance of payments depends on income and relative prices and where demand pressures do not necessarily have any inflationary consequence. The neoclassical approach allocates to 'Keynesian' factors a short-term role, but extends the analysis to allow for portfolio balance, which dominates the steady-state analysis.

The model

The logical structure of our model focuses on the principal variables:

the money supply, output and determination of wages and prices. It is cast in the context of fixed but adjustable exchange rates because the analysis of the EMS necessitates this. However, it may easily be re-expressed with floating rates.

The monetary theory of the balance of payments assumes a relationship between the domestic money stock (M), the world money stock expressed in world currency (Mw), the exchange rate (E), domestic GDP (Y) and world GDP (Yw). This relationship is implied by three assumptions. First, demand for money in the home country is homogenous in the price level (P) and depends positively on GDP in real terms (all variables here and in the following equations in this section are logarithms unless otherwise stated):

$$M = P + aY \tag{1}$$

Secondly, a similar relationship applies abroad:

$$Mw = Pw + a_w Yw \tag{2}$$

Thirdly, the domestic–foreign price ratio tends towards a constant (k) in common currency:

$$P + E - Pw = k \tag{3}$$

where k responds to shifts in real variables such as preferences or factor supplies. These assumptions imply the following relationship between money, GDP and the exchange rate:

$$M - aY + E - Mw + a_w Yw = k \tag{4}$$

Although Johnson [7] and others originally proposed this theory by assuming perfect elasticities of substitution between traded goods, it has since been shown (for example, Beenstock [2], Chapter 3) that the same result is robust with respect to a wide variety of specifications and is implied by a broad class of econometric models.

Equation (4) is an equilibrium condition which might not be satisfied in the short term. If the lefthand side of the equation is greater than k, the balance of payments will tend to move into deficit, so that M falls in an equilibrating fashion. M will tend to increase faster when DCE expands faster. Therefore the change in the money supply will depend on a combination of domestic and external considerations:

$$\dot{M} = a_1 DCE - a_2(M + E + Yw - Y - Mw) \tag{5}$$

Assuming in the interests of simplicity that $a = a_w = 1$, since the change in the money supply is equal to DCE plus the balance of payments (B), equation (5) could be rewritten as a balance of payments equation. If the exchange rate is 'managed' so that the adjustment to monetary imbalances is spread between exchange-rate and balance of payments adjustments, equation (5) may be adapted as

$$\dot{E} + \frac{B}{M} = a_1' DCE - a_2'(M + E + Yw - Y - Mw) \qquad (5')$$

In equilibrium, as equation (1) implies, domestic output, the price level and the money supply are related. In a disequilibrium model the change in aggregate demand is therefore likely to depend upon the excess supply of real balances. In equation (6) we also assume that the rate of growth of aggregate demand depends upon that of real money balances. However, details such as this rarely alter the dynamics of the model; its steady-state character is unaffected.

In an open economy it will be necessary to take account of external influences on aggregate demand. As domestic prices rise relatively to world prices, net external demand and aggregate demand will fall. However, the opposite will occur when external economic activity grows faster. Therefore, our hypothesis is:

$$\dot{Y} = b_1(\dot{M} - \dot{P}) - b_2(\dot{P} + \dot{E} - \dot{P}w) + b_3(M - P - Y) + b_4\dot{Y}w \qquad (6)$$

In accordance with equation (1), equation (6) implies that external factors exert only a temporary influence on aggregate demand.

An alternative formulation is that external factors influence domestic economic activity in the long term as well as the short term, and that output is also determined by the long-run factors that determine supply. In this case equation (6) must be replaced by equation (6'):

$$\dot{Y} = b_1(\dot{M} - \dot{P}) - b_2(\dot{P} + \dot{E} - \dot{P}w) - b_3(Y - \bar{Y}) + b_4(Yw - \bar{Y}w) - b_5(P + E - Pw) \qquad (6')$$

so that in the long run Y depends upon $\bar{Y}$, Yw, $\bar{Y}w$, P, E, and Pw, where $\bar{Y}w$ represents the 'natural' rate of world output.

In our model inflation is assumed to reflect a wide variety of factors. If aggregate demand is above the 'natural' or full-employment level of output ($\bar{Y}$) demand-pull inflation will ensue. The same applies when world prices rise relatively to domestic prices and domestic goods become cheap relatively to goods produced abroad. In equation (7) this consideration is represented by $c_2(P + E - Pw)$, which may also be taken to represent cost-push inflation due to higher import prices. In addition to import costs it is assumed that prices must reflect domestic wage costs (W). Therefore, equation (7) represents a generalised demand-pull, cost-push inflationary process:

$$\dot{P} = c_1(Y - \bar{Y}) - c_2(P + E - Pw) - c_3(P - W) \tag{7}$$

Finally, the rate of change of wages is determined through an augmented Phillips curve:

$$\dot{W} = d_1(Y - \bar{Y}) + d_2\dot{P} \tag{8}$$

If $d_2 = 1$, money illusion does not exist and the Phillips curve will be vertical in the long run.

Integrating the model

The model is summarised in equation (9), where equations (5), (6), (7) and (8) are represented and where $D = d/dt$ is the differential operator

$$\begin{bmatrix} D + a_2 & -a_2 & 0 & 0 \\ b_3 + b_1 D & -b_3 - D & -b_3 - (b_1 + b_2)D & 0 \\ 0 & c_1 & -(c_2 + c_3) - D & c_3 \\ 0 & d_1 & d_2 D & -D \end{bmatrix} \begin{bmatrix} M \\ Y \\ P \\ W \end{bmatrix} =$$

$$\begin{bmatrix} a_2(Mw - E - Yw) + a_1 DCE \\ b_2\dot{E} - b_4\dot{Y}w \\ c_1\bar{Y} + c_2 E - c_2 Pw \\ d_1\bar{Y} \end{bmatrix} \tag{9}$$

the determinant of the system is:

$$-D^4 + \beta D^3 + \gamma D^2 + \delta D + \lambda \tag{10}$$

where:

$$\beta = a_2(b_1 - 1) - c_1(b_1 - b_2) - b_3$$

$$\gamma = (c_2 + c_3 - c_3 d_2)[a_2(b_1 - 1) - b_3] - c_1 b_3 - d_1 c_3(b_1 + b_2)$$
$$\delta = -b_3(d_1 c_3 + a_2 c_1) - a_2 d_1 c_3(b_1 + b_2)$$
$$\lambda = -a_2 d_1 c_3 b_3$$

Clearly (10) implies that the model may not be stable and, even if the stability conditions are satisfied, the underlying adjustment process could quite easily be oscillatory. Consider for example the sequence of events that follows a revaluation. Equation (5) implies that prices will fall. The critical question is whether real balances rise or fall. If they fall, output will contract because competitiveness has been adversely affected. The recession will put further downward pressure on wages and prices and a monotonic adjustment path will be generated.

But the constellation of elasticities could imply that real balances rise. This would happen if the elasticity of the price level with respect to the exchange rate (c_2) was greater than the elasticity of the money supply with respect to the exchange rate (a_2). In this case an oscillatory path might be generated, where initially output falls owing to loss of competitiveness, but after a point the positive real balance dominates and output rises. Thus revaluation may cause an expansion of aggregate demand and devaluation a contraction – an aspect of exchange-rate policy which is often ignored.

The steady state
The details of the dynamics of the model cannot be generalised and the length and profiles of the lags are an empirical matter. In contrast the steady-state properties of the model are simple enough. The steady-state solutions for the principal endogenous variables may be derived from equation (9) as:

$$M = Mw - E + \frac{a_1}{a_2}DCE + \hat{Y} - Yw \qquad \text{(i)}$$

$$Y = \hat{Y} \qquad \text{(ii)} \left.\right\} \text{(11)}$$

$$P = Mw - E + \frac{a_1}{a_2}DCE - Yw \qquad \text{(iii)}$$

This assumes the exogenous variables to be constant (that is, $Yw = 0$). The first equation states that revaluation results in a proportionate fall in the money stock, implying that exchange-rate changes do not have lasting balance of payments effects. An increase in the world money stock induces a proportionate increase in the domestic money stock, while an increase in relative income causes the equilibrium money stock to rise. The equation also implies that DCE has a permanent effect on the level of the money stock. However, this is an implication of the lags in the model – the more money the authorities pump into the system the higher will be the level of the money stock, since it takes time before DCE is fully reflected in balance of payments deficits. Since in equilibrium the rate of change of the money supply does not depend on DCE, we may conclude that the equilibrium balance of payments flow is equal and opposite to DCE

$$B = -DCE \qquad (12)$$

The second equation simply states that the economy will revert to the 'natural' rate of output in the steady state, that is, the model is self-equilibrating with respect to output. Finally, the third equation (11,iii) takes the same form as the first. Since the domestic money stock adjusts to world influences, so must the domestic price level. A revaluation eventually results in a proportionate fall in the price level through a mixture of adjustments implied by equations (5) and (7) in particular. Exchange-rate policy is neutral since it only affects nominal variables, not the real economy.

If instead of equation (6) the model is solved using equation (6'), its steady-state properties are directly affected. The basic difference is that equation (11,ii) becomes

$$Y = \hat{Y} + \frac{b_4}{b_3}(Yw - \hat{Y}w) - \frac{b_5}{b_3}(P + E - Pw) \qquad (13)$$

Since $(P + E - Pw) = k$ from equation (3), it follows that output equals its 'natural' rate when world output is at its natural rate.

Rational expectations and time lags
A growing body of theoretical and empirical research (for example, Beenstock [2], Fair [5]) shows that rational expectations will radically alter the dynamic structure of economic models. In general, rational expectations will quicken the responses of nominal variables and reduce those of real variables. In the limit lags may disappear completely so that instantaneous neutrality prevails. This tends to happen when an economic event becomes perfectly anticipated.

Expectations of the endogenous variables in the model were not specified; therefore the lag structures implied by equation (10) will generally be misleading. It is easy to see that they can vanish completely. The model implies that when the exchange rate is devalued by 5 per cent prices and the money supply both rise by 5 per cent. If agents fully anticipate the price rise they will tend to rise immediately, since everybody wishes to be on the right side of the market. Likewise, wage rates will rise instantaneously. Owing to transactions on the capital account of the balance of payments, the money supply will rise by 5 per cent too, for if it rises less interest rates will go up, which will generate capital inflows in anticipation of capital gains on domestic bonds. On this basis the money supply will immediately rise by 5 per cent.

In general, because of risk and risk aversion these responses are unlikely to be instantaneous. But the lags could be substantially curtailed by rational expectations. Indeed simulation exercises drawn from conventional econometric models which ignore rational expectations must be carefully qualified, as indeed is done below.

Empirical Estimates

In this section we present the empirical estimates of the key relationships. This is necessary as it is important that the reader examines the lag pattern of the equations. The equations have all been estimated with the error correction mechanism suggested by Davidson *et al.* [4]. (The elements of this methodology are set out in Appendix 1.) This enables us both to estimate the short-run dynamics of the relationship and to test certain long-run characteristics. The long-run characteristics of the equations are consistent with the model set out earlier. As will be seen these characteristics are reflected in the data and have not been obtained by imposing coefficients arbitrarily. We do not present alternative specifications, but concentrate on the final form of the model.

The model itself contains behavioural equations and identities. However, space does not permit a full description, which may be found in Beenstock and Burns [3]. Instead we focus on the elements identified in the previous section.

Prices

We report two price equations based on equation (7); one for wholesale prices (PIMO) and other for consumer prices (PC). (Appendix 2 contains a glossary of symbols; log means natural logarithm through-out.)

$$\Delta \log \text{PIMO} = -0.014 + 0.18 \Delta \log \text{PIMO}_{-1} + 0.1 \Delta \log \text{PIMI}$$
$$\quad\quad (1.3) \quad\quad (1.9) \quad\quad\quad\quad\quad (5.0)$$

$$+ 0.12 \Delta \log \text{PIMI}_{-1} + 0.38 \Delta \log \text{WPWVA}_{-2}$$
$$\quad (5.2) \quad\quad\quad\quad (4.5)$$

$$- 0.08 \Delta \log \text{E}_{-2} + 0.12 \Delta \log \text{ULCM}_{-1}$$
$$\quad (2.5) \quad\quad\quad (2.3)$$

$$- 0.064 \log \left(\frac{\text{PIMO}}{\text{WPW}\pounds} \right)_{-3} - 0.044 \log \left(\frac{\text{PIMO}}{\text{ULCM}} \right)_{-2}$$
$$\quad (3.1) \quad\quad\quad\quad\quad (1.9)$$

$$- 0.0123 \sum (\log \text{PIMO} - \log \text{PIMO*})_{-2}$$
$$\quad (2.6)$$

$$- 0.02 \text{ VAT} + 0.007 \text{ Q1} + 0.005 \text{ Q2} + 0.001 \text{ Q3}$$
$$\quad (5.1) \quad\quad\quad (4.1) \quad\quad\quad (2.7) \quad\quad\quad (0.7)$$

$$+ 0.0008 \text{ t} \quad\quad\quad\quad\quad\quad\quad\quad\quad\quad\quad (14)$$
$$\quad (2.4)$$

$$\bar{R}^2 = 0.941$$
$$\text{DW} = 1.94$$
$$\text{SE} = 0.0045$$
$$6401\text{--}7802$$
$$\chi^2_{12} = 8.4$$

Equation (14) was estimated on quarterly data, as indeed were all the equations reported in this section. It states that wholesale price inflation is influenced by a combination of cost-push and demand-pull. The former is represented by material input costs (PIMI) and unit labour costs in manufacturing and the latter by prices of foreign competitors expressed in sterling (WPW£). Equation (14) entails derivative, proportional and integral correction mechanisms as described in Appendix 1. Its steady-state solution is

$$\log \text{PIMO} = 0.6 \log \text{WPW}\pounds + 0.4 \log \text{ULCM} \quad\quad (15)$$

which suggests that in the long run world prices have a 60 per cent weight in wholesale price determination and domestic wage costs a 40 per cent weight. There is a time trend in (14) that does not appear in (15). This is because the time trend in the estimated equation reflects the method of computing the integral term PIMO* and does not imply that in the steady state United Kingdom prices tend upwards relatively to world prices in sterling and labour costs. This is explained in equations A(5) and A(6) of Appendix 1. The same issue arises later with equations (18) and (19), where a time trend appears in the estimated function but is not applicable to the steady-state solution.

Consumer prices are in turn related to wholesale prices, total unit labour costs and indirect taxes. In addition, the pressure of demand (represented by GDPTOX) directly affects consumer price inflation.

$$\Delta \log PC = \underset{(9.4)}{0.4264} \, \Delta \log PIMO + \underset{(8.7)}{0.1112} \sum_{i=0}^{2} \Delta \log ULC_{-i}$$

$$+ \underset{(5.0)}{0.0474} \, \Delta \log TEA^* + \underset{(2.9)}{0.0265} \, \Delta \log TEA^*_{-1}$$

$$+ \underset{(3.2)}{0.0982} \log GDPTOX_{-1} - \underset{(4.9)}{0.031} \log \left(\frac{PC}{PIMO} \right)_{-1}$$

$$- \underset{(3.7)}{0.064} \log \left(\frac{PC}{ULC} \right)_{-2} - \underset{(0.4)}{0.0000225} \, t$$

$$+ \underset{(4.9)}{0.0128} \, PTAXDMY - \underset{(3.3)}{0.0039} \, Q1$$

$$+ \underset{(2.4)}{0.0028} \, Q2 + \underset{(3.3)}{0.029} \tag{16}$$

$$\bar{R}^2 = 0.948$$
$$DW = 1.89$$
$$SE = 0.0034$$
$$6304\text{--}7802$$
$$\chi^2_{12} = 12.6$$

Unlike equation (14), equation (16) only contains derivative and proportional error feedback mechanisms and its steady-state solution is:

$$\log PC = 0.33 \, PIMO + 0.66 \, ULC + 1.034 \, GDPTOX + 0.000024 \, t \tag{17}$$

that is, wholesale prices have a 33 per cent weight in consumer prices. Although indirect tax rates (TEA*) disappear in equation (17), they have a short-term effect in equation (16).

Wages

The wage equation is based upon equation (8) and plays an important role in the determination of prices. However, as equation (18) indicates, prices play an important part in wage determination. Therefore, equations (14), (16) and (18) interact in a complex way and this interaction has a critical bearing on the transmission mechanism of the exchange rate to wages and prices. Once more the wage equation incorporates derivative, proportional and integral error feedback mechanisms.

$$\Delta \log \text{AEM} = \underset{(2.6)}{0.059} + \underset{(1.0)}{0.13} \Delta \log \text{PIMO} + \underset{(2.2)}{0.35} \Delta \log \text{PC}_{-1}$$

$$+ \underset{(3.7)}{0.3245} \Delta \log \text{PRDM} + \underset{(0.8)}{0.0547} \Delta \log \text{PRDM}_{-1}$$

$$+ \underset{(3.4)}{0.4351} \Delta \log \text{RNDI*} + \underset{(4.2)}{0.041} \sum_{i=0}^{11} \log \text{GDPTOX}_{-i}$$

$$- \underset{(3.9)}{0.0449} \text{DV3DWK} - \underset{(4.4)}{0.0113} \text{YDUM}$$

$$- \underset{(3.5)}{0.2017} \log\left(\frac{\text{AEM}}{\text{PIMO}.\text{PRDM}.\text{RNDI*}}\right)_{-1}$$

$$- \underset{(2.4)}{0.02026} \sum (\log \text{AEM} - \log \text{AEM*})_{-2} - \underset{(2.4)}{0.001077} \, t \tag{18}$$

$$\bar{R}^2 = 0.753$$
$$\text{DW} = 1.3$$
$$\text{SE} = 0.0086$$
$$6303\text{–}7802$$
$$\chi^2_{12} = 28.1$$

Earnings changes are responsive to the going rate of inflation measured by both the wholesale index (a measure of what employers can afford to pay) and consumer prices (a measure of the reduction in purchasing power). The ratio of real national disposable income to output is included to pick up the extent to which we would expect that an increase in prices resulting from an adverse movement of the terms of trade would not lead to wage increases as firms could not afford to pay such increases. The dummy variable YDUM is an incomes policy dummy which takes the value of unity in 6603 to 6903 and again in 7503 to 7703. Because of the operation of the stabiliser term this implies that incomes policy effects would only be temporary, as once they cease to be operative the stabiliser term acts as a 'catch-up' variable and the integral mechanism will lead to some overshooting.

The long-run relationship is

$$\log \text{AEM} = \log (\text{PIMO} . \text{PRDM} . \text{RNDI*}) + 2.44 \log \text{GDPTOX} \tag{19}$$

This implies that in the long run earnings move in line with the average value of sales per head in manufacturing (prices multiplied by productivity) corrected for changes in the terms of trade and in the pressure of demand.

Given that unit labour costs in manufacturing are earnings divided by productivity, combining the long-run relationships (15), (17) and (19) implies that eventually, with unchanged pressure of demand and productivity, wholesale prices, consumer prices and earnings will move in line with world prices in sterling. The equations determine the dynamic path, while the pressure of demand variables modify both the consumer prices and manufacturing earnings relationships.

Balance of payments

An equation based on equation (5′) which assumes that a given monetary disequilibrium with respect to k in equation (3) will be reflected under fixed exchange rates in a proportionate change in the money supply via a balance of payments adjustment (BOF) took the form:

$$\frac{100 \text{ BOF}}{M_{-1}} = -\underset{(2.2)}{19.14} - \underset{(1.4)}{18.37} \log \left(\frac{M . E . WIP}{\text{GDPOX} . Mw} \right)_{-1}$$

$$- \underset{(2.0)}{61.4} \log\left(\frac{\text{GDPTOX}}{\text{WIPT}}\right)_{-1} - \underset{(2.3)}{47.25} \log\left(\frac{\text{PIMI}}{\text{PIMO}}\right)$$

$$- \underset{(1.9)}{49.47} \left(\frac{\text{DCE}}{\text{M}_{-1}} - \Delta \log \text{Mw}\right)$$

$$- \underset{(2.2)}{1.32} \sum \log\left(\frac{\text{M}.\text{E}.\text{WIP}}{\text{GDPOX}.\text{Mw}}\right)_{-2} + \underset{(1.4)}{0.318}\, t + \underset{(2.6)}{2.16}\, \text{QI}$$

$$- \underset{(0.0)}{0.0027}\, \text{Q2} - \underset{(1.3)}{1.11}\, \text{Q3} \tag{20}$$

$$\bar{R}^2 = 0.72$$
$$\text{DW} = 1.72$$
$$\text{SE} = 1.55$$
$$6403\text{–}7104$$
$$\chi^2_{20} = 17.6$$

The principal features of equation (20) are that changes in DCE have a moderately high short-term impact on the balance of payments – half of DCE is reflected in the balance of payments instantaneously. The proportional corrective factors are the relative income velocity of money for the United Kingdom and the world, the relative deviations from trend of output in the United Kingdom and the world, and the ratio of United Kingdom manufactured input to output prices. When velocity in the world rises relatively to velocity in the United Kingdom, pressure builds up in the foreign-exchange market and leads to a balance of payments outflow under a fixed exchange-rate regime. The relative output deviations from trend reflect the pressures that influence the current account when domestic demand rises relatively to world demand. As the ratio of PIMI to PIMO rises, the current account of the balance of payments tends to deteriorate, since sterling costs of imported raw materials and fuels tend to rise relatively to manufactured export prices. This will tend to generate J-curve effects as the exchange rate and relative prices interact. That these effects may be quite pronounced is shown by the large co-efficient in equation (20). The steady-state solution for the money supply from equation (20) is

$$\log M = \log\left(\frac{Mw \cdot GDPOX}{E \cdot WIP}\right) - 3.342 \log\left(\frac{GDPTOX}{WIP/WIPT}\right)$$

$$- 2.57 \log\left(\frac{PIMI}{PIMO}\right) \tag{21}$$

Finally, equation (20) has an integral feedback mechanism in the relative velocity term whereby accumulated deviations from the trend in the long-run ratio of United Kingdom income velocity of money are recycled into the balance of payments at a rate of 1.3 per cent per quarter.

Output
We report two equations for output based on equations (6) and (6′) respectively. In the former equation output is dominated by real balance effects in the long run, while external factors only exert a short-term influence on domestic economic identity:

$$\Delta \log GDPOX^* = -0.062 + 0.288 \Delta \log WIP$$
$$\qquad\qquad (1.6) \qquad (1.8)$$

$$+ 0.25 \Delta \log\left(\frac{M}{PGDP}\right)_{-2}$$
$$(2.1)$$

$$- 0.062 \log\left(\frac{GDPOX^* \cdot PGDP}{M}\right)_{-1}$$
$$(1.4)$$

$$+ \sum_{i=0}^{8} w_i \Delta \log PC_{-i} + \sum_{i=3}^{9} v_i \Delta \log\left(\frac{PIMO}{WPW\pounds}\right)_{-i}$$

$$- 0.013 \; VAT - 0.0681 \; DV3 + 0.01 \; Q1$$
$$(1.12) \qquad\quad (3.88) \qquad\quad (1.5)$$

$$+ 0.016 \, Q2 + 0.0056 \, Q3 \tag{22}$$
$$(2.5) \qquad\;\; (0.93)$$

$$\bar{R}^2 = 0.40$$
$$DW = 2.15$$
$$SE = 0.01$$
$$6502\text{–}7802$$
$$\chi^2_{12} = 4.2$$

Lag structures:

	0	1	2	3	4
w_i	-0.248	-0.185	-0.121	-0.055	-0.013
				(0.6)	(0.1)
v_i	(1.4)	(2.0)	(1.6)	0.043	-0.016
				(0.4)	(0.3)

	5	6	7	8	9
w_i	0.082	0.153	0.225	0.299	
	(0.9)	(2.4)	(2.4)	(1.6)	
v_i	-0.055	-0.074	-0.075	-0.057	-0.0191
	(1.1)	(1.3)	(1.3)	(0.9)	(0.2)

	$\sum$
w_i	0.163
v_i	-0.255

The lag structures were both estimated with second-order poly-
nomials. The dependent variable is the change in GDP excluding
North Sea oil and public expenditure. If world economic activity
rises by 1 per cent, GDPOX* rises by 0.28 per cent in the short run,
reflecting the share of exports in GDP. If United Kingdom prices rise
by 1 per cent relatively to world prices, GDPOX* falls by 0.25 per cent
in the short term (spread over ten quarters), which implies that the
sum of the price elasticities of demand for exports and imports is
slightly greater than unity. The change in consumer prices has a dual
function. The negative terms reflect the deflationary effects of inflation
on asset holdings, while the positive terms reflect the fall in the demand
for money when expected inflation increases.

Equation (22) implies that in the steady state the money demand
function is of the form:

$$\log M = \log GDPOX^* + \log PGDP - 2.63 \, \Delta \log PC \qquad (23)$$

that is, the demand for money varies inversely with the rate of inflation
but is linear homogeneous in economic activity and the price level.

Our representative result for equation (6') is:

$$\Delta \log GDPOX^* = 2.53 + 0.24 \, \Delta \log WIP + 0.36 \, \Delta \log \left(\frac{M}{PC} \right)_{-2}$$
$$ (3.4) \quad (1.8) \qquad\qquad (3.42)$$

$$- 0.069 \log \left(\frac{PIMO}{WPW\pounds}\right)_{-1} - 0.17 \log WIP_{-1}$$
$$\quad (1.4) \qquad\qquad\qquad\qquad (2.9)$$

$$- 0.233 \log \left(\frac{GDPOX^*}{WIP}\right)_{-1} + 0.00075 \, t$$
$$\quad (2.9) \qquad\qquad\qquad\qquad (1.2)$$

$$- \sum_{i=0}^{4} w_i \, \Delta \log PC_{-i} - 0.014 \, VAT - 0.064 \, DV3$$
$$\qquad\qquad\qquad\qquad (1.5) \qquad\qquad (4.4)$$

$$+ 0.0029 \, Q_1 + 0.012 \, Q_2 + 0.004 \, Q_3 \qquad\qquad (24)$$
$$\quad (0.6) \qquad\quad (2.3) \qquad\quad (0.8)$$

$$\bar{R}^2 = 0.543$$
$$DW = 2.12$$
$$SE = 0.0131$$
$$6402\text{--}7802$$
$$\chi_{12}^2 = 6.01$$

Lag structure:

w_i	0	1	2	3	4	Σ
	0.223	0.163	0.104	0.045	−0.014	0.522
	(1.8)	(2.2)	(1.8)	(0.5)	(0.1)	

In this case $\Delta \log PC$ represents the deflationary influence of inflation on expenditure due to the erosion of the value of financial assets. The role of real balance effects is only modifying, rather than stabilising as in equation (22). Economic activity now depends upon supply trends and external factors in the steady state:

$$GDPOX^* = 0.27 \, WIP - 0.296 \frac{PIMO}{WPW\pounds} + 0.0032 \, t \qquad (25)$$

The parameters in equation (25) are similar to their modifying counterparts in equation (22). It is also noted that the standard error of estimate in equation (24) is significantly below its value in equation (22). It is equation (24) that we use in the following section.

Simulating Exchange-rate Objectives

The control run

Our full model is described in Beenstock and Burns [3]; however, we have described its main logical structure and its empirical structure above. In so far as we treat the money supply as endogenous, relate the level of economic activity to monetary factors and introduce an augmented Phillips curve, we extend the analysis of exchange-rate adjustment that was presented in Ball, Burns and Laury [1].

Table 5.1   Assumptions in the control run

End-year	Index of wholesale prices: UK/competitors'	Index of effective exchange rate	Differential inflation rate (%)
0	1.00	1.00	—
1	1.04	0.96	+4.0
2	1.08	0.93	+3.8
3	1.12	0.89	+3.7
4	1.16	0.86	+3.6
5	1.20	0.83	+3.4
6	1.24	0.81	+3.3
7	1.28	0.78	+3.2
8	1.32	0.76	+3.1
9	1.36	0.74	+3.0
10	1.40	0.71	+2.9

In this section we simulate the effect of less flexible exchange rates. If the United Kingdom were to join the EMS it would have to keep its exchange rate in line with its European partners'. For argument's sake we assume that inflation in the United Kingdom is above the European average so that the exchange rate has to depreciate. Details of the control run are given in Table 5.1, which takes an initial inflation rate in the United Kingdom 4 per cent greater than the European rate, although by the end of the control period this differential is reduced to 2.9 per cent. In the control run we assumed that sterling depreciated at a constant rate to maintain relative prices, so that the effective exchange rate fell from unity to 0.71 by the end of the period. Thus, if the United Kingdom is to stay in the EMS and have a constant exchange rate its exchange rate will have to be higher than that shown in Table 5.1 – 40 per cent higher by the end of the period. Details of this profile are given in Table 5.3 below.

Effects of the exchange-rate shock
First, however, we examine reactions to an appreciation of sterling by 5 per cent in comparison with what might otherwise have been the case. The results are presented in Table 5.2. This shows the response to a single once-and-for-all movement in the rate. The appreciation leads to a fall in foreign prices expressed in sterling of 4.8 per cent. The fall in wholesale input prices causes a cost-push reduction in wholesale prices. At the same time the fall in world prices expressed in sterling exerts downward competitive pressure on wholesale prices. This leads to an initial reduction in consumer prices, which in turn leads to lower wage settlements, as both the inflation rate and firms' ability to pay are reduced. In turn, the lower level of wage settlements exerts a downward cost pressure upon prices.

5.2   *Simulation 1: exchange rate appreciates by 5 per cent*
(changes relative to control run)

End-year	Wholesale prices (%)	Mfrg earnings (%)	Money supply (%)	GDP (%)	BOF (£b.)	Competi-tiveness (%)
1	− 2.0	− 0.9	+ 2.0	+ 0.1	+ 0.7	− 3.0
2	− 2.9	− 2.1	− 0.2	+ 0.1	− 0.8	− 1.9
3	− 3.6	− 3.4	− 2.6	− 0.2	− 1.2	− 1.2
4	− 4.3	− 4.5	− 5.0	− 0.1	− 1.3	− 0.4
5	− 4.9	− 5.4	− 7.4	− 0.1	− 1.2	+ 0.2
6	− 5.3	− 5.9	− 7.9	—	− 0.9	+ 0.5
7	− 5.5	− 5.9	− 8.4	+ 0.2	− 0.3	+ 0.7
8	− 5.5	− 5.7	− 8.0	+ 0.2	− 0.2	+ 0.7
9	− 5.4	− 5.2	− 7.3	+ 0.2	− 0.3	+ 0.6
10	− 5.0	− 4.8	− 6.3	+ 0.2	− 0.2	+ 0.3

This interaction results in a fairly rapid fall in prices and earnings such that 90 per cent of the appreciation has been offset after four years and the whole of it after five. Prices and earnings overshoot the fall in the exchange rate because of the integral mechanism. The initial loss of competitiveness and the gain in real wages resulting from the time lags lead to a portfolio disequilibrium between the personal and company sectors which is restored by some over-adjustment of the long-run equilibrium in wages. Prices follow in part because of lower wage costs and because of the need to compensate for some of the cumulated lost competitiveness that will have affected firms' sales and assets positions.

The balance of official financing (BOF) is initially positive after the revaluation. This is due to the declining ratio of import prices to output prices and the implied J-curve. By this mechanism the current account initially improves, which leads to some speculative capital flows. This is only temporary because of the monetary stock disequilibrium that emerges as a consequence of the appreciation, lower prices and the J-curve. Outflows begin in year 2 and peak in year 4. Hence, with a given rate of DCE, the stock of money declines relatively to the control. This decline is moderate initially but eventually overshoots. At its lowest point the money supply is $8\frac{1}{2}$ per cent lower than its control, although by the end of the period it is moving back to its equilibrium, which is 5 per cent lower. The overshooting again occurs because of the initial lags in adjustment.

This pattern of adjustment of money supply and prices means a large increase in the real money stock in the early period, as the money supply is higher and prices are lower. As outlined above the effect of the revaluation in these circumstances is ambiguous. Competitiveness has declined, real incomes have risen and real money balances are above equilibrium. The last is in part due to the J-curve and in part to price adjustment initially faster than monetary adjustment. In the simulation, output is slightly higher than in the control for the first two years – the real balance dominates the effect of competitiveness. Then output becomes negative. The real money stock becomes negative because of the fast monetary outflow, while the competitive loss, although reduced, is not removed. Later, competitiveness actually improves owing to overshooting, but the overall effect is that output does not move a great deal from its control level.

After the first year there is a large deficit for official financing. The equilibrium result is that with given DCE the cumulative reserve outflow will be equal to 5 per cent of the money supply.

Effects of inflexible exchange rates
The mechanisms of wage and price behaviour are the same in the simulation shown in Table 5.3 as in Table 5.2. While wages and prices adjust to the lower level of world prices in sterling, time lags are involved. It is not until year 5 that United Kingdom prices fall

as fast as world prices, although afterwards the overshooting referred to in simulation 1 leads to a greater rate of decline. The time lags therefore mean that competitiveness declines in the early years; the peak loss is 6.1 per cent after four years, but by the end of the period it is reduced to 2.5 per cent.

Table 5.3   Simulation 2: EMS exchange-rate strategy
(differences from control run)

End-year	Exchange rate[a] (%)	Wholesale prices (%)	Manufacturing earnings (%)	Differential inflation (%)
1	4	− 1.1	− 0.4	+ 2.8
2	8	− 3.1	− 1.7	+ 1.7
3	12	− 5.6	− 3.9	+ 0.9
4	16	− 8.5	− 7.0	+ 0.3
5	20	− 11.6	− 10.6	—
6	24	− 15.0	− 14.5	− 0.6
7	28	− 18.3	− 18.2	− 0.8
8	32	− 21.5	− 21.5	− 0.7
9	36	− 24.3	− 24.3	− 0.6
10	40	− 26.8	− 26.7	− 0.3

	Competitiveness (%)	BOF (£b.)	Money supply (%)	Output (%)
1	− 2.9	+ 0.6	+ 1.7	—
2	− 4.6	+ 0.4	+ 2.3	+ 0.2
3	− 5.7	− 0.6	+ 0.9	+ 0.1
4	− 6.1	− 1.7	− 2.5	− 0.1
5	− 6.0	− 2.5	− 7.6	− 0.2
6	− 5.3	− 3.4	− 12.5	− 0.2
7	− 4.5	− 3.4	− 18.3	—
8	− 3.6	− 4.1	− 23.1	+ 0.1
9	− 2.8	− 5.6	− 27.3	+ 0.1
10	− 2.5	− 7.1	− 30.4	+ 0.1

[a]A 40 per cent rise in the exchange rate leads to a 28 per cent fall in world prices expressed in sterling.

The balance of official financing improves for two years. A succession of J-curves leads to almost a £1 billion surplus over the two years as revaluation improves the terms of trade. This means that with given DCE the money supply grows faster in the initial stages and by the second year it is almost 2½ per cent higher than in the control run. The pressures of the money disequilibrium then build up and a very large outflow of reserves takes place. This contracts the money supply, which by the end of the period has been reduced to the full extent of the fall in world prices in sterling.

This combination of wage and price reductions, together with some initial monetary expansion followed by the subsequent fall, implies a large initial *real* monetary expansion. This reaches a peak of 6.5 per cent after three years and then declines; by year 8 it becomes negative as the monetary contraction exceeds the price reduction.

The forces operating on real output are therefore substantially offsetting. Initially there is a large real monetary gain and real earnings are boosted. At the same time competitiveness deteriorates. The balance of weights used here produces an initial small expansion of output as the effect of the real balance dominates. From year 2 onwards real balances are declining (although the level is still higher than in the control) and the competitive effect is bigger. The result is a period when output is depressed.

Tightening monetary policy

The cumulative loss of reserves in Table 5.3 is very large with DCE unchanged; at the end of the period it is equal to 30 per cent of the stock of money. This suggests that on its own this is not a feasible course of action unless the initial level of reserves is very high; if the outflow is to be avoided DCE must be reduced. Table 5.4 shows the effect of reducing it by a quarterly amount equal to 1 per cent of the money supply; such a policy has a marked effect on the balance of payments (BOF). Indeed, the inward balance of payments adjustment is sufficiently rapid to insulate the money supply from the credit contraction. By the end of the first year the money supply falls by 1.4 per cent relatively to the control and by the end of year 3 it has fallen to its lowest level. Thereafter it rapidly adjusts to its equilibrium as the monetary stabilisation process asserts itself.

Since the money supply falls, output falls initially as real balances fall (in relative terms) because the pressure of demand is reduced and lower wage costs are eventually reflected in lower prices. It is for this reason that competitiveness is adversely affected in years 3–7, although the magnitudes are not very large. In the long run the effects of the credit squeeze on these aggregates tends to zero, since in the model that we have proposed monetary policy is neutral in the long run, but not of course in the short run.

Table 5.4 Simulation 3: DCE reduced quarterly by 1 per cent
of money supply (differences from control run)

End-year	Wholesale prices (%)	Money supply (%)	GDP (%)	BOF (£b.)	DCE (£b.)
1	—	−1.4	−0.1	+0.7	−1.2
2	—	−1.7	−0.2	+1.3	−1.5
3	−0.1	−1.8	—	+1.7	−1.9
4	−0.1	−1.6	—	+2.1	−2.0
5	−0.2	−1.5	—	+2.0	−1.9
6	−0.1	−1.1	—	+2.4	−2.2
7	−0.1	−0.7	—	+2.5	−2.3
8	—	−0.3	—	+2.7	−2.5
9	—	—	—	+3.0	−2.8
10	+0.1	+0.2	—	+3.6	−3.4

EMS exchange-rate objectives and reduction in DCE

In Table 5.5 we look at a combination of simulations 2 and 3, where
we hold the exchange rate within a system where competitors' inflation rates are lower than the United Kingdom's, while DCE is
contracted to offset the balance of payments loss. The impact upon
the inflation rate and earnings is almost exactly the same as in simulation 2, where no additional policy measures were taken. The initial

Table 5.5 Simulation 4: EMS exchange-rate strategy and
reduced DCE (differences from control run)

End-year	Wholesale prices (%)	Money supply (%)	GDP (%)	BOF (£b.)	DCE (£b.)
1	−1.0	+0.3	—	+1.3	−1.2
2	−3.1	+0.7	—	+1.7	−1.5
3	−5.7	−0.9	+0.1	+1.2	−1.9
4	−8.7	−4.2	—	+0.4	−2.0
5	−11.8	−9.2	−0.1	−0.5	−2.0
6	−15.1	−13.7	−0.2	−1.0	−2.2
7	−18.4	−19.2	+0.1	−0.9	−2.3
8	−21.6	−23.7	+0.1	−1.4	−2.5
9	−24.4	−27.8	+0.3	−2.8	−2.8
10	−26.8	−30.8	+0.3	−3.8	−3.4

increase in the money supply that took place in simulation 2 is now much reduced, although from year 5 the effect is similar. The major difference is upon the balance of official financing. The initial gain to the reserves is increased, while the deficit in later years is reduced. The cumulative impact upon the reserves of the changes in official financing in simulation 4 is however small.

Conclusions

If the United Kingdom chose to join a fixed exchange-rate system against the background of a higher inflation rate initially and underlying depreciation of the exchange rate, our conclusions as to the results for the United Kingdom economy are as follows:

(a)   The United Kingdom's rate would fall towards a rate consistent with that of trading partners. However, this could take time because of lags between the fall in the exchange rate and the response of wages and prices to lower world prices expressed in sterling. Our estimate is that rates of inflation would be reduced by the extent of the rate of appreciation after five years, although the shortfall in years 3 and 4 would be modest.

(b)   The price level in world currency would for many years be higher than it would be otherwise. If the initial inflation gap is 4 per cent, we estimate that the consequential loss of competitiveness for manufacturing industry would reach 6 per cent after four years. From then on the gap would probably close.

(c)   Initially there might be a short-lived gain of reserves through the operation of the J-curve, but if no accompanying monetary changes were introduced a major loss of reserves would follow. To avoid loss it would be necessary to reduce DCE as a percentage of the money supply by an amount equal to the reduction in the inflation rate that is desired. Although we have not calculated this here, it would certainly involve a lower government financial deficit and probably tax increases or lower levels of government spending.

(d)   Real incomes would benefit if no deflationary action was taken. Even if there was some deflation, domestic expenditure would be higher than it otherwise would have been because real money balances would be raised above their equilibrium level. This is because prices adjust more rapidly than money supply to exchange-rate appreciation.

(e) Because competitiveness would suffer initially, export industries and manufacturing generally would lose sales. On the other hand domestic expenditure would be higher. The net effect on output and employment would be close to neutral.

It is important to stress the uncertainty of these calculations based on historical reactions to exchange-rate changes. If the changes were fully anticipated the speed of response might well be increased, the loss in competitiveness would be reduced and so would the increase in domestic expenditure. The distortion to the balance between different sectors of the economy would be less serious. We consider that the lags estimated in this paper are towards the longer end of the range of possibilities if the move to the EMS were judged over the long term and the appropriate policies were pursued.

Our principal concern has not been with normative issues of whether fixed exchange rates are desirable in the light of welfare analysis, but with the positive or descriptive issues of how the United Kingdom economy is likely to behave with a fixed rate. Because monetary and exchange-rate policies are neutral in the long run, it may not be concluded that currency independence is irrelevant. A fixed exchange-rate system replaces a price-adjustment mechanism by a quantity-adjustment mechanism, which seems to conflict with Paretian principles of economic welfare and efficiency. Indeed, postwar evidence (see Beenstock and Burns [3]) points to faster adjustment under flexible than under fixed exchange rates. Renunciation of an efficient degree of freedom may only be justified if some economic benefit is obtained in consequence, for example, greater market integration or monetary control. We have not addressed these matters in the present paper; the ultimate case for fixed rates lies beyond its bounds.

Appendix 1: Estimation Methodology

In the main text we use an estimation methodology suggested in Davidson *et al.* [4]. This note summarises the methodology in so far as is necessary to enable empirical estimates to be understood. For illustrative purposes we assume that in equilibrium Y depends on two exogenous variables x_1 and x_2 with the weights summing to unity

$$Y = a_1 x_1 + (1 - a_1) x_2 + a_0 \qquad \text{A}(1)$$

where all variables are expressed in logarithms. If Y does not equal the value that is implied by equation A(1) it may adjust towards the equilibrium value according to

$$\Delta Y = a_0 + a_1 \Delta x_1 + a_2 \Delta x_2 + a_3 \Delta x_3 - a_4 (Y - x_1)_{-1}$$
$$- a_5 (Y - x_2)_{-1} \qquad A(2)$$

The terms in Δx_1 and Δx_2 are *derivative feedback* mechanisms which relate changes in x_1 and x_2 with changes in Y, while the terms in $Y - x_1$ and $Y - x_2$ are *proportionate feedback* mechanisms which relate the levels of Y, x_1 and x_2 to changes in Y. x_3 is a *modifier* which modifies the adjustment process between Y and x_1 and x_2. However, x_3 will not influence the equilibrium or steady-state solution for Y. This may be seen by setting all terms in Δ to zero and solving for Y as

$$Y^* = \frac{a_0}{a_4 + a_5} + \frac{a_4}{a_4 + a_5} x_1 + \frac{a_5}{a_4 + a_5} x_2 \qquad A(3)$$

which is exactly in the form of equation A(1). The terms in $Y - x_1$ and $Y - x_2$ are referred to as *stabilisers*, since they stabilise Y around its equilibrium solution given in equation A(1). Equation A(2) enables us to distinguish between short-run and long-run factors. For example, x_3 only has a short-term influence if terms in Δx_3 are significant while terms in x_3 itself are not.

One might wish to add to equation A(2) an *integral stabilisation* feedback mechanism where the change in Y also depends on the cumulative deviation of Y from its equilibrium value Y^* (Hendry and von Ungern-Sternberg, [6]). This extra term would take the form

$$a_7 \Sigma (Y - Y^*)$$

as, for example, in equations (14) and (18) in the main text. This was done by rewriting A(3) as

$$Y^* = B_0 + B_1 x_1 + (1 - B_1) x_2 \qquad A(4)$$

The integral form is estimated as

$$a_7 \Sigma (Y - Y^*) = a_7 \Sigma [Y - B_1 x_1 - (1 - B_1) x_2] - a_7 B_0 t \qquad A(5)$$

where the cumulated constant term appears as a time trend in the equation.

With integral stabilisation feedback the estimating form of A(2) becomes:

$$\Delta y = a_0 + a_1 \Delta x_1 + a_2 \Delta x_2 + a_3 \Delta x_3 - a_4 (Y - x_1)_{-1} - a_5 (Y - x_2)_{-1}$$
$$- a_7 \Sigma [Y - B_1 x_1 - (1 - B_1) x_2] + a_8 t \qquad A(6)$$

where

$$B_1 = \frac{a_4}{a_4 + a_5}$$

Since B_1 has to be calculated from equation $A(4)$ it is necessary to estimate the coefficients iteratively. We tended to find that convergence across the parameters was achieved after about four iterations.

The integral stabilisation term implies that past deviations from equilibrium influence current behaviour, which may be a proxy for the influence of unmeasured stock disequilibrium. For example, in equation (18) if earnings are held down below their equilibrium value, that is if log AEM has been less than log AEM*, workers' assets will tend to be eroded and they will then try to make up for past shortfalls in earnings. In this case Σ(log AEM – log AEM*) represents the asset position of the workforce, so that by-gones are no longer by-gones under integral stabilisation.

Appendix 2: Glossary of Symbols used in Empirical Estimates

AEM	average earnings in manufacturing industry
BOF	balance of official financing
DCE	domestic credit expansion
DV3DWK	dummy for three-day week
E	effective exchange rate
GDPOX	GDP minus North Sea oil output
GDPOX*	GDPOX less public sector current and capital expenditure
GDPTOX	ratio of output (excluding North Sea oil) to its trend
M	UK money supply in sterling
Mw	index of world money supply expressed in foreign currency
PC	index of consumer prices
PGDP	deflator of GDP
PIMI	wholesale input prices to manufacturing industry
PIMO	index of wholesale prices of manufactured output
PRDM	productivity in manufacturing industry

PTAXDMY   dummy for the anticipation effects of the 1968 budget
Qi   quarterly dummies
RNDI*   ratio of real national disposable income to GDP
t   time trend
TEA*   indirect tax rates
ULC   unit labour costs
ULCM   unit labour costs in manufacturing industry
VAT   dummy for the introduction of VAT in 1973
WIP   index of world industrial production
WIPT   index of trend WIP
WPW£   world wholesale prices in sterling
WPWVA   world wholesale price of value-added output measured
            in foreign currency
YDUM   incomes policy dummy

References

[1] Ball, R. J., Burns, T. and Laury, J. S. E., 'The role of exchange rate changes in the balance of payments adjustment – the United Kingdom case', *Economic Journal*, March 1977.

[2] Beenstock, M., *The Foreign Exchanges Theory, Modelling and Policy*, London, Macmillan, 1978.

[3] Beenstock, M. and Burns, T., 'An aggregation monetary model of the UK economy' (London Business School, mimeo, 1979).

[4] Davidson, J. E. H. *et al.*, 'Econometric modelling of the aggregate time series relationship between consumers' expenditure and income in the United Kingdom', *Economic Journal*, December 1978.

[5] Fair, R. C., 'An analysis of a macroeconometric model with rational expectations in the bond and stock markets', *Journal of Political Economy* (forthcoming, 1979).

[6] Hendry, D. F. and von Ungern-Sternberg, T., 'Liquidity and inflation effects on consumers' expenditure' (London School of Economics, mimeo, 1979).

[7] Johnson, H. G., 'The monetary approach to balance of payments theory' in M. B. Connolly and A. D. Swoboda (eds), *International Trade and Money*, London, Allen and Unwin, 1972.

Comment

by G. D. N. Worswick

Introduction

Fixity in the exchange rate between two national currencies is a matter of degree. The currency may be tied to another, or to some unit of account with no margin for fluctuation, as was the case with colonial currencies in the British Commonwealth, or until recently the Irish pound and the pound sterling. But in many cases nominally fixed exchange rates can in fact fluctuate. The exchange rate between two currencies on a gold standard could deviate from the ratio of their par values according to the cost of transporting gold from one centre to the other and present-day systems may permit quite a wide margin of fluctuation between a currency and some common unit, or between pairs of member currencies. For instance the EMS allows a margin of ± 2.25 per cent for all members, with a wider range of ± 6 per cent for some. Apart from these fluctuations round a parity, the parities themselves can be altered infrequently, as under the gold standard, or quite frequently, as in the European snake. Changes may occur singly or there may be a general realignment.

At the opposite extreme, pure floating does occur, although it is comparatively rare for it to last long. In most cases the authorities will intervene to iron out 'short-period fluctuations'. The chart of a floating currency where there is substantial intervention may be indistinguishable from that of a pegged currency where the peg is adjusted fairly frequently.

The whole complex of international currency arrangements rarely conforms closely with either of the polar opposites. Although we characterise present arrangements as floating or 'managed' floating, in contrast with the fixed exchange-rate regime set up at the end of the second world war, most currencies are still pegged to another currency or to the SDR. On 31 October 1978, 95 out of 134 members of the IMF had pegged rates: 64 to a single currency, 13 to the SDR and 18 to some other composite of currencies. Members with floating currencies included six maintaining common margins, five adjusting exchange rates according to a set of indicators and 28 maintaining other types of arrangement, including those described as independent floating (IMF [2], p. 7) However, it is estimated that four fifths of world trade takes place between countries whose currencies are not pegged.

Complete fixity of rates among EMS members (which is not at present contemplated) would cover only two fifths of British trade. Nearly 15 per cent of imports and nearly 13 per cent of exports in 1978 came from or were sent to Japan and North America, where currencies would probably continue to move independently. Thus, general conclusions about fixed versus floating rates must be applied with care to the particular context. Finally, judgements about relative merits must take account of parallel arrangements concerning migration of labour, capital and technology, and trade in goods and services. On the face of it balance of payments adjustments might be made either by altering exchange rates or, given fixed exchange rates, by altering tariffs and subsidies. Will greater fixity of exchange rates be likely to encourage protectionism?

General Principles

Beenstock and Burns observe that: 'A fixed exchange-rate system replaces a price-adjustment mechanism by a quantity-adjustment mechanism which seems to conflict with Paretian principles of economic welfare and efficiency.' But the dimension of the balance of payments is price × quantity and adjustment with either fixed or floating rates will, I think, affect both, though in varying proportions. I am not sure, therefore, that I fully comprehend the meaning of this statement, but I can appreciate its emotive appeal. Let me, therefore, restore the emotive balance.

A visitor from another planet would surely opt for rigidly fixed exchange rates, preferably in the form of a single worldwide currency. If told that costs of changing monies or hedging in futures markets were small, he might still ask why they were necessary. And, if he had read a little history before setting off, he would point out that at Bretton Woods the world contrived a predominantly fixed-rate system under which production and trade in the industrial world grew at rates faster than ever before, but, since it has allowed this system to crumble and be replaced by predominantly floating rates, production and trade have grown only half as fast and there has been considerable unemployment in most industrial countries. If fixing rates conflicts with Paretian principles of economic welfare and efficiency,

unfixing them has been accompanied by altogether poorer performance for the industrial world. If pure theory points to flexible rates,
recent experience points the other way. Both arguments seem to me
about equally convincing (or unconvincing).

The theoretical case for a separate national currency is that, according to the size and structure of the economy, it permits pursuit of
monetary policies which can improve economic performance. It may
also, some sceptics argue, give scope for policies which can make things
worse. One difficulty in appraising alternative monetary systems is
that they, and the policies they allow, may benefit or harm different
sectors of society in different degrees. Account needs also to be taken
of the extent to which policies will be tolerated by other countries
and not be frustrated by retaliatory action.

A recurrent theme in British thought about exchange rates in the
past half century has been the fear that adherence to the gold standard,
or a system of rigidly fixed rates, would sooner or later force the
authorities into deflationary policies. While ideally such policies would
simply reduce prices and nominal incomes, encouraging exports, discouraging imports and thus restoring the balance of payments, in
practice prices of manufactures and money wages might be sticky and
the main consequence of monetary contraction might be reduced output and higher unemployment. The alternative method of adjustment
by devaluation seemed, by contrast, attractive, especially if there was
already unemployment, as a possible way of restoring the trade
balance while increasing output and employment. Because it seemed
so comparatively painless the Bretton Woods system included rules
intended to allow necessary adjustments, while precluding the obvious danger of competitive devaluations which 'exported unemployment'.

The greatest pressure to break out of fixed exchange rates undoubtedly came from deficit countries. But there was also criticism
from countries with no balance of payments difficulties complaining
that they were being obliged to import inflation. Advocates of
exchange-rate flexibility have argued that such a country has merely
to let the exchange rate rise. The difficulty is, however, that while
some interests would benefit from lower prices others, notably export
industries, could suffer.

Out of this wide range of issues underlying the choice between fixed
and flexible rates we have been asked to concentrate on two. First,
would greater fixity reduce inflation and, if so, at what cost? Secondly,

is it nowadays more difficult to make a change in the exchange rate effective as an instrument of policy?

Beenstock and Burns give explicit and implicit answers to both questions, but they differ according as we are concerned with the short or the long run. Moreover, the evidence to support the short-run and long-run answers differs substantially in kind.

Econometric Results

While Beenstock and Burns set out to model short-run behaviour, they constrain their model to have certain required properties in the long run. The influence of the basic postulates on their results for a 5 per cent appreciation can clearly be seen in Table 5.2 in the run of numbers from year 6 onwards when, after about five years ending in some overshooting, there is a return towards the long-run position in which the number 5 would appear in the first three columns and zero in the remainder.

The model was, in fact, designed to accord in the long run with the monetary theory of the balance of payments. The present National Institute model, though best described as eclectic, evolved from a Keynesian national income approach and, in its treatment of the exchange rate, makes use of import and export elasticities. It is thus of interest to see what it will deliver on the same assumption of a 5 per cent appreciation.

For this simulation the control run was taken to be the actual course of the economy from the first quarter of 1974 until the last quarter of 1978. All exogenous variables such as world production, prices and trade and United Kingdom public expenditure and tax rates have been assumed to remain the same. It is supposed that in each quarter the effective exchange rate is 5 per cent higher than it actually was, and the impact of this difference on the main endogenous variables is then computed. Table 5.6 shows the resulting divergencies from history.

The higher exchange rate at once begins to reduce exports and increase imports in volume terms, thus contracting GDP. Real disposable income and real consumers' expenditure expand (partly because of monetary effects via the credit term in the consumption function, and partly because in the simulation income tax allowances have been left unchanged in nominal terms). However the contraction of the real current balance is stronger than the expansion in consump-

Table 5.6   Exchange-rate appreciation in the NIESR model[a]

End-year	Wholesale prices (%)	Average earnings (%)	Real GDP (%)	Current balance (£b.)	Competitive-ness[b] (%)
1	− 1.1	− 0.1	− 0.4	+ 0.3	− 3.3
2	− 2.7	− 1.1	− 0.2	− 0.1	− 1.6
3	− 3.2	− 1.9	− 0.1	− 0.2	− 1.3
4	− 3.5	− 2.6	+ 0.1	− 0.4	− 0.9
5	− 3.8	− 3.0	+ 0.2	− 0.4	− 0.6

[a]Differences from actual values from 1974 to 1978 if effective exchange rate had been 5 per cent higher each quarter than in fact it was.
[b]Relative export prices of manufactures.

tion, so that the net effect is a reduction of GDP, which gradually gets less. As compared with history, import prices fall at once, wholesale prices with a lag and average earnings with a further lag. In the third year wholesale prices are 3 per cent lower and average earnings 2 per cent lower than they would otherwise have been. The relative fall in prices comes very quickly for imports but more slowly for exports, and the last column shows that competitiveness falls by over 3 per cent in the first year but then begins to improve, so that by the fourth year it is less than 1 per cent worse than in the control run. The current balance improves in the first year but thereafter worsens.

The Beenstock–Burns and National Institute simulations are not exactly comparable. The control run is different and there may well be differences in particular assumptions. Both show the same direction of change for wholesale prices, average earnings, competitiveness and the current balance, with a J-curve effect in the first year. For real GDP the National Institute shows an initial worsening followed by a slight improvement in years 4 and 5, while Beenstock and Burns show a slight improvement to start with, followed by worsening later, although the scale of movement is small both ways. (An important question is how far the smallness of the Beenstock–Burns changes in GDP comes about because of their 'natural' rate of output postulate.)

The consequences indicated by both models of a 5 per cent devaluation are obtained by simply reversing the signs of the differences given for the appreciation case. Devaluation raises earnings and prices (in sterling – in foreign currency, of course, it lowers them) and, in the National Institute case, increases output. The initial gain in competitiveness is eroded over time.

I have reservations about the evidence derived from both these simulations. They are different in kind.

My reservation about the Beenstock and Burns model concerns methodology. It may sometimes be useful to impose *a priori* restrictions on parameters of equations in a model so that, under specified conditions, they will behave in a certain way (for example, when there exists a lot of evidence about, say, elasticities of demand for exports, which would not get used in the estimation of the model itself). But the *a priori* restrictions imposed by Beenstock and Burns concerning how their model should behave in the long run are not of this kind. They are theoretical postulates about which direct evidence does not exist.

Consider booms, slumps and the 'natural' level or output. Time-series over long periods for GDP or industrial production for most industrial countries show fluctuations about a generally rising trend. For postwar Britain until the 1970s the cycles have been shorter and fluctuations smaller than in the interwar period in particular, or before the first world war. It has been much debated whether this greater stability is due to structural changes and how government intervention has affected it. Many other industrial countries have experienced less instability since the war, although nearly all of them recently encountered the deepest and most prolonged recession since the 1930s. What then is the point of assuming that output tends towards a 'natural' level? Indeed what meaning can be attached to such statements? The same question can be asked about the proposition that in the long run 'the domestic–foreign price ratio tends towards a constant in common currency'. This proposition is similar to the so-called 'law of one price'. The price predictions of the elasticity and monetary theories of balance of payments adjustment have lately been compared with actual price behaviour by Kravis and Lipsey [3]. They conclude: 'Price behaviour differs more from the relatively demanding monetary approach in that price levels and price movements for GDP as a whole and for specific types of export goods varied substantially even among major industrial countries. As for the elasticity approach, price levels tended to rise with appreciations and fall with depreciations as expected.'

I am extremely uneasy about assuming behaviour 'in the long run' which is inconsistent with actual behaviour over quite long periods.

One can see that if a projection shows British export prices rising faster than those of competitors, such a state of affairs cannot persist indefinitely. Something will ultimately have to give. The volume of exports may fall or the exchange rate may have to be altered; there are many possibilities. However, we have no more reason for postulating that in the long run the rate of increase of British export prices must be identical with that of others than that a period during which they rise faster will be followed by another during which they rise less fast.

My unease is compounded by the suspicion that on membership of the EMS Beenstock and Burns have postulated that their long-run requirements should also be observed in the short run. To the question what would happen to the exchange rate if the United Kingdom did not join, their answer is to make it fall so as to keep United Kingdom inflation in line with the European rate (incidentally begging a question about the non-European rate). But it is already apparent that for a number of years the actual exchange rate will be very much influenced by North Sea oil. The assumption makes the effective rate begin to fall at once, whereas we know that it has begun by standing higher than it would be had the United Kingdom joined the EMS in March.

My reservation makes me highly suspicious of the figures in later years of Beenstock and Burns' simulations as evidence of anything other than their long-run assumptions. Only detailed work on their model will show how far have these distorted the projections in earlier years; in particular one would want to look at the virtual constancy of GDP.

My reservation concerning the National Institute simulation is much more specific and concerns its augmented Phillips earnings equation. It is sensible to suppose, as this equation does, that nominal earnings will in general react to prices. However that does not mean that we have got a good relationship which has proved equally reliable in forecasting whether price increases are slowing down or speeding up. In recent years we have had more experience of the latter than of the former. For simulation purposes we have chosen the least bad of many earnings equations that we have estimated, but I feel less confident that a higher exchange rate will reduce inflation than that it will reduce output and employment by way of reduced exports and increased import substitution, and I am even more sceptical of Beenstock and Burns' stronger counter-inflation effect. In fact after nearly two years of a 'high' exchange-rate policy inflation in 1979 seems more likely to accelerate again than to slow down further.

To sum up: evidence from two distinct econometric models is that exchange-rate appreciation may reduce inflation only at the expense of the current balance, and in the case of the National Institute model with a loss of output and employment in the first two or three years. Both models agree that competitiveness of exports would deteriorate substantially and that this gap would not be closed for some years. This conclusion is of considerable significance. One of Beenstock and Burns' major postulates is that exchange-rate changes have 'no lasting balance of payments effect', but according to their simulation it is only by the fourth year that the competitive edge lost by the original appreciation has been restored; meanwhile in the four years taken together the balance of official financing has worsened by a cumulative £2.6 billion. If, after four years, there was a further appreciation there would, with these models, be an approximate repetition of the process. One could sensibly postulate that effects might diminish as expectations about successive devaluations became stronger and an enthusiast for 'rational expectations' might imagine that all time lags would vanish and everything adjust at once. But others need not jump to this extreme conclusion.

Neither model sheds direct light on the 'virtuous circles' of improved industrial efficiency which, it has been claimed, might follow exchange-rate changes. In the 1960s it used to be argued that devaluation would promote export-propelled growth. More recently, the Green Paper on the EMS has argued that appreciation would exert pressure to keep down costs which might stimulate cost saving. 'Once a virtuous circle of exchange rate stability, lower costs, greater stimulus to efficiency has been established, the effect of any initial loss of price competitiveness may be removed.' (Treasury [5], para. 39).

At the root of this question is whether, following a period in which profit margins have been especially low by historical standards, growth of exports is more likely to be stimulated by further squeezing of profits or by some restoration of margins such as would follow devaluation. My own view is that, while the comparatively high exchange rate may have contributed a little to slowing down inflation, it has been doing so at the cost of the non-oil current balance and of the level of output. The virtuous circle of the Green Paper is wishful thinking (see also NIESR [4], pp. 7–10).

Are Exchange Rates Any Longer a Policy Instrument?

In both models the question whether a change in the nominal exchange rate would lead also to a real change is answered in the affirmative. The change in the exchange rate causes the real rate to move in the same direction to a lesser extent; this change is gradually eroded but persists for some years.

The results so far have applied only to the United Kingdom. The 1977 IMF report noted that movements in exchange rates had tended to dampen the impact of differential inflation rates on the competitive positions of different countries, and in 1978 evidence is given from fourteen industrial countries that changes in competitiveness have been in the direction required for elimination of persistent current account imbalances (IMF [1]). The IMF also notes that natural gas and North Sea oil have strengthened the guilder and sterling respectively and led to declines in industrial competitiveness in the Netherlands and the United Kingdom. They find that relative price changes have a strong influence on volumes of exports and imports, but that only some fraction of the full effect, say a quarter to a half, should be expected in the first year.

Doubts have been expressed whether, in a system of floating rates, the authorities could choose one nominal rate rather than another. At first sight these doubts seem very odd. First, most currencies are still pegged. Secondly, there is ample evidence for those currencies classified as floating of substantial intervention by the authorities, who clearly fix exchange rates for periods of varying duration. Ah, yes, it is said, they can be fixed, but once fixed cannot be moved to another preselected point. Behind this idea, there are, I suspect, two quite different lines of argument, of which the first is largely bogus and the second genuine.

The Germans have not wished their exchange rate to go up for fear of hurting their export industries, but their persistent current account surplus has brought an influx of reserves. This has increased the money supply, which worries them because they do not like inflation. Most economists would advocate stimulation of demand, so as to reduce the trade surplus either by increasing the volume of imports or by pushing up prices and inhibiting exports. Which would actually take place would depend on various propensities and elasticities. If these are such that an unwanted rise in prices would ensue, then the exchange rate should be allowed to rise. Another recent instance was the alleged inability of the British authorities to keep the sterling exchange rate down because this caused reserves to flow in and the money supply to increase. Allowing the money supply to expand in such circumstances would have no direct effect upon inflation. It could have had indirect effects upon aggregate nominal demand through lowering of interest rates, which in turn might have stimulated investment and consumption. Given the slack in the economy, such expansion might well have been desirable, especially since the lower exchange rate would have protected the balance of payments. This sort of argument that the exchange rate cannot be lowered often stems from a very crude monetarism, which makes price changes proportional to money supply changes, irrespective of any other aspect of the economy, domestic or external.

The more serious argument is that exchange markets behave in accordance with catastrophe theory. If small interventions are undertaken to start pushing the exchange rate in the required direction, its initial response may be small. Gradually more and more agents perceive what is going on and, suddenly, all the passengers rush to one side of the ship and the exchange rate starts plummeting. This is, I believe, a genuine argument, the more so since such catastrophic falls are still fresh in people's memories. In theory, people should remember past instances of overshooting and not panic again. The persistence over long periods of 'excessive' fluctuations suggests, however, that this lesson is never fully learned. This raises the very wide question of whether any set of orderly exchange rates can be sustained for any length of time when vast amounts of capital are completely free to move at very short notice.

In the current mythology there was a period up to the late 1960s in which output and employment responded directly and smoothly to demand management changes and trade balances adjusted smartly to exchange-rate changes. Now, somehow, things have changed, so that real variables no longer respond to fiscal, monetary and exchange-rate changes. In truth, the picture of the past is too rosy and of the present too dark. Perhaps it is more difficult to set the exchange rate exactly where it is wanted, and perhaps prices and earnings now respond faster than before. Even so, rates can be changed, with consequences for real variables and for prices and earnings which have not changed their character.

Concluding Remarks

Two rather different mechanisms are suggested by which raising the rate could reduce inflation. The first would work by lowering import prices, and hence the cost of living, so that a smaller increase in nominal wages could secure any given objective for real wages. The second is based upon expectations. If firms and workers know that the exchange rate will not change, that will set limits on export prices and wage demands in export industries. However the learning process may be prolonged, with serious consequences for exports and employment. A newly fixed rate can always be changed, however vehement a Chancellor may be in asserting that it will not be. A single act can destroy confident expectations – a single statement cannot restore them. Lord Parmoor's famous remark after the national government left gold in 1931: 'Nobody told us we could do this', suggests that Labour leaders in the 1920s might have believed that the return to gold was irrevocable. But ever since then the possibility that the exchange rate could be changed has remained. It will only be precluded, if ever, after a very long period of actually unchanged rates. A higher rate may assist a counter-inflation policy; it is certainly not such a policy in its own right.

Will a low rate promote adjustment? Despite evidence that non-price factors play a large part in export competitiveness, a lower rate may encourage exports through higher profitability. The higher price of imports, however, will start eroding the competitive advantage if no effective incomes policy is in place.

Thus the right conclusion seems to be that the power of the exchange rate as an instrument of policy, whether to reduce inflation at the cost of output and the trade balance, or to improve the trade balance at the cost of greater inflation, is limited if there already exists a well-established wage–price spiral. To the extent that an incomes policy could bring the spiral under control, the power of the exchange rate might be increased.

References

[1] IMF, *Annual Report 1977* and *1978*.
[2] —, *Finance and Development*, March 1979.
[3] Kravis, I. B. and Lipsey, R. E., 'Price behaviour in the light of balance of payments theories', *Journal of International Economics*, May 1978.
[4] NIESR, *National Institute Economic Review*, February 1979.
[5] Treasury, *The European Monetary System*, Cmnd 7405, London, HMSO, 1978.

6 Symmetrical Treatment of Surplus Countries

by J. H. Forsyth

Introduction

Disillusionment with the international adjustment process is now widespread, not least because expectations had been so high in the early 1970s. In practice, adjustment has proved painful and has had distinctly limited success. This paper deals with a particular aspect of the problem, namely the way in which surplus countries appear, at least to the deficit countries, to bear less of the burden of adjustment. While the bulk of the paper is concerned with the relationship between this problem and more general questions relating to the adjustment process, it should be remembered that the concern of the deficit countries over what they perceive as unfairness is not unimportant. For the whole fabric of international economic cooperation must depend on all the countries concerned believing the system is a fair one which is not disadvantageous to their national interests.

The Problem of Asymmetry

The constraints on the behaviour of countries in current surplus are not particularly onerous; if the surplus is to be sustained for long enough for the country to move across the line which divides countries which happen to be in surplus from the surplus countries, a financial counterpart to the current surplus must be allowed to emerge. The nature of the counterpart is, however, largely at the discretion of the countries concerned and, although such concepts as scarce currency provisions have been discussed, in practice it is difficult to instance any surplus country which has come under sustained international pressure over the financing of its current surplus. The countries concerned have from time to time come under pressure from their trading partners to reflate or from the exchange markets to revalue, but pressure from the former has rarely been effective, while the costs of exchange-market intervention bear principally on the domestic market. Thus a surplus country is largely free to determine what it is prepared to pay in terms of exchange-market intervention to maintain a particular rate, although ability to absorb inflows within the domestic capital market depends on keeping domestic borrowing requirements well within the normal flow of funds through the capital markets.

Constraints on deficit countries are, in contrast, both onerous and effective. A sustained current deficit requires a sustained inflow of funds to finance it, and few industrial countries during the postwar period have benefited from major long-term private capital inflows.

Financing has thus come largely from public sector borrowing in the international markets, the use of central bank and IMF credit, and reserves. Foreign-exchange reserves have in no case been sufficient to finance a sustained current deficit, although a historically high level of reserves has sometimes provided a substantial cushion. The general pattern has, however, been the reverse of this, as the high levels of inflation and the growth of trade have led most countries to increase their reserves substantially, involving many of them in heavy borrowing in international markets.

The volume of lending in international markets has grown substantially over the last decade, and both the banking and bond markets are now major sources of funds for countries with external financing requirements. For any individual deficit country, however, there are distinct limits to the volume of funds available. Sustained and heavy borrowing will typically lead to a sharp deterioration in terms and there is a long list of major countries which have at one time or another been forced to rely less on these markets as a source of finance and more on central bank and IMF credit. These have always been regarded explicitly as short-term or medium-term facilities which enable the borrower to adopt policies aimed at restoring the current account position in an orderly manner. As such they are always implicitly conditional sources of finance; in the case of the later tranches of IMF credit they are, of course, explicitly conditional.

Thus, when a deficit country is pressed to correct its external position, the pressure comes from those able to apply direct financial sanctions so as to limit the country's access to credit. Such pressure has rarely failed to secure substantial changes in policy. The one exception to this general rule is, of course, the United States, which, as the sole remaining reserve currency country, enjoys the perhaps dubious privilege of an automatic financing of its deficit as long as the surplus countries choose to accumulate reserves as the capital counterpart to their current account position.

With this one exception, however, the adjustment process is asymmetrical, because pressure on deficit countries to adjust is backed up by effective financial sanctions, while pressure on surplus countries is not. This asymmetry in the financial power structure is, of course, part of a wider asymmetry in other areas such as defence – the countries with a strong resource position are typically in a stronger bargaining position.

It is worth noting that, while the pattern of deficits within OECD countries has shifted constantly as a result of adjustment policies, the pattern of surpluses has been far more consistent – a clear reflection of the asymmetry in the adjustment process. It is also significant that the major deficit within OECD countries is now that of the United States, which is the country least immediately susceptible to external financial pressures.

This lack of symmetry in the nature of the adjustment process causes considerable resentment in the weaker countries, which, not unnaturally, consider that an international economic system which depends on mutual cooperation should lead to a fairer distribution of costs and benefits. There are, however, more objective grounds for concern over the workings of the adjustment process.

The first of these is that a system which constrains deficit countries to deflate while not imposing a parallel constraint on surplus countries to reflate imposes a deflationary bias on the international economy. In the period before the oil price increase of 1973, when the OECD countries as a group tended to be in small surplus, the bias was perhaps not unhealthy, but latterly it has become a matter of more general concern. It was symptomatic of this that in 1978 the BIS in its Annual Report observed: 'Adjustment policies last year had, on balance, a net depressive effect on world economic activity. There are two obvious reasons for this. Firstly, the oil imbalance, although shrinking was still there: the sum of current account deficits was therefore bigger than that of adjustable surpluses. Secondly, domestic demand did not expand sufficiently in the surplus countries ... and while restrictive demand management undertaken by deficit countries proved to be highly effective, its expansionary counterpart in the surplus countries did not.' (BIS [1]). While the BIS went on to express the hope that this pattern would be reversed during 1978–9, it is difficult to believe that the pattern of adjustment which it described was accidental, for to do so would be to argue that the deficit countries were more successful at macroeconomic management than the surplus countries. A more convincing hypothesis is that the deficit countries were under the greater external pressure. If the adjustment process is indeed imparting a deflationary bias to the international system, it does not necessarily mean that the world economy is entering a recessionary spiral, but it does suggest that the cost of adjustment in terms of growth forgone is increasing and this must be a matter for international concern.

The second and more practical reason for concern over the asymmetry is that the longer the surplus position of the strong countries is sustained the more deeply embedded it becomes in their industrial structures and the more intractable the adjustment problem becomes. For in practice the export orientation of Swiss and German industries is such that it is difficult to sustain a reflation in these countries without an export boom. Thus, while the pressures of the adjustment process have militated against the emergence of structural deficits among the industrial countries, they have also been markedly unsuccessful in preventing the emergence of structural surpluses. Moreover, the development of such surpluses poses fundamental problems for adjustment policy.

There are two possible reactions to this situation. The first is to resort to more vigorous exhortation to the surplus countries to expand, coupled with a greater willingness to urge reflation on those countries 'which have succeeded in restoring their external balance' (BIS [1]). The problem with this approach is that there is no reason to expect it to be more successful in the future than in the past. Indeed, there are substantial reasons for thinking it may be less successful, for the industrial structures of these countries are already such that it is difficult for them to accept current account equilibrium as a policy target. When the Swiss National Bank intervened to hold the Swiss franc down, the action reflected concern amounting to desperation among Swiss exporters. The intervention did not imply that the franc had reached a level at which Switzerland would run an unfinanceable current account deficit, but rather that the level imposed an intolerable strain on a number of Swiss companies. The criteria for currency valuation are thus moving away from considerations of current account balance and towards a more industrial basis.

The other possible reaction to the problem of asymmetry is to re-examine the workings of the adjustment process since the war and consider whether the concept which has been used is practicable. This must, by implication, involve an analysis of the basic assumptions on which international economic policy has developed.

The Postwar International Economic Order

The international economic system that has developed since the war has three outstanding features. The first is the concept of a cooperative international policy: the experience of the 1930s, when unilateral attempts by individual countries to correct external and internal imbalances proved futile and destructive, led to a consensus after the war that trade and adjustment policies should be based on cooperative decisions by the industrial countries. This consensus, which was fundamental to the Bretton Woods agreement, has been maintained ever since, despite major changes in the techniques employed and radical shifts in both the volume and the pattern of trade. The OECD and IMF have given an institutional form to this policy, and the influence of these bodies and of the regular international policy meetings has served to maintain a remarkably uniform approach to the problems of trade and adjustment policy, to which the exceptions are few but instructive.

The most obvious point on which there has been a uniform approach among the industrial countries is trade restriction. Through the various GATT rounds, and more specific regional arrangements such as the EEC, there has been a sustained attempt to reduce barriers to trade in terms both of tariffs and of non-tariff restrictions. There have, of course, been important exceptions to this trend, both in specific kinds of traded goods such as agricultural products, where the autarkic practices of the prewar period have been maintained, and in particular countries such as Japan and Canada, which have been remarkably successful in maintaining a special status for themselves. While this trend towards a freer international market in goods, and to a lesser extent in services, is now taken for granted, it is worth remembering that it involved reversing the whole trend of trade policies in the earlier part of the century and a complete change of face for political parties which had historically favoured protection.

Since the mid-1970s this consensus in favour of free trade has been under sustained attack and there are now important restrictions on the growth of trade in many areas. However, the pattern of international trade still reflects the shift to a more liberal international trading order, while the impact of trade restrictions, although important for the future, has as yet been only marginal.

The third, and less obvious, feature of the postwar economic order has been the concentration on the current account as the criterion by which international adjustment should be judged. As Junz observed in a paper presented to the American Financial Association in December 1977: 'The emphasis on current account transactions is reflected in the discussions on the balance of payments adjustment process during the sixties. The question of what, in fact, one ought to be adjusting towards, was answered in terms of current account aims. Discussion focused on early identification of the extent to which such goals were internationally compatible and to what extent they indicated the need for adjustment, internally or externally.' (Junz [2]). The experience of the 1970s has in no way diminished support for this view of the adjustment process. Indeed the BIS recently observed, 'balance of payments financing policies' . . . normal function [is] complementing and facilitating current account adjustment instead of substituting for such adjustment. For the clear lesson to be drawn from the last few years is that, apart from the traditional transfer of real resources from highly developed countries to developing ones, long lasting substantial current account imbalances lead ultimately to a painful reckoning whether for the deficit countries or the surplus countries, or both.' (BIS [1]).

The vigour with which this view of the adjustment process is maintained is, perhaps, surprising in a historical perspective. For during the nineteenth century 'long lasting substantial current account imbalances' were a normal feature of the international economy, and indeed were seen as playing a major role in promoting economic growth.

However, this view of the adjustment process as a current account phenomenon had certainly immense influence on international policy in the postwar period and thus, by extension, on the structure of the international economy. The concomitant to this view was necessarily to downgrade the importance of the capital account. Thus as Junz observed: 'while emphasis was placed . . . on freeing trade flows . . . there was much less reluctance to accept restrictions on capital flows. The interaction between current and capital account transactions was not necessarily misunderstood but rather neglected.' (Junz [2]). The logical consequence of this view was that countries enjoyed far greater latitude with respect to policies affecting the capital account than to policies affecting the current account. Thus both inward and outward capital controls have proliferated and official intervention has played a major structural role in international capital movements.

The three fundamental features of the postwar international economic order outlined above have combined to produce a system whose most remarkable feature is a general bias towards free movement of goods and against free movement of capital. The question which the experience of the past decade would seem to raise is whether such a system is sustainable in the longer term or is inherently unstable. For if it is unstable there can be no alternative to fundamental reform aimed at either restricting trade or restoring the capital account to a major position in the system.

In considering this question it is perhaps worth analysing the likely development of a system in which goods are freely traded but capital flows restricted to discretionary official interventions in the exchange market. In such a system prices in the internationally traded sector must tend to equate within each national market and, depending on pricing behaviour, between national markets. There will, however, be no mechanism for equating profit levels. Thus, if for some reason costs in one of the countries concerned fall below the level in other competing countries, profits in that country will rise sharply, leading both to higher investment overall and a shift of investment into the internationally traded sector. Similarly, a country where costs have risen would suffer a decline in profits and a shift of investment out of the internationally traded sector. Countries which had become more competitive would therefore tend to develop a structural surplus of capacity in the internationally traded sector and increased official external assets, whereas countries which had lost competitiveness would tend to develop a shortage of capacity in the internationally traded area and large official external liabilities. In such a situation the imbalances in capacity in the internationally traded sectors must tend to grow with time and so must the costs of achieving equilibrium on current account through the management of domestic demand.

The process would be avoided in so far as the discretionary exchange-market interventions were always made at exchange rates set so as to equate profitability, but in so far as an imbalance in capacity had built up in the past it would be necessary to set the rate so as to produce lower profits and investment in the country with excess capacity than in the country with deficient capacity. This imbalance would have to be maintained until sufficient excess profit and investment had been generated in the country with deficient capacity to bring its capacity into line. Until then an imbalance in trade would persist and the country with excess capacity would continue to accumulate financial assets, even though its structural surplus was being eroded. However, the restoration of equilibrium would depend on the surplus country being prepared to allow its exchange rate to be maintained at a level at which profits and investment in the internationally traded sector were below the international average. Again it is important to note that the larger the imbalance in capacity which developed while profit and investment levels were out of line, the greater the rise in the exchange rate needed to reverse the imbalance must be, for profit levels on the larger investment stock in the surplus country will have to fall very low before profit levels on the smaller stock in the deficit country are sufficient to generate a higher level of investment in that country.

The above analysis gives a highly simplistic account of the workings of an international system in which goods are able to move freely but capital movements are limited to official interventions. In practice we have an international system in which neither movements of goods nor movements of capital are wholly free or wholly restricted. The most that can be said is that the present system has a general bias towards the free movement of goods and against the free movement of capital. However, if the foregoing analysis is correct, such a bias might be expected to produce imbalances and strains of the type outlined above, albeit in an attenuated form.

The evidence would seem to be compatible with such a hypothesis. First, the three major surplus countries, Japan, Germany and Switzerland, are all now generally admitted to have gone through periods when they had substantial cost advantages over their international competitors, and in consequence very high levels of investment in their internationally traded sectors. Secondly, all three have intervened heavily in the capital account of their balance of payments either by direct controls or intervention.

Japan has always discouraged direct inward investment by insisting that any company wishing to invest in Japan should do so in partnership with a Japanese company. This has proved to be an extremely effective control in that, although there has been a general awareness that growth and profitability in Japan have been exceptionally high, inward investment has been largely restricted to substantial portfolio flows, which Japan has allowed since the 1960s. It should be noted, however, that although restrictions on foreign inflows into the domestic bond and money markets have been eased substantially in recent years, they are still a significant factor in the market. Japan has also, of course, intervened in the exchange markets substantially over the years, accumulating over $80 billion of reserves during the last decade. The figures for reserve accumulation understate the official influence on the level of capital inflows, as the Japanese authorities have, from time to time, prevailed on both the Japanese banks and the trading companies to engage in substantial capital exports. For this reason the figures for Japanese capital exports provide a poor measure of autonomous outflows.

The position in Germany is rather more straightforward. Inward capital controls in the form of official restrictions on the acquisition by foreigners of short-term Deutschemark assets have been a feature of the German market and, at times of upward pressure on the exchange rate, differential reserve requirements and 'Bardepots' (non-interest-bearing cash deposits required when borrowing from non-residents) have been used to discourage inflows. Direct investment has been relatively unregulated and, particularly from the United States, not insignificant. The main policy instrument on the external side has therefore been exchange-market intervention: German reserves rose by $44 billion between the end of 1968 and the end of 1978, so that the main financial counterpart to the German current account surplus has been reserve accumulation, with official capital exports playing a not insignificant role. In this situation the exchange rate has been determined by official policy over intervention, rather than moving the rate to a level at which private capital outflows would offset the current account position. Indeed, during the earlier part of the period unofficial intervention held the rate at a level where Germany ran a surplus on both current and private capital accounts. The effect of such intervention has, of course, been to keep up the levels of profits and investment within Germany, and in particular within the internationally traded sector.

The Swiss position has been similar to that of Germany, the main difference being that the process has been taken to greater extremes. Swiss inward capital controls have in general been more draconian and the direction of the bond market more influenced by a desire to secure capital outflows. Exchange-market intervention has been pro-portionally greater than in Germany, with reserves accumulating by $17 billion between the end of 1968 and the end of 1978.

Thus in all three countries the capital account has been dominated by official intervention directed towards holding the exchange rate at a level at which profitability was at least sufficient to prevent private capital outflows. In these circumstances it is hardly surprising that domestic investment has produced an extremely strong capacity posi-tion in the internationally traded sectors. Measures of capacity are notoriously unreliable, but it is worth noting that in all three countries the manufacturing sector is abnormally large and an unusually high proportion of its output goes to export markets; in this context it is significant that the BIS [1] cited structural imbalances as a factor preventing the surplus countries from restoring external balance through reflation. More significant, perhaps, is the fact that all three countries have defended their exchange-market interventions by claiming that without them the exchange rate would have risen to a point at which profits in the internationally traded sector would have fallen dangerously low – an observation which is entirely consistent with excess capacity in the internationally traded sector.

The most compelling evidence for the structural nature of the Japanese, German and Swiss surpluses is, in the last analysis, their consistency. Germany has registered a substantial surplus on goods and services in every year since 1965, when it ran a small deficit; Japan has had three deficits on goods and services since 1965 – a minimal one in 1967 and a substantial one in 1974 (following the rise in the price of oil and other commodities), which was substantially reduced in 1975 and reversed in 1976; Switzerland has not run a deficit on goods and services since 1964.

The consistency of the current account positions of these countries would seem to rule out an explanation in terms of demand. For if the surpluses were due to depressed demand it would be logical to expect low growth and abnormally high unemployment, neither of which is a feature of these economies (although it must be admitted that immigrant labour has been an important factor in Switzerland and, to a lesser extent, in Germany). Equally, if the surpluses were caused by a shift in demand reflecting undervaluation of the exchange rate, it might have been expected that the substantial rise in real exchange rates, as measured by unit costs in manufacturing (see OECD [3]), would have eliminated the current account surpluses.

Structural imbalances affecting the supply side would, however, be consistent with the pattern of surpluses which these countries have experienced. They would also make the elimination of such surpluses through either reflation or revaluation difficult. For if supply factors are in imbalance within the economy, reflation sufficient to bring the external account into equilibrium must tend to produce excess demand in the domestic sectors. Revaluation may shift profits dramatically but, once supply imbalances are embedded in the economy, its effect on the external balance must be limited in the short term, for on this analysis the main impact of exchange-rate changes will be through profits and investment affecting capacity. Exchange-rate-induced shifts in demand *per se* will have only a limited impact on trade patterns.

The pattern of deficits in the international economy has been far less consistent than the pattern of surpluses, as might be expected in a system with such marked asymmetry in its adjustment process. It is, however, worth noting that the countries most closely approximating to structural deficit countries have the following characteristics: first, they have all used outward exchange controls and accumulated official liabilities as a result of exchange-market intervention; secondly, they have exhibited low rates of investment, particularly in the internationally traded sector; thirdly, they have experienced relatively intractable unemployment problems.

The overall cost to the industrial countries of bringing these current accounts into equilibrium is tending to grow even where no structural imbalances exist. For the imbalances between the OECD countries have grown substantially as a proportion of GDP. A measure of this can be obtained by taking the average OECD surplus or deficit expressed as a proportion of GDP as a norm and then aggregating the difference of each country's actual position from the norm. If these differences are taken as a proportion of GDP it is possible to gauge the degree of maladjustment within the OECD. The results of doing so are shown in Chart 6.1. It will be seen that there has been a substantial rise in these imbalances since the mid-1960s, even though both exchange-rate and demand management have been used more actively to secure external balance. This trend towards increasing imbalance appears to be more closely related to the overall growth in trade than the growth in GDP and there seems little evidence that a trend towards better adjustment has emerged. This would seem to suggest that, even if the problems of symmetrical adjustment and structural imbalances could be resolved, the costs of pursuing current account equilibrium as a policy target will tend to grow if trade continues to grow faster than GDP.

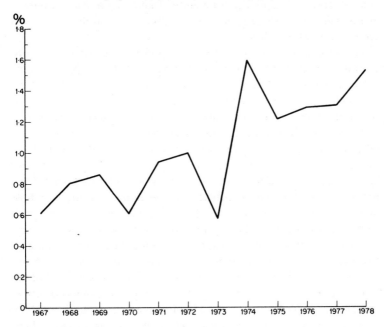

Chart 6.1   Aggregate imbalances of OECD countries as a proportion of OECD GDP, 1967–78

Source: *Morgan Grenfell Economic Review,* August 1978.

Potential Constraints on Surplus Countries

It is evident that existing constraints on surplus countries are ineffective and that their willingness to accept them is, if anything, diminishing. I have suggested that the reasons for this are twofold: first, there are no effective financial constraints on surplus countries to parallel those on deficit countries; secondly, the structural nature of the imbalances means that adjustment through conventional demand and exchange-rate management is likely to be expensive and ineffective, so that countries which are not constrained to do so are unlikely to adopt such policies.

In the long term, if constraints on the surplus countries are to be effective they must be constraints which deal with the underlying problem of structural imbalance. The argument of this paper has been that the root cause of such imbalances is the dichotomy between the free movements of goods and the restricted and directed movements of capital in the international economy. If this is correct, it follows that in principle a solution may be found by restricting movements of goods or by freeing movements of capital, and these solutions are not mutually exclusive.

The revival of trade restriction as a policy in recent years, both in practice and in theory, can hardly be regarded as surprising. The policy has the attraction of acting directly on the problem and, although radical on the trade side, has the additional advantage of remaining firmly within the tenets of postwar financial orthodoxy.

There are, however, significant problems which are dealt with more fully in other papers. In this context it is important to note that existing capacity imbalances can only be corrected by high investment in the countries with deficient capacity, which must be financed by profits or taxation unless private capital inflows occur, and low investment in the surplus countries. The problem with the protectionist approach is that as long as the present structural imbalances remain and present capital account policies are maintained the surpluses will tend to be diverted. Thus, if Japanese motor companies are excluded from the car markets of Europe, they are bound to devote more of their efforts to the faster-growing markets of the third world; indeed restrictions on Japanese car exports to Europe, by reducing upward pressure on the yen, must tend to increase their competitive edge in third world markets, while at the same time reducing the competitiveness of European-based producers.

To put it another way, as long as the capital account is subject to official manipulation, to manage one area of trade will simply place further pressure on other areas. If it was possible to achieve a comprehensive series of trade agreements this problem could be overcome, but in recent years the dispersion of economic power from the old metropolitan countries has made it much harder to impose international agreements throughout the free world. The key factor here is the emergence as major forces in international trading of a number of third world countries which, in certain cases, seem set on policies that will create structural surpluses of capacity in a manner paralleling Japanese development.

This shift away from a simple pattern of developed and developing countries to a more complex pattern, in which the international economy consists of countries with a wide range of growth rates and development levels, also undermines one of the principal assumptions behind the use of current account balance as a policy target, namely that the problem of international resource allocation could be resolved by an agreement to adopt a simple rule of thumb that the developed countries should devote a certain proportion of their GNP to transferring resources to the poorer countries. In a world in which countries could be neatly classified as 'haves' and 'have nots' such a principle may have been workable, but in the world we live in it is not.

The case for attaching greater importance to the capital account does not, however, depend on the emergence of the third world as a major factor in the world economy, but rather on the realisation that autonomous international capital flows have a major role to play in both preventing and correcting imbalances; for as long as deficiencies of capacity in the deficit countries have to be corrected by a faster internal generation of investment funds than in the countries with a surplus of capacity, the process of adjustment must be longer than in a system where investment funds can flow freely between countries.

The role of the capital account should be to distribute resources efficiently, rather than to facilitate current account adjustment or provide help to the developing countries. In this context exchange-rate changes are important for the effect they have on relative rates of return and the pattern of capital flows. As most recent research on exchange-rate changes indicates that they work through profitability rather than pricing, it follows that they will only work effectively if external capital is allowed to move to areas of high profitability.

This argument suggests that the most effective constraint which could be applied to the surplus countries concerns the structure of their capital accounts. In practice they have been able to finance sustained current account surpluses by official short-term capital exports which would have been more appropriate to short-term speculative inflows, without attracting any significant international criticism.

They were able to do so because it was conventionally assumed that their surpluses were temporary in nature. The consequence is that the official capital exports from these countries, although notionally transferring resources, have not in practice shifted investment. Indeed, by obviating the need for autonomous private capital exports they have prevented the shift in the pattern of private investment which might otherwise have been expected. In this sense intervention in the exchange markets by the authorities, both as transactors and as regulators, has tended to militate against effective long-term adjustment.

If capital flows are to be seen as a dynamic element in the adjustment process, it is important to note that reliance on the exchange rate as a policy mechanism will, if anything, be less than under the present system, as both fiscal and interest-rate policies can be used to encourage autonomous capital flows.

For the deficit countries the attraction of imposing constraints on the capital accounts of the surplus countries is twofold: first, such a system could be used to apply financial constraints on the official accumulation of short-term and medium-term financial assets parallel to those affecting the accumulation of official liabilities; secondly, it should lead to an increased flow of investment within their domestic economies. However, it would not be without cost, as it would necessitate raising the return on capital to at least the international level.

References

[1] BIS, *48th Annual Report 1977-78*, Basle, 1978.
[2] Junz, H. B., 'The balance of payments adjustment process revisited' (paper presented to the American Financial Association, December 1977).
[3] OECD, *Budget Indicators – the international competitiveness of selected OECD countries*, Paris, 1978.

Comment
by M. J. Balfour

John Forsyth's paper, 'Symmetrical Treatment of Surplus Countries', contains a lucid analysis of the asymmetrical nature of the adjustment constraints which fall on surplus and deficit countries; it gives a perceptive view on how the international economic system in the postwar years has been moulded by certain characteristics, with the consequences that flowed from them; finally, it offers some signposts –

prescriptions would be too strong a word – to the route along which progress might be achieved.

This note discusses key points in the paper and then considers possible ways in which symmetry might be improved.

The Problem

Few would question that the expectations of the early 1970s have not been fulfilled. One must, however, be clear about the nature of those expectations and who most believed in them. 1971 saw the last effort to keep the Bretton Woods system going and in official circles at that time it was obviously hoped that the steps taken then would shore up the old structure. John Forsyth's paper, however, evidently has in mind the subsequent move to generalised floating of exchange rates, which began in 1972 and was consolidated by the oil crisis at the end of 1973. What is important for understanding the subsequent developments he traces out is that, while a body of eminent academic opinion greeted the arrival of floating as a rational and much more sensible solution to the problems of external payments imbalances, in official circles only the American authorities saw it wholly in that light. Germany also saw certain advantages in floating, but the other leading industrial nations were generally driven to it by force of circumstances rather than choice, and by and large non-industrial countries continued to peg their currencies to whatever unit seemed best suited to their particular trade patterns and ties. Few countries apart from the United States were predisposed by conviction to give floating the full benefit of the doubt and, after many countries had suffered painful experiences, the innate inclination of most monetary authorities to try to maintain order in their own foreign-exchange markets came more and more to the surface. There is therefore the paradox that since 1973 the volume of interventions in the exchange markets by the main industrial countries has probably been considerably greater than when the Bretton Woods system was still functioning adequately.

All this underlies the points made in John Forsyth's paper about the problems of asymmetry and rather than repeat them here it is more useful to examine other considerations which are only implicit in his argument. The first point is that, whereas there is a lack of symmetry in the pressures to adjust felt by deficit and surplus countries, there is all too much symmetry in the effects of exchange-rate adjustment by the two sets of countries. Countries with depreciating currencies are exposed still more to the inflation which no doubt was a prime cause in driving down their exchange rates, whilst countries with appreciating currencies enjoy the significant benefit of a stabilising or downward force on their internal price level. In a period like the 1970s, when inflation has been experienced by even strong economies at levels undreamt of fifteen years ago, it is little wonder that governments have increasingly come to the view that, even if they could engineer it to their own satisfaction, a step devaluation which caused a significant decline in their real exchange rate is not the advantageous policy instrument which it was when fixed but adjustable exchange rates were the rule.

Reluctance to aim for real depreciation of exchange rates (which, incidentally, was not foreseen in 1973 when the international community's response to the oil crisis was, *inter alia*, a mutual undertaking to avoid 'beggar-my-neighbour' devaluations) has certain side-effects. To illustrate these by *reductio ad adsurdum*, if the world consisted of two currency zones each resolutely opposed to devaluation, neither could appreciate against the other. In the actual world this still holds partially true, since the ability of a whole set of countries deliberately to appreciate in 'effective terms' must depend on the willingness of the remaining set of countries to depreciate by whatever amount is required. The more evenly balanced the two sets are and the more the second resists real depreciation, the more difficult it becomes for the first to appreciate in real terms.

Secondly, the problems of adjustment between industrial countries were compounded by the 1973 oil crisis and, though its international effects had been considerably mitigated by last year, they have begun to reappear since the events in Iran. The aspect to stress here is that after 1973 (and again today) the current account 'norm' of each industrial country should have been a deficit which bore some correlation with its share of the OPEC countries' unavoidable surpluses *vis-à-vis* the industrial world. Consequently, the persistent surpluses of certain countries could no longer appropriately be measured against the old standard of, say, $\frac{1}{2}$–1 per cent of GNP (to allow for aid and other long-term capital flows), but rather against a standard deficit of the same order of magnitude. Thus, the adjustment needed if the financing of the OPEC surpluses was to be evenly distributed amongst the industrial countries had to be very much greater than appeared at first.

The third point is to draw attention to a simple but telling phrase in John Forsyth's paper where he speaks of 'the line which divides countries which happen to be in surplus from the surplus countries'. This distinction is important in relation to the points listed above. The fact is that the only persistent surplus countries are the three he mentions, though until recently the Benelux countries would also have been candidates for inclusion however special the case of the Netherlands. It follows that, though the aftermath of the 1973 oil crisis has produced some polarisation of weaker and stronger economies, the distribution has been very one-sided, a fact which observers of the United Kingdom with its particularly severe problems in the mid-1970s are apt to forget.

Because of this one-sidedness and the long attachment of the United States authorities to the doctrine of free floating, the problem inherent in the first point made above has not prevented quite major changes in real exchange rates.

The Postwar International Economic Order

The second part of John Forsyth's paper demonstrates that the postwar trading and payments systems created a bias towards the freedom of current transactions and against free capital movements, and that balance of payments adjustment was consequently seen in terms of the current account rather than of the current and capital accounts combined. More specifically, the accepted use of capital controls after the war militated against adjustment by redressing international imbalances of capital investment in the traded goods sector.

That there was some bias of the kind described is undeniable, but it should be remembered that:

(a) Throughout the late 1950s and 1960s the industrial countries made considerable and largely successful efforts to liberalise capital movements (both in the EEC and more widely in the OECD).
(b) All countries were committed to defending fixed but adjustable exchange rates and it was necessary for credibility that exchange-rates changes should not be an instrument of easy resort.
(c) For much of the period, the industrial countries, apart from the United States, were concerned to accumulate gold and foreign-exchange reserves.

Because of (b) it always remained 'respectable' for industrial countries to control as best they could short-term capital movements, but those countries which maintained control on capital movements judged to be of fundamental importance (such as direct investment) came under constant pressure to grant greater freedom. The effects of (c), together with a streak of mercantilism in most countries, no doubt left the system open to the criticism that upward exchange-rate adjustments were 'too little and too late'. But the system was certainly intended to give maximum scope for the benefits of cross-frontier capital investment and the rise of the multinationals was proof of its happening. These, however, are debating points which probably do not invalidate the thesis that it was because of the way that the postwar order developed that, in the hostile environment after 1973, the problems of the structural surplus countries proved so intractable.

The real question, however, is whether in this new environment the conclusions drawn by John Forsyth could do the trick. To answer it is necessary to consider more closely how the desired shifts in investment would take place. The first and obvious point is that only very limited categories of capital movement would contribute. If German investors buy City of Copenhagen Deutschemark bonds, it will help Denmark's external financing problem but will do nothing for its traded goods sector.

Secondly, flows of direct (and to some extent portfolio) investment between countries will, in the absence of trade restrictions or other barriers, be determined primarily by judgments about relative profitability. This indeed is the kernel of the argument in John Forsyth's paper. These judgments will depend on a host of factors which change slowly if at all – geographical position, local raw materials, labour relations, etc. – but also crucially on domestic cost and exchange-rate expectations. The problem is that, in a world where monetary authorities no longer intervened in exchange markets, the movements in exchange rates required to clear the markets would be violent and erratic. It is difficult to see on what rational basis any potential direct investor could then count on durable conditions for his investment. Conversely, it is easy to see that on short-term considerations temporary buyers of financial assets would continue to judge that a particular country was a profitable haven for their funds for a short period, even when its longer-term economic prospects were not rosy. The experience of the dollar in the last five years clearly demonstrates the violent swings to which a currency can be subject when little official intervention is being undertaken to stabilise it and how disordered or even perverse in those circumstances capital flows can be. In practice, of course, the authorities of most industrial countries have tried during the period of floating to moderate fluctuations in their exchange rates. Therefore, although their actions were much more unpredictable than in the Bretton Woods era, markets were not left in total uncertainty.

Table 6.1   Changes in cost competitiveness and in gross fixed capital formation in OECD countries

	Cost competitiveness,[a] change 1973–7 inc. (percentages)	Gross fixed capital formation		
		Change 1968–72 inc.	Change 1973–7 inc. (percentages p.a.)	Change in change
United Kingdom	+17	2	−1	−3
France	−4	7	2	−5
Germany	−14	7	−1	−8
Italy	+26	4	—	−4
Japan	−16	14	2	−12
United States	+19	3.5	0.5	−3
Canada	+3	4	4	—
Belgium	−5	3	3	—
Netherlands	−9	4	1	−3
Sweden	+2	2	—	−2
Switzerland	−6	7	−5	−12
Total OECD	—	6	1	−5

Sources: IMF, *International Financial Statistics*; OECD, *National Accounts of OECD Countries* (various issues).
[a]Inverse of relative normalised unit labour costs.

Thirdly, supposing that exchange-rate changes and other factors did encourage the necessary shifts in capital investment, the results would be slow to appear. There are examples enough of how slow can be the demise of a declining industry faced with increasing foreign competition and the converse is also likely. Consequently, for this mechanism to work much time would be required, during which problems of balance of payments maladjustment would subsist. To parry these the classic recipes would still be needed – demand management in both surplus and deficit countries, and encouragement by interest-rate and other policies of non-volatile capital flows to finance the disequilibria and exchange-rate changes however imperfectly controlled. It should here be mentioned that, in spite of the oil crisis, most OECD countries have managed since 1972 to avoid being either deficit or surplus countries within John Forsyth's definition; that is to say, they have achieved very large swings in their current accounts and have done so chiefly through 'old fashioned' demand management. So while the costs, in terms of extra demand or output lost or needed for a given adjustment, may have grown in the 1970s, relative changes in demand are still one of the most potent factors in balance of payments adjustment.

However, there is evidence that fixed investment in the main industrial countries has in fact responded to the changes in recent years in real exchange rates, and hence in competitiveness. Table 6.1 suggests that the slower growth in fixed capital formation observed in most OECD countries in the years 1973–7 was particularly marked in those countries which were simultaneously in persistent surplus and had lost most in cost competitiveness. Thus it may be that the process advocated by John Forsyth has been at work.

Concluding Remarks

John Forsyth's paper examined the *types* of action by surplus countries which would best bring about adjustment, while this note has suggested that, though capital movements could and should play a more useful role, they cannot always be counted on to be benign and will in any case be structurally slow-acting. Consequently it may be concluded that adjustment will have to continue to take all the varied forms of the past.

There remains, however, the interesting question *how* pressure can be brought to bear on surplus countries so that the onus of adjustment falls more evenly between them and the deficit countries. By inference, John Forsyth's paper sees this coming about through international persuasion in the numerous bodies which discuss or monitor countries' economic policy and performance. This certainly is a possibility that should not be discounted – witness the Bonn 'summit' last year which, whatever cynics may say, did lead to a tangible effort by Japan and Germany; witness the new Article IV of the IMF Agreement and so on. This approach, however, differs entirely from the pressure put on persistent deficit countries, which are required to pursue stabilising policies as a condition of obtaining finance from official sources (which sooner or later they will need). Would it be possible, therefore, to introduce an analogous 'conditionality' on surplus countries?

For there to be some kind of symmetry of this sort, it seems clear that the point of leverage would have to be the counterpart to official borrowing, that is the official settlements received by creditor countries. Since the international monetary system no longer has binding rules about convertibility of currencies (as guaranteed by the par value system), the general notion of asset settlements is now elusive, to say the least. At first sight, therefore, there seems little prospect of applying pressure by this method. Nevertheless, there are two areas which might allow some scope for it. The first is the EEC and the second is the Group of Ten and Switzerland. The EEC has recently instituted the European Monetary System, which in its exchange-rate regime and associated elements is essentially a par value system with asset settlements tempered by credit facilities. The European Currency Unit 'divergence indicator', which is a wholly new feature of the system, has the makings of a pressure mechanism; even though its functions fall rather short of the uses to which certain countries, including notably the United Kingdom, had hoped it would be put, with time and experience it could become a more powerful tool. The Group of Ten and Switzerland have all subscribed to a facility to assist in the financing of large drawings on the IMF by members of their own group, namely the General Arrangements to Borrow, and in any case it is they, and especially those in surplus, that are called upon to meet the lion's share of other IMF financing. It could be conceived, therefore, that persistent creditors' claims on the IMF might attract 'reverse conditionality' in some way, either in the rate of interest they bear, or in their usability, or both.

The underlying idea in both these cases would be not to dictate the way in which surplus countries should adjust – that is their affair – but to create a disincentive for their not doing so. Is this fanciful?

7.1 Responses to Current Account Imbalance

by R. L. Major

Imbalances on Current Account

Persistent imbalances on current account are not a purely recent phenomenon. Canada recorded nineteen annual deficits in the twenty years from 1951 to 1970. At the other extreme the United States recorded nineteen surpluses and Germany eighteen in the same period. In the 1950s and 1960s surpluses were recorded for Belgium, the Netherlands and Switzerland and deficits for Australia and Norway with almost equal regularity. The scale of the imbalances appears, however, to have increased recently, not only in absolute figures but in relation either to national reserves or to national output (Table 7.1).

Over the four-year period 1974–7 four of the seven major OECD countries (Canada, France, Italy and the United Kingdom) each had an annual average current deficit exceeding 30 per cent of the average levels of their reserves at the end of each year. The same was true of the smaller OECD countries as a group, even though two of them, Switzerland and the Netherlands, were running big current surpluses. Moreover, in both 1977 and 1978 the United States and Canada ran deficits approximately equal to their reserves. Nor is this due merely to a greater tendency towards deficit since the big increase in oil prices in 1973–4. The United States swung to massive deficit from a substantial surplus from 1973 to 1976, while the Italian balance of payments swung in the opposite direction on a scale even more remarkable in relation to GDP.

Direct Investment and Other Capital Flows

All major countries have responded to upward or downward pressure on their exchange rates arising from developments on current account

Table 7.1   Current balances in relation to reserves and GDP/GNP

	1960–6	1967–73	1974–7	1977	1978[a]
	($ billion, annual average)				
Current balance					
United Kingdom	−0.1	+0.3	−3.6	+0.5	+0.5
France	−0.1	−0.3	−3.9	−3.3	+4.1
Germany	+0.1	+2.0	+5.3	+3.7	+8.8
Italy[b]	+0.7	+1.3	−2.3	+2.3	+6.3
Japan[b]	—	+2.5	+2.3	+10.9	+16.6
United States	+4.2	+0.8	+3.0	−15.3	−16.0
Canada[b]	−0.9	—	−3.5	−3.9	−4.6
Other OECD[c]	−1.5	+0.1	−15.7	−21.8	−8.7
Total OECD	+2.5	+6.6	−18.3	−26.9	+7.0
	(percentages)				
Current balance/reserves					
United Kingdom	*−3.3*	*+5.7*	*−38.4*	*+2.4*	*+2.9*
France	*−2.3*	*−4.3*	*−44.8*	*−35.8*	*+31.0*
Germany	*+1.0*	*+13.3*	*+16.5*	*+10.0*	*+17.7*
Italy	*+20.2*	*+24.6*	*−31.0*	*+19.7*	*+43.4*
Japan	*+0.3*	*+31.1*	*+14.9*	*+50.4*	*+50.9*
United States	*+26.5*	*+5.8*	*+21.3*	*−105.7*	*−86.1*
Canada	*−35.7*	*−0.7*	*−74.4*	*−103.9*	*−114.9*
Other OECD	*−10.8*	*+0.5*	*−33.0*	*−42.6*	*−12.5*
Total OECD	*+4.9*	*+7.9*	*−13.0*	*−15.8*	*+3.2*
Current balance/GDP or GNP					
United Kingdom	*−0.1*	*+0.2*	*−1.6*	*+0.2*	*+0.2*
France	*−0.1*	*−0.2*	*−1.2*	*−0.9*	*+0.9*
Germany	*+0.1*	*+1.0*	*+1.2*	*+0.7*	*+1.4*
Italy	*+1.5*	*+1.3*	*−1.3*	*+1.2*	*+2.7*
Japan	—	*+1.1*	*+0.4*	*+1.6*	*+1.7*
United States	*+0.7*	*+0.1*	*+0.2*	*−0.8*	*−0.8*
Canada	*−1.9*	—	*−2.0*	*−1.9*	*−2.2*
Other OECD	*−1.0*	—	*−2.2*	*−2.6*	*−1.0*
Total OECD	*+0.2*	*+0.3*	*−0.4*	*−0.5*	*+0.1*

Sources: OECD, *Balance of Payments of OECD Countries, National Accounts of OECD
  Countries* and *Main Economic Indicators; National Institute Economic Review.*
[a]Estimated.
[b]Excludes reinvested profits.
[c]Excludes reinvested profits for most countries.

by varying their regulations governing or influencing capital flows.

In the United States the first direct controls, which were mandatory for direct investment though voluntary for financial flows, were introduced in 1968, as the war in Vietnam whittled away the current surplus almost to vanishing point. This system was, however, gradually phased out and, with the current balance returning to massive surplus in 1973, all controls over capital outflows were effectively abolished in the following year. Similarly in Japan, where the regime had been more restrictive, big current surpluses in 1971 and 1972 were followed by the virtual removal of controls on outward investment as such, though the degree of freedom for domestic borrowing for the purpose has subsequently varied and inward direct investment has been liberalised only gradually.

French controls on direct investment, both inward and outward, were relaxed gradually during the 1970s. Other forms of inward investment are, with minor qualifications, permitted freely, as is outward portfolio investment. From August 1971 to March 1974 there was a dual exchange market, with the official market accommodating only visible trade and trade-related or official invisible transactions. From January 1973 to March 1974 Italy also operated a dual exchange market, but in this case the official market handled all current transactions. The aim of discouraging capital outflows has subsequently been achieved mainly by the requirement of a lira deposit by residents transferring capital for investment overseas.

The United Kingdom operates the most restrictive regime of all the major countries. During most of the 1960s direct investment outside the sterling area had normally to be financed by foreign currency borrowing or through the investment currency market (the latter involving purchase from another resident at an effective premium which has at times been very high). There were also voluntary restrictions from May 1966 on investment in developed sterling area countries. With the current balance initially in substantial surplus, the mandatory controls on outward investment were somewhat relaxed in the early 1970s and the programme relating to the developed sterling area was terminated by the 1972 budget.

In Germany and Switzerland it is, with only minor exceptions, capital inflows that controls have been designed to restrict. In Germany these have been concentrated on the financial sector, particularly since 1974. Borrowing from non-residents other than by banks had previously been subject to Bundesbank approval and to payment of a non-interest-bearing cash deposit. Interest payments on non-residents' bank balances were often prohibited during the early 1970s and other weapons against speculative inflows have included tax on interest earned by non-resident holders of fixed-interest securities, minimum reserve requirements which discriminate against liabilities to non-residents and a requirement that banks should make deposits with the Bundesbank in respect of such liabilities. The rates involved have varied according to the degree of upward pressure on the Deutschemark, but in 1972 reserve requirements on new external liabilities were raised to 90–100 per cent, at which point negative interest rates were imposed by some banks. This device has been regularly used in Switzerland, which has also relied heavily on reserve requirements to discourage short-term inflows and varied the degree of non-residents' freedom of access to the long-term capital market. The policy of the other most persistent surplus country, the Netherlands, has been to allow inward transfers of foreign capital only if they constitute direct investment, while capital exports have been liberally permitted.

It is probably not mere coincidence that the three countries which have most conspicuously combined surpluses on current account with discouragement of private capital inflows have another characteristic in common. In each case a rise in the share of domestic output absorbed by the foreign balance has had as its main counterpart a reduction in the share devoted to gross fixed investment, while in OECD countries generally the distribution of output between the major sectors of demand has changed relatively little since the early 1960s. On the other hand manufacturing industry's share in GDP has fallen much more slowly in Germany than in the other major industrial countries except Japan and Italy and since the early 1960s it has been higher in Germany than elsewhere.

Government Non-monetary Capital

Of the major countries, the United States, Japan, France, Germany and the United Kingdom are normally net exporters of official non-monetary capital, with Canada a net borrower, mainly through issues of securities, and Italy varying from year to year. Japan has, however, become a substantial net lender only in the last ten years or so and special factors have turned a number of the other countries into net borrowers on several occasions in recent years. Even Germany figures as a net borrower in 1976 and, to a lesser extent, 1975, largely because of foreign (including OPEC) buying of notes issued by public authorities, and since the mid-1960s the main counterpart of the German surplus on current and private capital accounts has been official accumulation of monetary assets rather than outflows of non-monetary capital on official account (Table 7.2).

The Asymmetry in the Adjustment Process

The problem of how to equalise the pressure to correct balance of payments disequilibria between debtor and creditor countries has periodically exercised the minds of the experts for nearly four decades. Under Keynes' 'Proposals for an international clearing union', first drafted in 1941, member states were to agree to accept payment of currency balances due to them from other members by establishing credit balances in their favour in the books of the union and in return were to be entitled to overdraft facilities. Unless otherwise agreed on the grounds that unduly expansionist conditions were impending in the world economy, interest was to be charged on credit as well as debit balances as 'a significant indication that the system looks on excessive credit balances with as critical an eye as on excessive debit balances, each being, indeed, the inevitable concomitant of the other'. Subsequently, however, discussions between Keynes and Mr White of the United States Treasury, led to the publication of a 'Joint statement by experts on the establishment of an International Monetary Fund', in which those of the clearing union proposals that had, in the words of the British commentary, 'introduced certain provisions for placing on creditor countries, as well as on debtor countries, some pressure to share the responsibility in appropriate circumstances for maintaining a reasonable stability in the balances of international payments' were replaced by 'a different, but perhaps more far-reaching, provision with the same object in view'. After minor amendment this provision later became Article VII, the 'scarce currency' clause, of the IMF Articles. Section 1 of the Article provides that if the Fund finds that a general scarcity of a particular currency is developing it may make recommendations to bring it to an end. Section 3 requires the Fund to declare a currency scarce if it finds that the demand for it seriously threatens the Fund's ability to provide it and thereafter to ration the Fund's supplies. Any member is then authorised, after consultation with the Fund, to impose temporary limitations on transactions in the scarce currency.

Table 7.2   Capital accounts, 1967–77 ($ billion, annual averages)

	Direct investment[a]		Other long-term capital[b]		Other capital[d]	Official settle- ments
	Inward	Outward	Private	Official[c]		
United Kingdom[e]						
1960–6	+0.5	−0.7	—	−0.2	—	+0.5
1967–73	+0.9	−1.6	+1.0	—	−0.2	−0.3
1974–7	+1.6	−3.3	+3.2	+2.2	+2.8	−2.9
France						
1960–6	+0.2	−0.2	+0.2	−0.3	+1.1	−0.9
1967–73	+0.5	−0.4	−0.4	−0.1	+0.8	−0.1
1974–7	+1.3	−1.1	+0.3	−0.1	+3.8	−0.3
Germany						
1960–6	+0.5	−0.3	+0.1	−0.3	+1.1	−0.9
1967–73	+1.1	−1.0	+0.7	−0.5	+1.2	−3.5
1974–7	+1.7	−2.3	+4.4	+0.1	−7.6	−1.6
Italy						
1960–6	+0.3	−0.1	−0.4	—	−0.2	−0.3
1967–73	+0.5	−0.3	−1.0	+0.2	−0.7	—
1974–7	+0.6	−0.3	+0.3	+0.2	+1.5	—
Japan						
1960–6	—	−0.1	—	—	+0.2	−0.1
1967–73	+0.1	−0.6	−1.3	−0.8	+1.5	−1.4
1974–7	+0.1	−1.9	+0.8	−0.3	+1.5	−2.5
United States						
1960–6	+0.3	−3.7	−0.9	−1.2	−0.4	+1.7
1967–73	+1.2	−7.2	+2.0	−2.0	−2.9	+8.0
1974–7	+3.8	−11.8	−3.2	−1.2	−4.2	+13.6
Canada						
1960–6	+0.5	−0.1	+0.5	−0.1	+0.1	−0.1
1967–73	+0.7	−0.3	+1.0	−0.1	−0.9	−0.3
1974–7	+0.4	−0.7	+5.3	−0.7	−0.4	−0.4

Source: OECD, *Balance of Payments of OECD Countries*.

[a]Direct investment excludes reinvested profits for Italy, Japan and Canada.

[b]Among the transactions classed as private are: for Germany transactions in bonds of German public authorities, for the United States transactions with non-official agencies in certain US Treasury securities, and for Canada transactions in securities issued by Canadian public authorities.

[c]Excludes special transactions.

[d]Includes errors and omissions.

[e]Direct investment excludes investment by oil companies and most investment by insurance companies.

The hopes placed in Article VII proved, however, to be unfounded and the Article has never been used. The Executive Board did in August 1947 consider whether it was appropriate for the Fund to declare under Section 1 that a general scarcity of dollars was developing, or to decide under Section 3 that the demand for dollars seriously threatened the Fund's ability to supply them. It concluded, however, that neither action could be justified. The Fund's holdings of dollars were almost intact and the wider scarcity of dollars was not due to contractionary policies in the United States but to shortage of productive capacity elsewhere. The fact that the Board never subsequently had recourse to either section is attributed in the Fund's official history partly to aversion from any form of discrimination and partly to the fact that after the major currencies became convertible it was doubtful whether limitations on operations in the scarce currency would be effective. The Article seems in fact to have been designed for a world of balance of payments bilateralism which for twenty years at least has not existed.

A more realistic attempt to devise a system for exerting pressure on surplus countries followed the establishment in 1972 of the IMF's Committee on Reform of the International Monetary System and Related Issues (popularly known as the Committee of Twenty). This body in turn set up 'technical groups' including one on 'adjustment', which in its report suggested five possible means of applying pressure. In what the majority of its members regarded as ascending order of severity these were:

(a)   forfeiture of SDR allocations;
(b)   charges on reserve accumulations;
(c)   a compulsory deposit with the Fund, possibly subject to negative interest, of 'excess' reserves;
(d)   publication of a report (which, it was thought, could have internal political repercussions and might stimulate speculative flows which would reinforce its impact);
(e)   authorisation of discriminatory exchange controls.

The group also referred to an Italian proposal for a progressive system of charges to be applied unless otherwise decided if a country's reserves reached a 'first point' and for an automatic requirement that all reserve accumulations above a 'second point' should be deposited with the Fund and all interest accruing on them forfeited.

The Committee agreed that a reformed international monetary system should include 'an effective and symmetrical adjustment process' and 'an appropriate form of convertibility for the settlement of imbalances with symmetrical obligations on all countries', and that under the surveillance of the Fund both surplus and deficit countries should 'take such prompt and adequate adjustment action, domestic or external, as may be needed to avoid protracted payments imbalances'. The Executive Panel of the Fund would 'where appropriate call upon the country concerned to adopt or reinforce policies to correct its imbalances' and if suitable action were not taken would 'have available graduated pressures to be applied to countries in large and persistent imbalance, whether surplus or deficit'.

The Committee stated, however, in its report of June 1974 (published in 'International Monetary Reform: Document of the Committee of Twenty', from which the quotations are taken) that it would be some time before a reformed system could be finally agreed and fully implemented. In the interim, countries 'would be guided in their adjustment action' by the agreed general principles, but 'the pressures which may be applied to countries in large and persistent imbalance will continue to be those at present available to the Fund'. These are, of course, pressures which many would think have already proved inadequate, but the Second Amendment to the Fund's Articles of Agreement, which became operative on 1 April 1978, did not in fact increase them. It merely gave the Fund the duties of exercising firm surveillance of members' exchange-rate policies, based on specific principles, and ensuring that they comply with their obligations. These include a broad obligation to collaborate with the Fund and other members to ensure orderly exchange arrangements and promote a stable system of exchange rates.

7.2 The Management of International Trade

by S. A. B. Page*

The Change in Trade Restriction since 1974

In the last five years there have been two fundamental changes in the organisation of international trade. The resulting changes in its behaviour should alter the assumptions made by economists and governments. For a quarter of a century until 1973 there was an almost uninterrupted trend towards greater liberalisation from quantitative controls and tariffs. There was also an almost universal acceptance that trade and the restrictions on it should be governed by certain rules and that governments were not free to impose any constraints they wished. This assumption became so completely accepted that its novelty and its importance in promoting the growth of trade (Blackhurst et al. [3]; Long [16], p. 257) may not have been as fully appreciated as those of liberalisation. Departures from either were explicitly temporary and exceptional for those countries which accepted the discipline of GATT, unlike the Comecon and some developing countries. The increase in protection in the last five years is not a temporary emergency measure, but a long-term change, made in the belief that the costs of free trade exceed its benefits; no account has been taken of the costs of destroying the system of rules. The world recession has brought not only a search for new methods of promoting growth, which could explain some pressure for trade controls, but greater concern for stability and orderliness as goals in themselves and fear of disruption caused by change, even if it is ultimately beneficial.

The countries imposing restrictions have not left GATT or other international organisations; they are either ignoring the rules or attempting to evade them, for example through bilateral 'voluntary' agreements. This may explain delay in recognising the fact and extent

* This note is a shortened version; the longer version is available on request from the National Institute of Economic and Social Research.

of the shift to protection. This paper seeks to describe and measure what has been done to 'manage' trade in the last five years, to determine how far the conventional assumption that most trade is 'free' or controlled only by tariff barriers was true even before 1974, and to examine the reasons for the change to protectionism, especially whether they became important only because of the recession, or have longer-term implications.

1974, the year after the oil price rose and the recession began, was the turning point. In 1975 the IMF reported for the first time that increases in restrictions had been more important than decreases (IMF [12]); previously in the 1970s its reports had found growing liberalisation (except when the United States imposed temporary restrictions in 1971), but subsequently new restrictions have always been most emphasised, though many are informal and some semi-concealed. OECD countries first felt a need to declare they would not impose restrictions in 1974 (this has been renewed annually by most of them). The National Institute [18] noted the trend towards protection in February 1977. GATT, which has been the only international agency to give continued strong support to free trade, started issuing warnings in mid-1977 and surveys of exporters, including that by the CBI, began to cite protectionism as an important problem at about the same time, but public recognition of the problem is still incomplete.

In general, developing countries have intervened more both in domestic economic policy and, consequently, in trade than developed market economies, so that their growing share in world trade increases the proportion controlled. In the early postwar period many of them used extreme versions of traditional intervention, such as high tariffs and multiple exchange rates, but even before 1973 more were shifting to direct controls and import licensing; there was increasing state trading in imports (IMF [12], *1973*, p. 5) and it continued in exports in countries with a dominant export. The 'new international economic order' clearly needs international political intervention to secure a shift in income distribution.

The developed countries also have increased management of their domestic economies. Once this is considered to be within the proper sphere of government the effect of other countries' trade becomes a legitimate interest. The addition of stability – of incomes, economic structure and patterns of employment – to the conventional economic goals may have been particularly important in encouraging intervention in trade because it encourages changes between countries and, within a country, between sectors, regions and income groups. Intervention for both planning and stability has been stimulated by the recession of the last five years.

How Governments Manage Trade

Types of 'managed' trade

Managed trade is defined here as trade that is subject to some non-tariff control, by exporter, importer or both, and therefore not determined entirely by market forces. (All tariffs are excluded, although if tariffs are set at a deliberately prohibitive level they are very like direct controls.) It is not important to identify how each trade flow is controlled; countries switch from one means to another to increase effectiveness or to stay within the letter of international rules, or use the threat of one to enforce acceptance of a simpler alternative. It is important to identify all controls in use and draw some broad distinctions that may have implications for the permanence or nature of the restrictions.

One major classification is into international agreements, national controls on trade, and other national controls whose major effect is on trade. International agreements permanently modify the liberalised structure of trade rules. International cartels normally promote the interests of dominant producers. This is true of commodity funds and other agreements, such as OPEC, and some agricultural policy in the developed countries. Traditionally such systems have been based on a dominant economic position, but current proposals require reinforcement by political agreements. Although they promote stability by protecting against new entrants, their principal purpose is to redistribute income from consumers to producers. The type of trade management which is increasing most rapidly is market-sharing agreements among consumers with the (possibly forced) agreement of suppliers; these set permissible growth rates for imports by consumer and by supplier. They include the growing protection of textiles, steel and shipbuilding in developed countries. These must be implemented through political intervention, being designed to help declining or weak producers unable to protect themselves by economic means.

National controls on trade include quotas, anti-dumping duties, licences, certificates of origin or other administrative controls, price controls and restrictions on imports by the government or by industries in which it has an interest. They turn away from an international approach to trade regulation, as well as from liberalisation. The effect of discrimination in government procurement has risen independently of any protectionist motives because of the growing government share in most economies.

Though purely domestic in form, and so largely exempt from international control, price controls or subsidies for specific products or industries, government stockpiles, patent rules, and safety, health or other technical standards may all have trade implications similar to those of import controls. But to establish in each case whether the deterrent effect was intended or incidental would require analysis of all policies followed by any government, so no such restraints are included in the limited and preliminary measurements given here.

All these controls can be fixed or discretionary when they can be altered more quickly and may be only a potential limit. In practice 'voluntary' export agreements are not more temporary or more flexible than other controls (IMF [13], p. 64). The uncertainty that they can cause and the possibility of discrimination among suppliers or products may make their actual effect on trade at least as strong, but they may escape opposition because they are less obvious to those in the importing country whom they hurt. This could also be true of non-trade controls relative to trade controls, and possibly of national controls relative to international agreements. Which actually lead to more restriction is difficult to determine. International agreements have not pre-empted national controls on the same commodities; some countries that might not have imposed national controls may have found themselves included in international ones.

In principle, any of these types of control could be questioned under GATT (and, for members, EEC) restrictions on trade barriers. Under 'voluntary' agreements exporters renounce their rights to complain. Both organisations occasionally criticise, and the EEC has complained through the Commission and the European Court, but the weakness of their reaction indicates that they believe the measures have at least the tacit acceptance of most major countries and cannot be prevented through a conventional case-by-case approach.

Although it is not covered by this paper, it is arguable that trade by multinational companies is another form of managed trade. It may be 'managed' to avoid rapid adjustments between divisions of a firm for the same motives that influence government controls. Intra-firm trade is estimated at about a fifth of industrial countries' manufactured exports (all exports by multinationals may be as much as two thirds, see Morgan [17]), and 15 per cent of developing countries' manu-factured exports (Blackhurst *et al.* [2], p. 38). Most is in commodities not covered by other intervention.

Controls on trade

The particular frequency of controls on first food, then textiles and clothing, and, most recently, steel is partly a reflection of their import-ance in world trade. As other goods have grown in importance, restric-tions on them have increased. (Fuller details are given in Appendix 1.)

The EEC as a group and its members use almost all the standard types of restriction; the United States and Canada use a smaller variety including the strongest and most selective measures (Table 7.3). The main commodities controlled include food, steel, textiles and clothing, and fuels in both cases. The EEC also controls ships and air-craft. In the United States the effect on prices has been discussed with each new trade measure and anti-inflation policy has probably restrained protection, but except possibly in Germany this considera-tion does not seem to have influenced EEC measures.

Although Japan has used a variety of trade controls, characteristics of the domestic market and distribution system are probably the most effective restraints on manufactured imports. 'Encouragement' to exporters and importers to follow government policy is far stronger than in other industrial countries. It could be argued that all Japanese trade is 'managed'. It is clear that the estimates here, based only on known measures, are too low, but Japanese protection has probably not increased significantly in recent years; the measurements of the change may be less inadequate. Some controls, such as inspection and testing requirements, are being relaxed.

Controls have in general been similar to those of the EEC and North America in the other developed countries, but much more extensive in some of the poorer ones and in the developing countries. Greece, Turkey, New Zealand and South Africa control all imports, as do several of the poorer oil producers. Some Middle Eastern countries, including Saudi Arabia, have no import controls. The rest normally control at least some food and the more advanced some textiles, often steel and chemicals, sometimes machinery and cars. All oil exports are assumed to be controlled.

The large number of other developing countries that control all imports has not changed much in recent years, but the stringency of

Table 7.3   Use of non-tariff measures

	EEC[a]	Other OECD[b]	Other developed	Oil exporters[c]	Other developing[d]	World
Total in group	8	*14*	*3*	*15*	*82[e]*	*122*
A. National plan or import programme	—	2	—	5	18	25
B. State trading	2	5	—	5	28	40
C. Import ban	8[f]	2	—	5	27	42
D. Quotas	8[f]	11	2	2	15	38
E. Licensing	8[f]	5	3	7	27	50
F. Agreements with exporters	8[f]	3	—	—	4	15
G. Minimum prices	8[f]	2	—	—	—	10
H. Supervision	8[f]	1	—	—	—	9
I. Public procurement	2	2	—	—	6	10
J. Export controls	8[f]	6	1	15[f]	49	80

Sources: IMF [12]; Department of Trade [21]; press [24]; EEC press releases.
[a]National controls include France B, D, H, I, Ireland B, C and United Kingdom D, E, F, H, I, J.
[b]Canada D, H, J, Japan B, E, I, J and United States A, C, D, F, G, I, J.
[c]Algeria A, Iran A, C, D, Iraq A, E and Nigeria A, B, C, E.
[d]China (Taiwan) B, C, D, E, J, India A, B, C, E, Israel C, Korea (South) A, C, E, J and Mexico B, E, J.
[e]Includes Yugoslavia.
[f]Joint controls.

control has probably increased, as it varies with the balance of payments (as well as with the type of product). It is impossible to generalise about the rest, beyond saying that there seems to have been little net change in controls.

It is assumed that all the centrally planned countries' trade is controlled, and hence all imports from them by other countries; their own imports are not included in the world totals. Some commodities are included in the measures for every country because so many control either exports or imports that effectively all trade is controlled. These are petroleum (nearly 20 per cent of world trade in 1974), meat, sugar and dairy products (each about 1 per cent) and coffee, iron ore, alcoholic beverages, crude rubber and, in 1979 though not in 1974, gas, iron and steel scrap, and synthetic fibres (about $\frac{1}{2}$ per cent each).

Measures of managed trade

In this paper controlled trade is measured against total trade flows. It was assumed that the important distinction is between any control and none, not among different degrees of control. The method used was to take trade figures for 1974 and to find the ratio of the controlled sectors to the total, first under the restrictions in force at the end of 1974 and then under those in force now. (See Appendix 2 for a fuller description.)

After the analysis by individual country and commodity, those commodities for which at least 60 per cent of trade was controlled were identified as 'mainly managed' and used to analyse interregional trade flows, on the assumption that all trade in the mainly managed commodities and none of that in others was managed.

The structure of world trade

For the last decade, about 60 per cent of trade has been in manufactures, in which the share of the industrial countries has remained at about 80 per cent (Table 7.4), while the share of developing countries has risen slightly at the expense of the centrally planned. Manufactured exports are very important to the developing countries, making up about 40 per cent of their total exports. The industrial countries are much more specialised, as manufactures account for over three quarters of their exports. For both groups about 55–60 per cent of imports are manufactures.

About 80 per cent of industrial areas' primary exports are to themselves. They still supply about 88 per cent of their own manufactured imports, but this now represents only two thirds of their manufactured exports, down from almost three quarters in the early 1970s, as both oil producers and other developing countries have been rapidly growing markets. In each of the areas of 'industrial countries' – North America, Western Europe and Japan – developing countries are now a more important market than the sum of the other two groups (Blackhurst *et al.* [2], p. 35). The share of exports from non-oil developing countries going to the industrial countries has remained close to 70 per cent. Within this total, the share of manufactures rose between 1970 and 1973 to a peak of 40 per cent, but has fallen back slightly since.

Table 7.4   The structure of world trade (percentages)

	1955	1963	1970	1973	1974	1977
Shares in world trade						
Primary products	50	42	33	35	40	38
Manufactures	49	55	65	64	58	60
Shares in manufactured trade						
Industrial countries (IC)	82	80	82	81	82	80
Non-oil developing (DC)	7[a]	6[a]	7	8	8	8
Centrally planned (CP)	10	13	10	10	9	10
Shares in manufactured imports						
Of IC from DC	8[a]	6[a]	7	8	8	8
Of IC from IC	89	91	90	89	88	88
Of DC from IC	89[a]	83[a]	80	80	81	78
Shares of manufactures in						
IC exports	66	69	77	76	76	77
DC exports	13[a]	15[a]	35	40	37	40
CP exports	49	60	64	64	60	61
IC imports	41	51	63	62	55	57
Oil exporters' imports	n.a.	n.a.	78	78	76	82
DC imports	61[a]	63[a]	66	62	57	58
CP imports	51	60	69	69	71	69
Trade among IC	58	66	75	75	74	75
IC exports to DC	78[a]	77[a]	79	77	78	80
DC exports to IC	11[a]	14[a]	34	40	36	38
Trade among DC	17[a]	23[a]	43	45	44	47
IC exports						
To IC	63	70	75	75	72	70
To DC	} 28	} 22	{ 15	14	15	14
To oil exporters			{ 4	4	5	9
IC manufactured exports						
To IC	56	67	73	74	70	67
To DC	} 33	} 24	{ 15	14	15	14
To oil exporters			{ 4	5	6	11
DC exports						
To IC	70[a]	71[a]	69	70	68	67
To DC	25[a]	21[a]	18	18	19	19
Share of exports to IC in						
DC manufactured exports	62[a]	63[a]	68	69	65	64
IC primary exports	79	79	82	80	79	80

Sources: GATT [6] and [7].
[a]Including oil exporters.

The Increase in Controls on Trade

Non-tariff restrictions on goods
Under the definitions and assumptions specified here, control of
market countries' trade has risen from about 40 per cent in 1974 to
about 46 per cent. The rise for manufactures from 13 to 21 per cent
(Table 7.5) accounts for about 90 per cent of this. Most trade in
non-manufactures was managed in 1974; the rise since then has been
small.

Table 7.5 Managed trade by country, 1974 and 1979

	Import value, 1974		Percentage of total 'managed'			
	Total	Manu-factures	All trade		Manufactures	
	(billion dollars)		1974	1979	1974	1979
Belgium	29.4	18.9	28	33	1	8
Denmark	9.8	6.4	30	40	—	18
France	52.1	30.1	33	42	—	14
Germany	69.0	36.5	37	46	—	16
Ireland	3.8	2.4	27	32	2	9
Italy	40.7	17.7	44	52	—	15
Netherlands	32.4	19.3	32	39	—	13
United Kingdom	54.0	27.8	38	45	—	13
EEC (8)	291.2	159.1	36	43	—	14
Australia	11.1	8.7	18	34	8	30
Austria	9.0	6.4	21	30	—	13
Canada	32.3	24.6	22	18	11	6
Finland	6.8	4.4	33	34	3	4
Greece	4.4	2.5	100	100	100	100
Iceland	0.5	0.4	21	31	1	16
Japan	62.0	14.5	51	55	—	4
Norway	8.4	6.0	16	34	—	25
Portugal	4.6	2.7	26	28	10	12
Spain	15.3	7.2	32	37	—	4
Sweden	15.7	10.9	25	30	3	10
Switzerland	14.4	10.6	17	18	2	3
Turkey	3.7	2.4	100	100	100	100
United States	101.0	56.2	36	44	6	18
Other OECD (14)	289.2	157.5	36	41	8	16
TOTAL OECD (22)	580.5	316.6	36	42	4	15

	Import value, 1974		Percentage of total 'managed'			
	Total	Manu-factures	All trade		Manufactures	
	(billion dollars)		1974	1979	1974	1979
New Zealand	3.7	2.8	100	100	100	100
South Africa	7.2	6.2	100	100	100	100
Other developed (3)	11.2	9.3	98	98	98	98
Algeria	4.4	3.5	100	100	100	100
Indonesia	3.9	3.0	29	32	15	17
Iran	6.5	5.0	100	100	100	100
Iraq	2.4	1.6	100	100	100	100
Libya	2.8	2.1	16	48	8	43
Nigeria	2.8	2.3	17	100	8	100
Saudi Arabia	2.8	2.2	6	6	—	—
Venezuela	3.7	3.1	11	12	9	9
Oil exporters (15)	35.5	26.0	54	63	46	57
Argentina	3.6	2.6	5	6	—	—
Brazil	14.2	9.1	24	25	—	—
Chile	1.9	0.9	100	19	100	13
China (Taiwan)	7.0	n.a.	100	100	n.a.	n.a.
Egypt	2.4	1.1	100	100	100	100
India	5.2	2.5	100	100	100	100
Israel	4.2	2.8	21	20	—	1
Korea (South)	6.8	3.6	100	100	100	100
Lebanon	2.5	1.7	31	16	23	—
Mexico	6.1	4.2	16	20	14	14
Morocco	1.9	1.0	100	100	100	100
Pakistan	1.7	1.0	15	16	—	—
Peru	1.5	1.1	85	91	100	100
Singapore	8.3	4.7	32	32	—	—
Syria	1.2	0.8	100	100	100	100
Thailand	3.2	2.1	21	23	—	—
Tunisia	1.1	0.7	100	18	100	—
Non-oil developing (81)	106.9	60.3	50	49	25	23
WORLD (122)[a]	741.6	417.0	40	46	13	21
Alternative maximum estimates (see App. 2)						
OECD			36	43	4	15
Non-oil developing			54	54	32	31
World			41	47	14	23

Sources: United Nations [22]; OECD [19], series B; IMF [12], *Direction of Trade* and *International Financial Statistics*.

[a]Includes Yugoslavia.

As both sides control primary trade and developing countries control imports, trade between industrial countries and developing countries has always been more controlled than trade among industrial countries. The restrictions of the last few years have greatly extended the controls on developing countries' exports of manufactures, thus reducing their ability to avoid restrictions by diversifying out of primary products. The proportion of industrial countries' manufactured exports that is managed in other industrial countries, though much lower than that for the developing countries, is much higher than in 1974.

One implication is that changes in trade or apparent trends cannot be assumed to result from economic forces without analysis of institutional restraints. Another is that it has always been wrong to assume that tariffs are the only significant control on trade and it is now wrong to assume that non-tariff barriers are constant or declining. A fifth of trade in manufactures is now controlled; the industrial countries' controls have all been introduced in the last five years. Protectionism has not been successfully resisted in the recession and the increase has come from the industrial countries, not from the developing countries that were more seriously affected by the oil price rise and the subsequent recession in the developed countries.

Table 7.5 gives the proportions of trade controlled under the limits that existed in 1974 and at the end of 1978 or early 1979. The increases come only from changes in the number of items controlled as the 1974 composition of trade is used throughout. The main part of the table gives minimum estimates where there was uncertainty over the exact extent of a control.

For all goods, the increase in managed imports for EEC countries was slightly above average, but the level remains slightly below it. There were no large differences in the changes among EEC countries because most measurable trade policies were usually concerted. Differences in levels mainly reflect differences in composition. Only for Ireland is the proportion of managed trade under a third, with Germany, France and the United Kingdom all between 40 and 50 per cent, and Italy taken above a half by high oil imports. The figures for manufactures (which, unlike those for all goods, exclude trade with the centrally planned economies in goods that would otherwise be uncontrolled) show the largest change for any group (from almost zero to 14 per cent).

The United States raises the average for the rest of the OECD to about the same as that for the EEC (in both periods) and had an unusually large increase. Among the major countries only Japan's share is over a half because of the high proportion of primary goods in its imports. For manufactures Canada actually had a fall (because of lower restrictions on cars). The poorer countries, Portugal and Spain, had only a small increase.

For all trade and for manufactures the increase was about the same for the oil producers as for the OECD countries, but it was concentrated in Nigeria, which changed to complete control, and Libya. Despite many individual variations, there was almost no change for either the total or trade in manufactures for the other developing countries as a group. They control about half their total imports and about a quarter of their imports of manufactures. Both of these are still higher proportions than those for the OECD countries. Among the largest importers, Chile has removed all controls, and Lebanon and Tunisia have reduced protection, while Mexico and Peru have increased it. The larger Asian countries frequently control all imports, although those that have strong balances of payments may be reducing the degree of control. The Latin American countries have fewer controls (but this may be balanced by higher tariffs).

Table 7.6 shows the percentage of trade that is managed for commodities for which it was over 30 per cent. Most foods not already assumed to be wholly managed are normally subject to import controls. For other primary products, except fuels, the proportions rarely exceed a third. The main increase in manufactured controlled trade is in iron and steel. In chemicals, fertilisers are over a quarter, but no component reaches a third. Almost half of clothing imports and over a third of textile imports are controlled, with the proportions much higher for developing suppliers (for textiles over 60 per cent).

In Tables 7.7–9, the share of 'mainly managed' goods is presented for the main interregional flows. Comparison of Table 7.7 totals with Table 7.5 suggests that for OECD imports the approximation ('mainly' for actual managed) holds quite well. For all imports, with 1974 trade patterns the proportion mainly managed was 34 instead of 36 per cent and rises to 41 instead of 42 per cent. For EEC countries the figures are almost the same, and though GATT data (Tables 7.8 and 7.9) give higher proportions for the slightly different category of 'industrial countries', the size of the change is again about the same. The approximation does not, however, allow for countries that control all trade and the 'mainly managed' commodities were identified on

Table 7.6   Commodities in which importers controlled more than 30 per cent of trade in 1979

	Share in world trade in 1974	Share of commodity's trade controlled		Trade controlled by		
		1974	1979	EEC	United States	Japan
		(percentages)		(A = in 1974, B = in 1979[a])		
Live animals	0.3	64	64	AB		
Fish	0.8	30	31	AB		
Cereals	3.1	76	76	AB	(A)	AB
Fruit and vegetables	1.7	70	78	AB	(A)(B)	
Confectionery	0.1	43	43	AB		
Cocoa	0.3	56	56	AB		
Chocolate	0.1	62	62	AB		
Tea	0.1	66	64	AB		
Animal feeding stuffs	0.6	69	69	AB		
Misc. food	0.2	49	48	AB		
Non-alcoholic beverages	—	57	58	AB		
Silk fibres	—	6	71			B
Textiles	3.4	21	35	(A)B	AB	
Lime, cement, etc.	0.2	32	35			
Iron and steel	3.8	16	66	B	B	
Aircraft	0.8	12	83	B	B	B
Ships	0.7	18	82	B	B	B
Clothing	1.9	20	48	B	(A)(B)	
Footwear	0.5	1	32	(B)	(B)	
Travel	. .	24	21	(A)(B)		AB

Sources: United Nations [22]; OECD [19], series B; IMF [12] and *Balance of Payments Yearbook*.
[a]Brackets indicate part of category.

the basis of world trade and thus determined by the industrial countries' restrictions. Thus correspondence is poor for the developing countries. The results for the oil exporters are clearly unreliable, but the figures on the basis of the 1979 restrictions for imports by the other developing countries may give a reasonable indication for total trade (for manufactures they are much too low).

For all OECD countries and for the EEC, the discrimination against imports from the developing countries is clear and seems to be increasing. Only 24 per cent (15 per cent in 1974) of imports from other

Table 7.7   Shares of 'mainly managed' goods in OECD and
EEC trade (percentages)

	All trade				Manufactures, 1979 restrictions	
	1974 restrictions		1979 restrictions			
	1974	1977	1974	1977	1974	1977
OECD imports						
Total	34	33	41	39	13	12
From OECD	15	14	24	22	11	9
From DC	54	55	62	66	30ᵃ	33ᵃ
OECD exports						
Total	17	16	28	25	15	12
To OECD	13	13	23	22	12	10
To DC	12	9	30	24 }	21	16
To Middle East	10	7	25	17 }		
EEC imports						
Total	34	32	41	38	12	11
From EEC	17	17	27	26 }	11	9
From other OECD	14	13	20	20 }		
From DC	55	52	63	61	34ᵃ	39ᵃ
EEC exports						
Total	17	17	27	25	12	10
To EEC	17	17	27	26 }	11	9
To other OECD	10	9	19	17 }		
To DC	10	9	22	20 }	19	11
To Middle East	7	6	19	13 }		

Source: OECD [19].
ᵃIncludes Middle East.

OECD countries are controlled, compared with 62 per cent from the non-oil developing countries; for manufactures the figures are 11 per cent and 30 per cent because of the controls on textiles and clothing. Less than a third of all OECD exports and only 15 per cent of their manufactured exports are managed. If the commodity composition of trade in 1977 rather than 1974 is used, the share of mainly managed trade is lower in inter-OECD and total OECD trade, although it has risen in imports from developing countries. If managed goods are those that were likely to grow fastest, the controls have prevented this. The pattern for manufactures is the same. For exports the share of mainly managed products has also declined, in this case in trade with all areas,

Table 7.8   Shares of 'mainly managed' goods in world trade flows (percentages)

	1979 restrictions		1974[a]	1979 restrictions	
	1970	1973	A	1974	1977
Industrial areas' imports	36	38	*38*	46	44
From industrial countries	26	27	*18*	29	27
From non-oil developing	52	55	*47*	58	62
Share in total of:					
Industrial countries	54	52	*31*	40	40
Oil exporters	18	21	*43*	36	33
Non-oil developing	18	17	*15*	15	17
Centrally planned	10	10	*11*	9	9
Industrial areas' exports	27	29	*21*	31	29
To industrial countries	26	27	*18*	29	27
To oil exporters	23	25	*12*	29	22
To non-oil developing	24	27	*15*	29	24
Share in total of:					
Industrial countries	70	70	*62*	65	65
Non-oil developing	13	13	*10*	14	11
Centrally planned	14	16	*24*	16	16
Non-oil developing imports	38	42	*39*	47	46[b]
From industrial countries	24	27	*15*	29	24
From non-oil developing	48	40	*42*	45	47[b]
Share in total of:					
Industrial countries	42	42	*22*	36	30[b]
Oil exporters	17	23	*45*	37	40[b]
Non-oil developing	13	15	*15*	13	15[b]
Centrally planned	23	21	*17*	14	15[b]
Non-oil developing exports	54	54	*48*	56	58[b]
To industrial countries	52	55	*47*	58	62
To oil exporters	40	43	*43*	49	47[b]
To non-oil developing	48	40	*42*	45	47[b]
Share in total of:					
Industrial countries	68	72	*67*	70	69[b]
Non-oil developing	16	14	*16*	15	15[b]
Centrally planned	14	12	*13*	11	11
Oil exporters' imports	31	33	*22*	36	29[b]

Sources: GATT [6] and [7].
[a]A = 1974 restrictions.
[b]For 1976.

Table 7.9   Shares of 'mainly managed' goods in world trade in
manufactures with 1979 restrictions (percentages)

	Imports		Exports	
	1974	1977	1974	1977
Industrial countries (IC)	15	14	16	13
From/to IC	14	12	14	12
From/to DC	30	33	18	14
Non-oil developing (DC)	17	14[a]	22	26[a]
From/to IC	18	14	30	33
From/to DC	8	6[a]	8	6[a]

Sources: as Table 7.8.
[a] For 1976.

in manufactures as well as in total. Management of imports by the
developing countries has probably not increased enough to give this
result, which is consistent with the goods being those in which developing countries are increasing their production and have less need to
import from developed countries. The mainly managed goods seem to
be products where trade from the developed countries is declining.

Tables 7.8 and 7.9 confirm the discrimination against the developing countries. They also indicate that between 1974 and 1977 a fall
in the share of managed trade among the industrial countries outweighed a small rise in imports from the developing countries, while
for exports there were falls to every area, with a particularly large
one to the oil producers.

Between 1970 and 1973 mainly managed goods had been increasing
their share in import and export trade with both industrial and
developing countries, but especially in imports from the developing
countries. The rise in this share was only slightly greater from 1974
to 1977 than from 1970 to 1973; the controls probably prevented
an acceleration between the 1960s and early 1970s from continuing.

Almost half developing countries' imports from one another are
controlled (compared with under a third of imports from the industrial countries). This reflects the greater importance of primary
products in their mutual trade and is not true for manufactures. In
total about half of their exports and imports alike is now controlled,
and they have even less scope than industrial countries for changing
their trade. The share controlled is rather higher for their exports to

industrial countries, mainly due to new restrictions. About a quarter of their exports of manufactures is now controlled.

The proportion of managed goods in trade among the developing countries also appears to have risen slightly, though it has fallen in their imports from the industrial countries. Tables 7.8 and 7.9 both indicate that these changes apply to newly managed trade, although some also apply to previously managed trade.

Restrictions on services

There are three types of service where control is common and can be roughly measured. Most shipping is now allocated between importers and exporters. Aviation is controlled by IATA. Most countries limit spending on travel, but the share for the world is low because of the heavy weight of the OECD countries which do not (Table 7.6).

Changes in tariffs

Increased non-tariff protection has not been balanced by tariff reductions in GATT negotiations since the end of the 1960s, when the 'Kennedy' round of tariff negotiations brought cuts of about a third. These were spread over five years and are unlikely to have affected world trade prices by more than 5 per cent on average. By 1978 average tariff levels in the industrial countries were only 2 per cent for raw materials and 6 per cent for manufactures. This makes them relatively small in relation to price or exchange-rate variations, but quantitative comparison with the effective level of protection provided by non-tariff barriers is not permitted by the measures used here. The benefits which developing countries receive under the Generalised System of Preferences are unlikely to have outweighed losses from other barriers, as each industrial country can exclude certain producers and limit the quantities (IBRD [11], p. 58). The elimination by mid-1977 of tariffs on manufactures among members of EEC and EFTA reinforced the non-tariff discrimination against industrial–developing trade.

The 'Tokyo' round of GATT negotiations, which began in 1973 but has only just reached partial agreement, was initially intended primarily to continue the process of cutting industrial countries' tariffs on manufactures, with possibly some liberalising of agricultural trade, particularly between the United States and the EEC. There is still not full agreement on all tariff cuts, and the estimated final result for industrial goods, cuts of about one third (GATT [8c]) (the initial target was 60 per cent), would reduce prices by less than 2 per cent. The Japanese cuts may be rather larger and earlier, but the EEC hopes to be able to renegotiate some later stages of the programme. There were also tariff concessions on about a quarter of agricultural trade. The cuts again discriminate against developing countries. Their average was about 38 per cent on trade among industrial countries, but only about a quarter on imports from developing countries (only about 2 per cent on textiles).

The Arguments for Managed Trade

Arguments for long-term management of trade need to be examined against possible social, economic or political criteria and for their relevance to the controls actually imposed. The traditional free trade argument focuses on increasing income by reallocating inputs to more productive uses through extended specialisation and exchange. It thus accepts the income of a country, or of the world as a whole, as the criterion against which to measure the effects of trade policy, and defines increasing income in terms of relative market prices among goods within a country and between home and imported goods. It implicitly accepts that the most efficient way for any market system to operate is, almost by definition, for it to be guided by individuals and organisations taking decisions in their own interests and implementing them through economic actions not political pressure.

Countries could move away from free trade because they believe either that its conventional advantages do not apply to them, or that other, non-economic, benefits from controlling trade outweigh them. Although the former, structural, view explains some protection of infant industries by the developing countries, it has not been as important as interventionist arguments in recent pressure for protection. Either argument is conceptually acceptable. But, except perhaps as a new political goal, it is difficult to accept the argument which seems to be behind some current advocacy of managed trade, that there is a new economic benefit called 'stability', which is more important than high and growing income and which may not be promoted by free international trade.

Structure and development

Developing country arguments for intervention and the 'Cambridge' argument for the United Kingdom (discussed in the papers by Neild and Lal and in *Cambridge Economic Policy Review* [4]) postulate structural reasons limiting the benefits of free trade to particular countries. It is not entirely clear whether all market forces or only those transmitted through trade are supposed to operate too weakly or too slowly to change the structure of the economy. If the former, this becomes equivalent to an argument for general planning. For developing countries, the argument in the 1950s was that the relative decline in demand for primary products would restrict their volume of sales and produce constantly falling terms of trade. Their imports were held down by their exports; new industries could develop only with protection and government direction. Controls could allocate imports to the most effective use to change the structure away from dependence on commodities. The empirical basis for the trade argument might not be accepted now, but probably they have always had additional grounds for planning and this can best be considered under national intervention.

The view of the Cambridge Economic Policy Group is that the structure of trade produces imbalances: 'persistent structural trends in trade in manufactures are now a serious obstacle to growth of world trade and GNP'. They argue that for countries having 'current accounts vulnerable to persistent deficit' there is a balance of payments constraint on growth. They further argue that the ideal solution would be a change in the international rules, but consider that, in default of such a change, a country in a serious predicament should break them.

The analysis of current balances depends on constant relationships between imports and income, and between exports and markets (with no price effects for manufactures). These propositions are open to question in the light of changes in both import and export behaviour in recent years. It is also implicitly assumed in the model that the only constraint on growth in the 'constrained' countries is the balance of payments and that, if the constraint is eased by import controls, output will respond to increased domestic demand.

The specific criticisms that in the industrial countries trade is not promoting growth and is destroying some industries seem also to be based on a view that planning is needed because market responses cannot achieve changes in income. Raising income has been mistakenly identified with preserving and expanding the existing industrial structure. The discussion of the relationship between imports and inefficiency suggests that because trade can damage or destroy industries it cannot improve economic performance. In fact the reverse is the case. The argument for free trade is not that competition makes each industry more efficient (as it is assumed that each is operating efficiently given national conditions), but that imports replace the least competitive, allowing resources to be reallocated to the more competitive. Any structural differences in trade may mean that some countries have specialised in industries where demand is growing particularly fast. Their exports rise rapidly and their imports slowly; their terms of trade improve. A country that has done the reverse will have difficulty in increasing its relative income, even if it raises its rate of growth. In that case it needs to change the structure, whether by market or planning mechanisms, not to preserve its disadvantage.

The difficulties at international level of abandoning a market system without substituting any other are discussed later. The risks for a single country may be greater. If it obeys only the international rules it chooses, it cannot appeal to international support against other governments' actions. As the extent and form of any retaliation would be matters of bargaining not market forces the results cannot be calculated. They would not necessarily be limited to the trade sector.

International government intervention
Given that administrative or political processes may properly be used at national level to avert a threat to fundamental political or social objectives, two types of argument against free trade are possible. First, the same reasons can apply equally between countries, or between groups in different countries, and require intervention in trade. Secondly, intervention in domestic economies may be in sectors in which international flows are important. In this case intervention must also apply to them, and may indeed need to operate more strongly if they are more variable than domestic factors. The first is an argument for international intervention in trade; the second could justify unilateral action if all the objectives are seen in purely national terms. Neither would reject income as the chief economic objective.

Most countries now accept that governments have some responsibility for managing the national economy, either in the interests of economic growth or as necessitated by non-economic objectives. Intervention by GATT and other international agencies up to the 1960s can often be considered equivalent to traditional domestic policies to improve the functioning of markets through the removal of artificial barriers. Since the early 1970s, however, equivalents of domestic interventionist arguments have been used in international negotiations. After 1976 the developed countries shifted their interest in the GATT 'Tokyo round' almost entirely from tariffs to regulatory codes – on trade restrictions by developing countries, on discriminatory government procurement, on export subsidies and on safeguards against imports of particular goods from individual countries. New demands by the developing countries illustrate even more clearly the trend towards increased regulation. They wanted formal sanction for import restrictions to protect infant industries and for treating as an exception to the normal rules against discrimination the Generalised System of Preferences. Under this some of their manufactures are admitted with lower or no tariffs to some industrial countries; it also covers the access of some countries to EEC markets under the Lomé convention. The developing countries have also used redistributive arguments in other international negotiations, both non-trade, for example in demanding discriminatory SDR allocations, and trade, in particular on commodities. Their commodity proposals involve a clear shift from the earlier view that commodity agreements are exceptions. They now emphasise changing the structure of trade and distribution of its benefits, rather than using trade to increase world income or stabilising a single commodity.

Opposition to their line on commodity agreements, especially from Germany (Hermes [9]) and the United States (Bergsten [1]), is often based on objections to a link between aid and price stabilisation; either opponents do not accept international extension of interventionist arguments or they support direct rather than indirect redistribution. The latter line would be consistent with conventional arguments at national level, but the aid records of the two countries suggest that the former is at least as important. Any new commodity agreements are therefore likely to require economic power. The measures discussed in this paper have generally been taken unilaterally and have discriminated against the poorer countries. An international principle may explain the introduction of the relatively weak provisions of the Generalised System of Preferences, but it does not fully explain even the demands of the developed countries in the GATT negotiations.

National government intervention
Arguments from purely national criteria seem to be increasingly influential in the developed countries and have always been used by

the developing. The strongest version, adopted by the centrally planned economies and by developing countries with national plans, is that trade, equally with other elements of the economy, should conform with the plan. Provided international markets and other governments' policies permit the required imports and exports to be achieved by unilateral intervention, the practical difficulties differ little from those of national planning itself. In a mixed economy the problem is more complicated, because what is controlled may not exactly correspond with the government's objectives. Objectives for a particular sector that are ends in themselves may determine trade policy for it; where they are a means to national goals, the independent effect of trade on these overriding objectives must also be taken into account. For example, trade flows determined in part by external markets may make planning a sector more difficult, but this will not justify intervention if trade makes it easier to increase national income. Although economists have often made the case for not using trade policies for domestic purposes when domestic policy instruments are available, the practical and political benefits have always impressed planners more. In recent years non-tariff barriers have tended to replace tariffs because growing acceptance of government intervention has led to growing acceptance that it may take direct forms.

Intervention in agriculture stems in part from concern for the income of farmers and the poor (although pressure groups are also important) and is accepted even in the generally non-intervening countries, Germany and the United States. Another type of sectoral intervention is nationalisation. The reasons for it are likely to require government control over supplies from all sources and of inputs as well as competing products. More public ownership has brought an extension of trade controls from the traditional monopolies of alcohol, tobacco and salt to post offices and telecommunications, fuels, railways and airlines, and now steel and shipbuilding. Even governments that avoid intervention have traditionally bought their own supplies at home and many expect nationalised industries to do the same. Using trade controls to promote nationalised industries may, however, have indirect effects that weaken the national control of which they are a part, for example, the EEC's efforts to regulate output as a condition of import control in steel, textiles and oil refining, and the OECD agreement on shipbuilding.

While public ownership is not increasing much except in some developing countries, sectoral intervention is likely to spread as governments accept wider responsibilities. Once the possibility of intervention is accepted, the government must be prepared to accept responsibility for the results of intervention or non-intervention and to stand up to damaged pressure groups if it abandons the security of fixed international rules. Benefits from international trade are likely to be less concentrated than the costs to a few producers, so that intervention may be demanded when it would not increase national income.

The case for intervention for a general policy objective, such as changing the rate of economic growth, is stronger the greater is confidence in the government's ability to promote growth relative to the clear evidence of the advantages of trade in increasing income. The greater the restrictions on international trade, the less likely is the complete case for free trade to hold, but the greater are the difficulties of resolving inconsistencies among national policies. If there is no international framework, either of supra-national criteria or of accepted limits on national intervention, bargaining will be needed and may produce unstable and inefficient solutions or international conflict (Hirsch *et al.* [10], p. 15), possibly associating political with economic issues. Such linkages are still regarded by the market economies as unfortunate, though oil producers clearly use economic means for political objectives, and they have always been accepted by the centrally planned economies and to some extent by the market economies in dealing with them (for example, trade concessions have been tied to SALT talks or emigration). The growth of intervention in trade makes them more common.

Corden has argued ([5], pp. 2–4) that attitudes towards free trade have passed through three stages: first, perception of its benefits, secondly, acceptance, to promote domestic objectives, of limits analogous to those accepted for the market system at national level, and thirdly, recognition that domestic aims can be achieved more efficiently by domestic policies than by trade restrictions. The argument here is different. It is that unilateral planning of one country's trade cannot be a complete trading policy because, except for a small country in an otherwise completely free trading system, some non-market solution for inconsistent national objectives must be found. Therefore arguing from domestic planning to trade planning may be less reasonable than it seems when other countries' reactions are ignored.

Stability and security

Stability is acquiring acceptance as a welfare criterion in itself and not in need of explanation or defence (for example, Cambridge [4], p. 2). If it is really a permanent addition to economic goals, not only trade policy will need to be reconsidered. It can have various meanings. In domestic policy, it may be avoidance of external shocks to planned development. For output, it may be absence of the 'risk' of shortage or price competition presented by external supplies. In terms of traditional economic goals, the advantages of stability (of levels or rates of change) for planners and for producers of primary commodities or declining manufactures must be weighed against the costs of slower switching to new, more efficient producers of existing commodities or to new products.

It is debatable whether stability will be considered more or less important as incomes recover after the recession. One view is that people are less willing to change a structure of prices and output which is producing an adequate result (Lal [14] and [15]). The contrary argument is that in a recession people feel threatened by any change and will accept risks and uncertainties only when incomes are secure and rising. The move towards management of trade has certainly come mainly in the years since 1974, and has been most pronounced in countries like the United Kingdom and least in Germany and the United States, which have had higher incomes and a shorter period of slow growth. There may, however, be reasons other than the recession for current attitudes. Once a government has taken a major responsibility for the operation of the economy, past interventions or commitments may constrain it to maintain the relative or absolute positions of a growing number of sectors or groups, and thus steadily reduce the scope of the acceptable changes. Continued support for agriculture in the EEC can be partly explained in this way. More recently, government measures to assist steel and shipbuilding may stem from previous commitments, for example nationalisation. A wish to preserve industry in general has appeared in the United Kingdom.

A social criterion may be emerging that it is more important to preserve all existing incomes than to increase total income (Corden [5]). If redistribution would be difficult, this may lead to postponement of change, particularly when real incomes are growing slowly. Maintaining existing employment has also been an important motive behind protection of textiles, steel and shipbuilding. It seems to be thought that a loss of any jobs is unjustifiable whatever the potential gain in jobs in other sectors, for example from higher exports to the developing countries if they increase their own export income. It is not merely that the gains may be harder to identify; the assumption is that the cost of a loss of a job or reduction in income is greater than the benefit from the gain of a job or equal increase in income. (This attitude is common in purely domestic United Kingdom policies; an improvement is often introduced slowly, presumably because the pain from losing a benefit is believed to be worse than the pain, and possibly injustice, from not receiving the greater one immediately.) The rational or moral basis for this principle is not clear.

An argument for stability that applies particularly to trade restrictions on fuels and metals is national security, both on a narrow military definition and on a more general one of immunity from economic actions abroad. The industrial countries, particularly the United States, have always controlled some trade, by area or commodity, for such reasons. The argument is however being extended; for example, all national energy programmes explicitly include the goal of reducing reliance on imports to ensure security of supply. In a modern economy almost any product can be considered essential because of the interdependence of production, but it is not clear that foreign suppliers, of whom there may be many, are necessarily less reliable for a non-military commodity than a limited number of domestic suppliers. A remoter extension of the argument, that there is some level of dependence on all imports that is too high, has appeared in some Department of Trade statements, but does not seem to have influenced actual policies. It compounds two types of stability, national security and conserving existing industrial structures.

Even if stability is an objective, trade need not be destabilising. If countries are in different stages of cycles it may be stabilising, and it may change more slowly than government policies. Intervention may require breaking existing rules, but stable rules of behaviour may be at least as beneficial as stability of particular trade flows, especially for countries attempting to grow or change their economic structure. This may be more important for developing countries than for developed. It may also be more significant for a small country than a large, as it has less bargaining power in the negotiations that must take the place of rules.

Stability in the sense of preserving the existing structure of domestic industry is an important motive in some issues that the developed countries are pressing under the GATT negotiations and in the separate advocacy by France and the United Kingdom of what they call 'managed' trade. The latter may be associated with their preference for informal and administrative measures rather than clear legal guidelines as in Germany and the United States.

In the GATT negotiations on export subsidies the United States wants a ban on certain types of payment, while the EEC emphasises examining any payment, determining whether it is damaging trade and having consultations about abolishing it. The EEC also wants permission for safeguard measures that distinguish among suppliers (contrary to present GATT rules) and may be taken unilaterally without consultation (indicating that the important element in its demands is national discretion not restricting measures to cases of actual damage). The developing countries are particularly opposed to selectivity (of which they would be the principal victims) and are pressing for formal controls and surveillance of any measures. Their preference for formal controls is rational for weak countries that have had experience of 'voluntary' agreements. The EEC presumably believes that it is strong enough not to need the rules and procedures that can protect the weak. This does not mean that an individual member of the EEC could take such a position.

Neither France nor the United Kingdom has specified precisely what it means by managed trade. Like the United States and Germany, which support trade limits temporarily to permit adaptation without considering this a basic change in the trading system, France indicates that it wants gradual adjustment. The British emphasis has, however, been on postponing adaptation, perhaps permanently, to 'unfair competition' from imports. This can be seen most clearly in the textile industry, which has come to regard the MFA as permanent, though the explicit protection of the producer rather than the consumer cannot easily be justified on any grounds, economic or non-economic.

The Effects on Economic Growth and Structure of Restricting Trade

The first effect of trade restriction is to retard increasing specialisation among countries. This is its purpose and could explain the recent relatively slow growth of trade in sectors identified as 'mainly

managed'. Even in established (and therefore already slowing) industries, protection slows trade still further. In addition to the direct
effects, the growth of protection and acceptance of arguments that
point to further measures must make investors fear for future
opportunities. This effect is strongest in sectors already protected, but
the spread from sector to sector could discourage all investment. If
the changing rules help to explain the recent decline in investment
(Blackhurst et al. [2], p. 48), protection of existing industries may
have contributed to the length of the recession and, if this encourages
further protection, may be causing a circle of recession and protection.
It is quite clear that unexploited opportunities still exist. The
main growth of trade from 1950 to 1973 was among developed
countries and even there within each area (Blackhurst et al. [3], p.
19). The beginning of specialisation between industrial and developing countries is now being obstructed; there may also be some loss
because trade is frozen into blocs among the former. Japan is
developing an independent group in South East Asia to replace its
trade which is prevented from growing in Europe and the United
States. The EEC is potentially the weakest group as it does not
include any major suppliers of primary products. Preventing
specialisation will slow the growth of productivity that occurs by
switching out of relatively unproductive industries and possibly the
growth from introducing new ones. Raw-material controls may also
reduce efficiency by discouraging their use in favour of synthetics or,
in the case of fuel imports, of other factors of production. Growth in
the developed countries may therefore be slower, and both this and the
fall in investment may slow technical progress and thus potential as
well as actual growth. Productivity could be further reduced if protection reduces efficiency in individual firms. Protecting existing jobs
slows down movement into more skilled and productive ones, possibly
reducing the average desirability of the jobs available as well as
incomes. Intervention in trade alters distribution of domestic income
between old and new industrial sectors, towards those already
employed and against the potentially employed.

   Growth in developing countries facing restrictions will be slowed
by the reduced opportunity to shift into what should be their fastest-
growing industries. They may have to switch resources from exports
to import substitution, or to trade with other developing countries. As
most of their trade growth has been in exports to developed countries, this will require major shifts in investment and output. Even if

the restraints proved temporary, they would have suffered substantial costs of adaptation. Slower growth in the restrictive countries and in those whose exports suffer will of course produce the usual multiplier effects on each other and on countries not directly affected. Controls against one country can lead to controls by it against a third if it protects the products that have been forced out of export markets; Japan may be reacting in this way against other Asian countries.

Controls like any administration have a cost, particularly if they are detailed (and the history of steel and textiles shows how controls must become increasingly precise if they are to be complete). They also impose costs on the industry affected; traders that are not controlled may face new administrative requirements, while those that are must comply or find ways around the controls (Corden [5], p. 233). There may be unforeseen costs if importers decide that the new procedures are too expensive and end all imports.

The Future of Managed Trade

The changes in international trade in the last five years, particularly for manufactures and for trade between developed and developing countries, resulted from a shift towards intervention for national rather than international purposes and by unilateral action. There was no structural change in trade to explain the shift. The aim most important in explaining both the past and the most pressing demands for the future is not increasing income, but avoiding falls for any domestic group even at the sacrifice of potentially greater rises. This may have been in part a reaction against the risks of international inter-dependence after its apparent role in encouraging inflation and de-pression, but it was probably mainly an attempt to introduce stability into a situation of slow growth and general economic uncertainty. Protection did not increase within a coherent programme for better international or national planning. That United Kingdom actions are not based on consistent support for organised trade is indicated by its pressure on other countries, including Canada and Nigeria, to remove limits they have imposed on its exports; also by its simultaneous support for protection of EEC energy from low-cost imports and opposition to the same policy for agriculture. The refusal by national industries, public and private, to accept international regulation as a corollary of trade controls also indicates that what some countries call 'managed' trade is really protection of particular national interests. It differs from traditional protection in its methods, which are more direct and therefore stronger, and in the national policies pursued.

It is difficult to see how a new structure of international trade could be built on a foundation of disregard for international rules. The gains from breaking them depend on each country assuming that other countries will not intervene, so that unilateral intervention will produce predictable effects. The spread of controls to cover nearly half of all trade and over a fifth of trade in manufactures means that this is untenable. The growing number of controls imposed without regard to the rules and customs of international trade (re-established and strengthened after the disruptions in the 1930s and 1940s) is increasing uncertainty in international economic relations. The possible benefits of unilateral intervention may therefore be increasingly difficult to obtain, while the costs of abandoning free trade remain certain.

The spread of controlled trade may depend partly on the duration of the recession and of high unemployment in the developed countries. But substantial intervention appears likely to continue, both because of its traditional importance to developing countries and to primary products and because governments which have accepted a responsibility for trade performance will find it difficult to return to claiming impotence. Only acceptance of new international objectives which could be set against national goals might offer a way of returning to rules; there is no movement in that direction. Even developing countries' demands for trade rules and commodity agreements using international principles are based on self-interest. It might prove at least as difficult to persuade them to sacrifice their 'sovereign' rights of unilateral intervention as the developed countries. The prospect therefore is, at best, a slower increase in intervention if the recession ends, but little reversal of steps already taken.

Increased control of trade contrasts with other contemporary changes in the international framework. Capital has continued to gain greater freedom of movement. Floating exchange rates also represented a reduction in government intervention. It is possible that the shift away from fixed exchange rates and from use of exchange-rate policy to affect real output and growth, with the failure of the IMF efforts of the early 1970s to develop other methods to adjust international imbalances, may have encouraged development of new tools to control international transmission of economic influences, including intervention in trade. If exchange-rate changes have generally compensated for divergences in rates of inflation (IMF [13], p. 52), protectionism may have replaced gains in competitiveness. With floating exchange rates, tariffs may be less effective because the level of protection they offer is more fluctuating and less predictable than under fixed rates. Managed trade and floating exchange rates are in one way a similar development; for exchange rates as for trade governments must now choose between intervention and non-intervention. Fixed exchange rates are in principle the severest form of intervention; if however such rates are treated as immutable with rare exceptions (devaluations or revaluations), managed floating may increase perceived intervention and cause a new uncertainty in exchange markets in the way intervention has in trade. Like trade controls it follows no fixed rules and may be in pursuit of goals other than the conventional ones. Both reflect reduced willingness to allow economic events to escape political control.

It is not sufficient to follow some recent studies of protection and simply to note that the new structure of trade departs from free trade; there can be practical or social reasons for modifying market results. But there is no justification for doing this by unilateral intervention in clear breach of established rules. So that the reader can judge the practical value of the new trade policies this paper has nevertheless attempted to discover and assess their purposes, and to discuss the costs of restricting trade and, particularly for a small country like the United Kingdom, of abandoning the rules. Demonstrating how far the world now is from a liberalised system may not slow the move towards even more intervention, but it may at least draw attention to the changes that have been made without a coherent philosophy or public discussion of the new goals pursued at the expense of traditional ones.

Appendix 1: Controls on Trade

For the EEC all *food* imports are treated as controlled under the provisions of the EEC Treaty, which controls by some individual countries reinforce. At present the EEC effectively regulates all *iron and steel* trade collectively. The basis for this dates from the European Iron and Steel Community. Unlike food, steel is not internationally accepted as subject to control. Control began in early 1977, with an export limitation agreement for steel with Japan; by the end of the year there was also an agreement with Spain, and the United Kingdom, which, with some other members, had already introduced surveillance licensing for certain types of steel to monitor imports, was trying to control imports from the centrally planned economies, with the motive admitted to be poor markets and British Steel's losses, not simply anti-dumping. The latter provided the nominal justification for minimum EEC import prices from the beginning of 1978, but they were soon replaced by agreements on price and quantity restraints; these guaranteed imports a minimum market share since the minimum prices were below EEC producers' prices. These were also fixed, but some EEC producers soon cut them in order to increase their own share. To enforce the minimum prices, control became increasingly tight over all trade and pricing and there was no sign that it was regarded as temporary. The Commission of the European Communities has proposed restrictions on domestic aids to the industry, which has suffered particularly severely in recent years because of a switch to lighter substitutes as well as the recession. From 60 per cent at the end of 1977, use of steel capacity in the EEC had recovered to 70–75 per cent at the end of 1978, but a revival of demand would scarcely bring it to 90 per cent in the 1980s, even with import controls; by then exports will have been further reduced by a major increase in developing countries' rapidly rising capacity.

Collective intervention in other fields has not been as clearly part of the EEC's economic objectives, but it has led the move for ever tighter and more comprehensive limits on *textile* imports. There is controversy over whether the controls should be permanent or gradually relaxed; the latter would be consistent with their original justification, to permit the European industry to adjust to new suppliers. The European Clothing Industry Federation has already started pressure for permanent controls after 1982, supported by the United Kingdom Department of Trade. In 1974 only controls by Belgium and Ireland on textiles and by the United Kingdom on some categories were included, but the methods and growing scope of the MFA justify inclusion in the 1979 measure of all imports from outside the OECD and from Greece, Spain, Portugal, Turkey and Japan.

Over-capacity in *shipping* has led to substantial intervention from individual countries and attempts at EEC organisation of markets. The market for new *aircraft*, also badly hit by the recession, has become subject to effective regulation as well, enforced by government owner-ship of most airlines.

The rise in oil prices and the threat of shortages in 1974 led the EEC to consider a common energy policy; each member also took individual powers to regulate trade in *oil* and *natural gas*, a clear example of increased control as oil was already effectively controlled from the export side by the OPEC cartel. Some trade in *coal* has always been formally controlled; the largely state-owned coal companies probably effectively control a high proportion of the rest, although it is not included here. The EEC has tried unsuccessfully to use the controls to justify industry-wide planning, for example to control capacity in oil refining.

There are many other goods controlled by individual EEC coun-tries, with varying degrees of EEC assistance, compliance, or tolerance. By the end of 1978, restricted goods included *television sets* and other appliances (especially by the United Kingdom from Japan and other Asian countries). Japanese *motorcycles* (by Italy) and *cars* (by the United Kingdom), *shoes* from Taiwan and Eastern Europe (by the United Kingdom) and *tyres* (by Ireland). Most of these restrictions were first imposed in 1977. The French tobacco monopoly, giving government control of all *tobacco* trade, is included. Although not included in the measurements, safety and standardisation provisions for electrical goods and cars may have been tightened. Some operate even within the Common Market. EEC regulations in theory have prohibited discrimination in public procurement policies since mid-1978, but there are permitted exceptions and few signs yet of any change.

Although not included, there are some EEC controls on exports of food, fuels and some steel. There are none on raw materials, in order to protect processors against manufacturers abroad, though this is a common use in developing countries and has been demanded by leather manufacturers, whose foreign competitors can pay high prices for raw materials at least partly because they are themselves protected. This is an example of retaliation and escalation of controls.

The United States controls *wheat, meat* and *dairy products* and has imposed a variety of individual controls on food from specific countries. As in the EEC, this is an extension of a domestic agricultural programme. Canada also controls some trade in food. In *textiles* both have been members of the international agreements. Although the United States originally opposed selective bilateral controls, it has insisted on maintaining its right to impose them and its controls by 1974 may have already been more extensive than those of the EEC. Canadian textile restrictions have followed a similar pattern, with a shift to tighter quotas in 1976.

The United States began to control *steel* imports in 1967; voluntary controls were accepted by the EEC and Japan for 1967–71 and later extended to 1974, when, however, they were not renewed. (The measure for the United States for 1974 therefore gives an atypical picture.) After the 1974 Trade Act, importers no longer needed to show that a trade agreement was the major explanation for imports when claiming 'serious injury' to obtain protection (Riedel [20], p. 8). In 1976 controls were renegotiated with Japan and quotas for some products were imposed on all countries. At the end of 1977 a 'trigger price' system, based on Japanese production costs, was introduced for all products and the prices have been revised quarterly since then. The imposition followed complaints of dumping by EEC and Japanese producers, not of excess penetration. (EEC steel was being sold below the domestic price, another interaction of controls.) The trigger price was presented as a faster method of imposing anti-dumping duties without individual investigation (US Treasury [23]). It does not limit imports' share of the market or adjust the price in relation to domestic prices. Japan, however, imposed its own restraints on exporters to reduce their share, apparently fearing that the United States might impose formal quotas if the trigger price failed to reduce the share of imported steel. As it did not fall the Japanese merely lost share to European producers. At the end of 1978 a new anti-dumping investigation of EEC steel was announced because, although the price was above the trigger price, it was still below the EEC guidance price. There are quotas on some special steels.

Both the United States and Canada effectively control trade in *oil* and *natural gas*. The United States and Canada have participated in managing the market for *ships*, and since 1977 the United States has restricted by bilateral agreement imports of *television sets* from Japan and Taiwan and of *shoes* from Taiwan and South Korea, while Canada has imposed quotas on all suppliers of *shoes*.

Japan limits most *food* imports and exports. In addition *silk*, *tobacco* and *leather* are controlled. In current trade negotiations, the limit that has been most criticised has been on government procurement, particularly by the state industries, which prevents some imports completely (not measurable by the method used here).

Food, textiles and *cars* are frequently controlled by developing countries, but only a few (excluding those that control all imports) control all manufactures; most have few restrictions on *machinery*. Some restrict *chemicals*, particularly fertilisers, but most restrictions are on finished goods and consumer goods. A decreasing number of former French African countries restrict imports from non-EEC countries. Total prohibition of certain goods is more common than among developed countries. The more advanced tend to use the same methods as developed countries. Many also have export controls, to influence prices or ensure low-cost supplies.

OPEC first exerted real pressure on the *oil* price in the 1970s and has regulated quantity since 1973, initially for political reasons, thereafter mainly to enforce its prices.

Appendix 2: Method of Measuring 'Managed Trade'

Each trade flow subject to any type of trade control is defined as managed. These flows are aggregated, by importing country and by commodity, and compared with total imports by that country or of that good to estimate the share controlled. No allowance is made for changes in the type or tightness of control; the tightness has almost certainly increased with the number of sectors controlled. Comparison between countries (or areas) of the share of managed trade may, therefore, be misleading, as one may control more imports less tightly. Comparing controlled trade with the total presents the problem familiar from tariff studies that the more tightly a sector is controlled the lower is its weight. For this reason 1974 weights were used to measure post-1974 controls. Trade covered by existing restrictions in 1974 that was already 'lost' is not measured and the method does not fully solve the problem of measuring the increase in the share controlled; the assumption that shares would have been constant without control is most unlikely to be true, as fast growth, actual or anticipated, may well lead to controls. For some of the trade groupings, 1977 and 1978 weights were tried as well. Without complete knowledge of domestic markets (which may themselves be controlled) and of the relationships between traded and domestic products, these assumptions give approximate estimates of the scale of controlled trade. In most cases, they are more likely to have underestimated the effect of controls than the reverse.

In some industries the recent spread of regulations from one product to another may have caused suppliers to expect that any product which grows rapidly will be restricted. This may cut imports by restraining exports. It is arguable that the recent increase in protection has discouraged all exporters from rapid changes, so that all trade is restricted, but here only textile and clothing imports from developing countries and steel imports are assumed to have reached such a point. The measurements were made entirely from the import side. Goods controlled by commodity cartels are recorded as controlled imports for every country. (Export controls by individual countries are omitted from the measures.)

For the OECD countries data at the three-digit SITC level were available, with some at four-digit level, while for other countries two- or three-digit classifications were available (OECD [19]; UN [22]; GATT [6] and [7]). Only OECD countries' data permitted simul- taneous disaggregation by country and commodity. When the data were not as disaggregated as the restrictions, the basic estimate includes none of the partially controlled category, but the 'alternative maximum' (see Table 7.5) includes all of it. The 'mainly managed' commodities were identified from the minimum estimates and were almost all well above 60 per cent. Because of the heavy weight in total trade of the OECD countries, the difference between the low and high estimates was not large. Manufactures were defined as SITC categories 5–8. The principal source of data on controls was IMF [12] supplemented by press reports [21] and [24]. The information is very incomplete. Systems for monitoring trade restrictions are under discussion at the IBRD and GATT.

The only previous estimates of the increase in protection from 1974 were by GATT [8a and 8b]. These estimated that the 10 per cent of world trade represented by 'temperate agricultural products' had been 'restrained and distorted' since the war, and that trade in textiles and clothing had added a further 5 per cent since the early 1960s, and restrictions on steel, ships, ball-bearings and consumer electronics by the industrial countries a further 5 per cent between 1975 and 1978. The estimate for the increase since 1975 is slightly lower than the 6 per cent found here; the latter includes a further year's restraints on textiles. About 20 percentage points of the difference in the level estimated is explained by the inclusion here of oil.

References

[1] Bergsten, C. F. (US Treasury) speech 27 June 1977.

[2] Blackhurst, R., Marian, N. and Tumlir, J., *Adjustment, Trade and Growth in Developed and Developing Countries*, Geneva, GATT, 1978.

[3] —, *Trade Liberalization, Protectionism and Interdependence*, Geneva, GATT, 1977.

[4] *Cambridge Economic Policy Review*, no. 5, 1979.

[5] Corden, W. M., *Trade Policy and Economic Welfare*, Oxford, Clarendon Press, 1974.

[6] GATT, *International Trade 1977/78*, Geneva, 1978.

[7] —, *Networks of World Trade 1955-76*, Geneva, 1978.

[8] —, press releases:

    (a) no. 1199, 9 November 1977.

    (b) no. 1220, 3 October 1978.

    (c) no. 1234, 12 April 1979.

[9] Hermes, P., 'International raw material policy in the agricultural and industrial sphere', *Intereconomics*, no. 7/8, 1977.

[10] Hirsch, F., Doyle, M. and Morse, E., *Alternatives to Monetary Disorder*, New York, McGraw-Hill, 1977.

[11] IBRD, *World Development Report 1978*, Washington (DC), 1978.

[12] IMF, *Annual Reports on Exchange Restrictions*.

[13] —, *The Rise in Protectionism*, Washington (DC), 1978.

[14] Lal, D., *Poverty, Power and Prejudice*, London, Fabian Society, 1978.

[15] —, 'The wistful mercantilism of Mr Dell', *The World Economy*, June 1978 (see also Mr Dell's reply in *The World Economy*, May 1979).

[16] Long, O., 'International trade under threat', *The World Economy*, June 1978.

[17] Morgan, A. D., 'Export competition and import substitution: the industrial countries 1963 to 1971' in *Industrialisation and the Basis for Trade*, Cambridge University Press (forthcoming).

[18] NIESR, *National Institute Economic Review*, February 1977.

[19] OECD, *Statistics of Foreign Trade* (series A and B).

[20] Riedel, J., 'Monitoring trends in protectionism' (mimeo., IBRD, 1979).

[21] Trade, Department of, press releases.

[22] United Nations, *Yearbook of International Trade Statistics*.

[23] United States Treasury, press releases, 6 and 28 December 1977.

[24] Press coverage of protection, especially *Business Week, Economist*.

7.3 The Experience of Floating Exchange Rates

by S. J. Brooks*

Introduction

The object of this note is to describe and discuss some of the major changes in exchange-rate behaviour since the Smithsonian Agreement of December 1971. Any historical account will necessarily appear to imply certain patterns of causation between the events that are described. The third section presents the results of an attempt to test some of these questions of causation.

History

There is no single date which signals 'the end of the Bretton Woods system'. The establishment of the two-tier gold market in March 1968, the floating of the Deutschemark in September 1969 and again in May 1971, the suspension of the convertibility of the dollar into gold in August 1971 and the subsequent floating of the major currencies, the floating of the pound in June 1972, and the dollar crisis preceding the move to generalised floating in March 1973 can all claim to be important landmarks in the change from the relatively rigid exchange-rate system of the early 1960s to the vaguer arrangements of the late 1970s.

Whether the Smithsonian Agreement should be included in this catalogue of landmarks is open to question – since in fact it re-established fixity after a period of floating. What the Agreement did was formally and finally to establish that the value of the dollar in terms of gold could be changed.

Throughout 1970 and in the first half of 1971 the United States

* This note is a shortened version of a background paper, which included a review of balance of payments theory, here omitted. The longer version is available on request from the National Institute of Economic and Social Research.

current account had been weak; at the same time interest rates in the United States had been low compared with those in continental European markets. Capital flows favoured the European currencies – in particular the mark – and particularly heavy selling of the dollar precipitated the suspension of official dealing on the Continent in May 1971. When the markets re-opened the mark and the guilder were floating and the Swiss franc had been revalued; at this stage the pound and the Japanese yen stayed pegged, so that the appreciation of the mark against the dollar shows up in the mark–pound exchange rate (Chart 7.1). With continued weakness in the United States current account there were further substantial flows of capital into European currencies. Expectations were validated when on 15 August the United States suspended the convertibility of the dollar into gold – the French were expected to convert $191 million the following day – and imposed an import surcharge. Subsequently all major currencies were floated; the yen soon caught up with the mark, while the pound fell more or less in line with the dollar (Chart 7.1).

These months of general floating were marked by the proliferation of controls on trade and capital movements; the fear that these would continue and that competitive depreciation would become rife spurred the meeting at the Smithsonian Institute in December 1971 to realign and re-fix the rates, but to allow wider margins. The dollar was devalued by 7.9 per cent against gold; the pound sterling and French franc maintained their gold values; the mark and yen were revalued. In early 1972 there followed an interlude of exchange-rate stability (Chart 7.1). In April 1972 the 'snake' was established among the members of the European Communities, thus implementing the first step on the road to monetary union that had been postponed the previous year when the mark and guilder had been floated.

The United Kingdom did not stay in the snake for long; in June 1972 the pound was floated and proceeded to depreciate rapidly. In the light of past balance of payments figures this depreciation was perhaps surprising; there had been large current account surpluses in 1970 and 1971, and foreign-exchange reserves had doubled in the year to May 1971. It was perhaps expectations which led to the depreciation, based on current high wage settlements, the adoption of a 5 per cent growth target and the view – reinforced by the Chancellor's statement – that a fixed exchange rate would not be allowed to be an obstacle to economic growth. At the same time as the floating of sterling, exchange controls on transactions with the

Chart 7.1   *Sterling exchange rates^a 1971–8 (1970 = 100)*

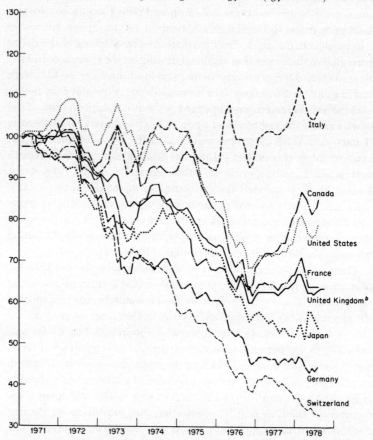

Sources: CSO, *Financial Statistics*; IMF, *International Financial Statistics*.
^{a}Units of foreign currency per £; monthly averages of daily rates.
^{b}Effective rate.

sterling area were substantially extended; the sterling area ceased to be of importance in the international payments system.

For some time the pound's was the only breach in the façade of the Smithsonian realignment; in the summer of 1972 the dollar was firm when high United States interest rates coincided with an apparent improvement in the domestic economy. This strength gave the European and Japanese central banks the opportunity to unload some of the dollars accumulated perhaps less than willingly in earlier support operations. Optimism was short-lived, however, as in the autumn it became clear that a worsening of the balance of payments and an increase in the rate of inflation were likely to accompany the rapid growth in output in the United States. At the same time interest-rate differentials began to favour outflows from the United States as Germany and Japan raised interest rates for domestic reasons. Political crisis in Italy precipitated the floating of the financial lira in early 1973, further weakening confidence in the Smithsonian system. After heavy sales of the dollar a further devaluation of 10 per cent against gold was announced in February 1973. At the same time the yen and the commercial lira were floated, so that of the major currencies only the dollar and the currencies of the 'snake' were attempting to maintain fixed parities. The second devaluation of the dollar failed to restore confidence that the new rate could be maintained and the dollar was soon at its floor against all the 'snake' currencies – upward pressure on the mark being particularly strong. Early in March the 'snake' finally gave up the struggle – its members opting to float jointly against the dollar and at the same time to revalue the mark against the other currencies in the scheme.

The oil price rise at the end of 1973 led to a major reassessment of the relative desirability of currencies (Chart 7.1) – for instance, the yen weakened because of Japan's heavy dependence on imported fuel, but sterling held up well through most of 1974 in spite of the three-day week, the political crisis and the election; a significant part of OPEC surpluses was being deposited in London. In 1975 and 1976 the main feature of exchange-rate movements was the rapid and sustained fall in sterling – so marked that in Chart 7.1 it masks relatively large changes in the bilateral exchange rates of other countries. The pound's rapid depreciation against the dollar in 1975 reflects in great part the strength of the dollar – following a decline in the United States GNP, an associated current account surplus and an improvement in interest-rate differentials in favour of the dollar – and its depreciation against the mark and the French franc was much milder. The United Kingdom's inflation rate was much higher than that of other industrial countries and, with the falling exchange rate, sterling holdings of OPEC and other countries were drawn down.

The decline of the pound was eventually arrested at the end of 1976 when agreement was reached with the IMF. Subsequently the pound started to strengthen and the United Kingdom authorities reacted by pegging its level at $1.72, bringing down interest rates and rebuilding the exchange reserves. At this time the dollar itself was weak; a constant pound–dollar rate meant sterling depreciation against the strong currencies, in particular against the yen and the Swiss franc. By the autumn of 1977 the pressure on the dollar had intensified; it was widely doubted whether the $1.72 peg could be held and short-term capital moved into the United Kingdom. It became clear that continued pegging of the rate was incompatible with the money supply targets that had been adopted; pegging was abandoned and the pound appreciated generally, peaking in February 1978 before declining.

The Prevalence of Floating Exchange Rates

The IMF has estimated that in 1978 more than 80 per cent of world trade was between countries the bilateral exchange rates of which were not fixed. However, small countries continued to peg their exchange rates; at no time since the Smithsonian Agreement could more than about a quarter of countries be said to have been floating their currencies (Table 7.10). The response of the smaller countries to disarray in the world's financial system has been to discover new rules of pegging; while most countries maintain the single currency peg, some have changed to pegging their currencies to a composite – often the SDR – while some in South America have continued their crawling peg system of frequent devaluations against the dollar in the light of domestic price developments.

The choice of a currency peg by the small countries is on the whole a matter for them alone as they are unlikely individually to affect the monetary policies of the 'host' country. The joint float of the European currencies differs because decisions about the relative values of currencies within the arrangement are supposed to be taken after consultation and because, in the EMS, the pegging arrangements are supplemented by borrowing facilities (see IMF [4]). Discussion about the United Kingdom's membership of such a system has generally been analysed in terms of a movement back to exchange-rate fixity (see NIESR [5]; Corden [2]). In practice the 'snake' experienced several realignments (see Appendix 1). A major problem for the United Kingdom would seem to be assessing how the world's system is likely to evolve if, on the one hand, sterling is drawn into the EMS and if, on the other hand, it remains outside.

*Table 7.10   Adherents to various exchange-rate systems
(numbers of currencies[a])*

	1972[b]	1973[c]	1975	1976	1977	1978
Single currency peg						
US$	42	53	52	48	44	41
£ sterling	} 44	{ 12	10	4	5	5
Fr. franc		{ 14	13	13	14	14
Other	26	8	4	5	5	3
Total	n.a.	87	79	70	68	63
Composite peg						
SDR	—	—	5	11	14	15
Total	—	—	5	11	31	32
Rates adjusted to a set of indicators	—	8[d]	6	5	7	5
Other arrangements[e]						
'Snake'	—	8	7	7	7	6
Total	3	30	37	40	25	34
All classified	115	125	127	126	131	134

Sources: IMF, *Annual Reports* and *Annual Reports on Exchange Restrictions*; Helleiner [3].
[a]Of IMF members plus Switzerland.
[b]This year's figures show reactions to the Smithsonian realignment; 'other' here includes all currencies which changed their parities relative to the US$.
[c]Developing countries allocated as by Helleiner, because the IMF classifies many exchange rates for this year in terms of par values or central rates.
[d]Includes IMF members said to 'periodically adjust exchange rate'.
[e]Includes currencies notified to the IMF as floating or floating jointly and a few not classified elsewhere.

Some Questions of Causation

The simple models of received balance of payments theory suggest several variables the behaviour of which is likely to be related to that of the exchange rate. A simple technique for analysing relations between a pair of time-series has been made popular by Sims [7] (see also Pierce and Haugh [6]). It is well known that regression analysis reveals nothing about the direction of causation between the dependent and independent variables. However when the independent variable appears in the equation with lags it is natural to interpret the result as showing the effect of past values of the independent variable on the dependent variable. Sims attempts to give content to this interpretation by arguing that causation can be examined by regression if a series X can be said to cause a series Y when predictions of Y made with the help of X are superior to those made without X. Using this definition of causation Sims has shown, given certain assumptions about the behaviour of X and Y, that, if and only if Y does not cause X, future values of X will fail to be significant in a regression of Y on current, past and future values of X. Intuitively one might argue that effects cannot precede their causes, so that if X causes Y the entire causal influence of X on Y is contained in current and past values of X and so future values of X will not be useful in explaining the current value of Y. If, on the other hand, Y causes X then regressing Y on future values of X evaluates the extent of the causation of soon-to-be-past Y on soon-to-be-current X. Thus a full analysis of the relations between X and Y requires that four regressions be run: Y regressed on current and past values of X and on current, past and future values of X, and X regressed on current and past values of Y and on current, past and future values of Y.

Certain technical problems complicate the implementation of such a test (for details see notes to Table 7.11). The most important of these is concerned with the difficulty of drawing inferences in regression analysis when the series are dominated by trends; to get round this difficulty the tests have been recast to examine the relationships between the deviations of the variables from their trends. Further, there are circumstances in which the test can be misleading. If the two series are independent but both are caused by a third variable, if certain conditions are met the test may spuriously suggest a causal relation. Secondly, if one variable is affected by expectations of another – without a causal link existing between them – then, if the expectations are reasonably accurate spurious causation may again be indicated. Finally, if one variable which causes another is subject to discretionary control, depending on movements in the controlled variable, the test may indicate bidirectional rather than unidirectional causality.

Most theoretical models imply that under managed exchange rates movements in the rate will have repercussions on the domestic price level and, conversely, under flexible rates exogenous changes in domestic costs and prices will affect the exchange rate. Casual examination of Charts 7.2 and 7.3 shows that, while the value of the pound has declined against both the dollar and the mark, the United

Chart 7.2   The United States and the United Kingdom: exchange rates, and relative money supply, price levels and interest rates, 1971–8

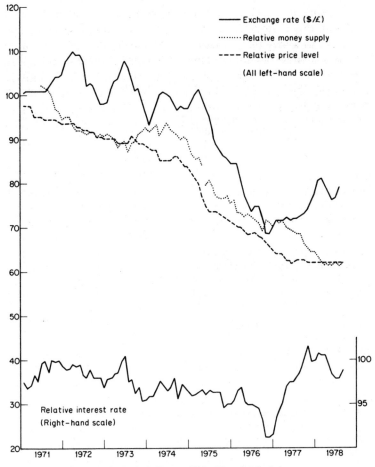

Sources: OECD, *Main Economic Indicators*; CSO, *Financial Statistics*.

Notes: (i) Exchange rate as in Chart 7.1.

(ii) Relative money supply is ratio of US M1 to UK M1, both series seasonally adjusted and scaled so that May 1970 = 100.

(iii) Relative price level is ratio of US consumer price index (all items) to UK consumer price index (all items), both series seasonally unadjusted with 1970 = 100 (not rescaled).

(iv) Relative interest rate is ratio of (1 + US 3-month Treasury bill rate) to (1 + UK 3-month Treasury bill rate).

Table 7.11   Results of tests of causality

	F_1	F_2	R^2
Germany: June 1971–January 1978			
Relative price level on exchange rate	1.091	1.169	0.199
$(1 - B)(1 - 0.417B - 0.285B^2 - 0.173B^6)$	(13,57)	(6,51)	
Exchange rate on relative price level	1.091	0.871	0.205
$(1 - B)(1 - 0.277B + 0.214B^2 - 0.210B^7)$	(13,57)	(6,51)	
United States: July 1971–January 1978			
Relative price level on exchange rate	0.449	1.575	0.081
$(1 - B)(1 - 0.106B - 0.187B^2 - 0.225B^3)$	(13,66)	(6,60)	
Exchange rate on relative price level	1.117	0.549	0.183
$(1 - B)$	(13,65)	(6,59)	
Germany: August 1972–October 1976			
Relative money supply on exchange rate	1.002	2.353*	0.260
$(1 - B)(1 + 0.412B)$	(13,37)	(6,31)	
Exchange rate on relative money supply	2.521‡	0.107	0.463
$(1 - B)$	(13,38)	(6,32)	
United States: July 1972–February 1978			
Relative money supply on exchange rate	1.091	0.802	0.218
$(1 - B)(1 + 0.200B - 0.183B^2 - 0.236B^3)$	(13,51)	(6,45)	
Exchange rate on relative money supply	1.102	0.998	0.219
$(1 - B)(1 - 0.240B + 0.152B^2)$	(13,51)	(6,45)	
United States: May 1972–January 1978			
Relative interest rate on exchange rate	2.471†	0.543	0.236
$(1 - B)(1 + 0.133B - 0.117B^2)$	(7,56)	(6,50)	
Exchange rate on relative interest rate	1.827*	1.733	0.178
$(1 - B)$	(7,59)	(6,53)	
United Kingdom			
Balance of trade on effective exchange rate	1.653	1.501	0.301
$(1 - B)(1 + 0.768B + 0.287B^2)$	(13,50)	(6,44)	
Effective exchange rate on balance of trade	0.680	2.324*	0.150
$(1 - B)(1 - 0.405B + 0.299B^2)$	(13,50)	(6,44)	

Sources: Price indices and money supplies: OECD, *Main Economic Indicators*; exchange rates and interest rates: CSO, *Financial Statistics*; Bank of England *Quarterly Bulletin*; effective exchange rate: IMF, *International Financial Statistics*; balance of trade: Department of Trade.

(Seasonal adjustment: ratios of price levels and the United Kingdom balance of trade were adjusted using seasonal dummies; ratios of money supplies used published adjusted series; all other series were unadjusted.)

Notes: (i) In the implementation of the tests the methodology of Williams and others [8] has been followed. All series were transformed into lags and stationarity was induced by differencing in the manner of Box and Jenkins [1]; in all cases first differences were eventually considered satisfactory. Next one series (Y) was regressed first on current and past values of the other (X) and then on current, past and future values of X. A compromise auto-regressive model was then estimated to account simultaneously for serial correlation in the two series of residuals. Y and X were transformed by the compromise filter and the equations re-run. The residuals of these equations were checked for serial correlation by comparing residual auto-correlations with their theoretical standard errors, using the Box-Pierce 'portmanteau' test (Box and Jenkins [1], Chapter 8) and running auto-regressive equations. If these tests were passed it was concluded that the F-tests reported would be valid and could be used for assessing causation. To complete the test the process was repeated with the roles of X and Y reversed.

(ii) F_1 is the F-statistic for a test of current and lagged values of the explanatory variable and F_2 for the additional significance of its leading values (with degrees of freedom in brackets below); * indicates significance at the 10 per cent level, † significance at the 5 per cent level and ‡ significance at the 2.5 per cent level. R^2 refers to the explanatory power of the current and lagged values together with the constant. The final filter used in estimation, in terms of the lag operator $B(B^i x_t = x_{t-i})$, is shown in brackets below the side-headings.

(iii) The money supply results for the United States and Germany do not bear close comparison. The estimation periods differ because a consistent series for Germany was available only up to April 1977, so that those results do not cover the appreciation of sterling in late 1977; also, the German exchange rate used is the monthly average of daily rates while the American rate is that at the end of the period.

(iv) F_1 was significant but F_2 was not in the regressions of interest rates on exchange rates; thus exchange rates (over the period of the test) seem not to have been caused by changes in interest rates. A similar pattern emerged in regressions of exchange rates on interest rates and, as examination of t-statistics suggested that only the first leading value might be at all significant, the other leading values were dropped, when F_2 became very significant, implying that exchange rates cause interest rates but not the other way about.

(v) Problems encountered in the test for the significance of the balance of trade included selection of 'the' exchange rate (the IMF's effective rate was used) and of the balance of trade variable (the United Kingdom balance in 1970 prices was used). Inflation has caused the balance of trade in current prices to become more erratic, but the use of 1970 prices plays down the importance of oil. These results are based on an *a priori* lag of twelve months only and must be interpreted with caution; the maximum lag was determined in part by the regression package and in part by the 1970 price data being available only until the end of 1977. Only F_2 for the balance of trade is significant at the 10 per cent level, but here F_1 for the exchange rate is very nearly significant.

Chart 7.3   Germany and the United Kingdom: exchange rates, and relative money supply, price levels and interest rates, 1971–8

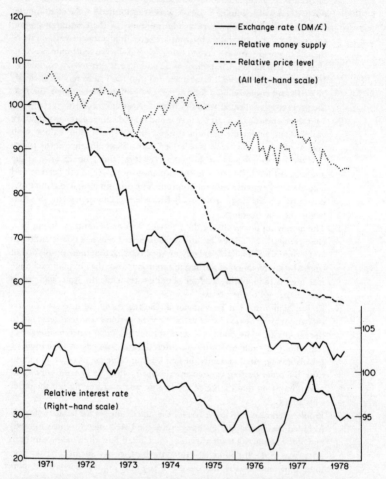

Sources: as Chart 7.2; *Monatsberichte den Deutschen Bundesbank*, Table V.5.

Notes: (i) Exchange rate, relative money supply and price level as in Chart 7.2 (equivalents for Germany instead of US).

(ii) Relative interest rate is ratio of (1 + Frankfurt money market rate) to (1 + UK 3-month Treasury bill rate).

Kingdom consumer price index has risen faster than either the German or the American. Formal tests of the causality between the ratio of consumer price indices and the mark–sterling and dollar–sterling exchange rates failed, perhaps surprisingly, to reveal any causal relation (Table 7.11). It was, however, only possible to test for the influence of variables up to one year previously, so a true causal relation might remain undetected.

The second set of tests concerned the relationship between the money supply and exchange rates. In these tests M_1 was used rather than M_3, on the grounds that M_1 was less likely to have been subject to discretionary control. The test of the relationship between relative money supplies and the mark–sterling exchange rate did indicate evidence of causation running from the money supply to the exchange rate. The relative money supply movement appears to explain a high proportion of the variation in the exchange rate and the twelve-month elasticity of the exchange rate to the relative money supply is about 0.7. For the United States, however, there is no evidence of a causal link (some of the inevitable differences in the estimation procedure are discussed in the notes to Table 7.11).

On the relation between relative interest rates and the exchange rate, the test was restricted to a comparison between the United States and the United Kingdom (Table 7.11). The tests provide some evidence that movements in the exchange rate cause changes in interest rates, but not the other way round; quantitatively, they suggest that a 1 per cent depreciation of the dollar will lead, after one month, to a 0.23 per cent rise in the United States interest rate relative to that of the United Kingdom. This might suggest that such an exchange-rate change leads to a movement of capital into the United Kingdom, so raising interest rates in the United States and lowering them here. It is less likely that the test is picking up government action to alter interest rates in order to moderate the movements of the exchange rate; if that were the case, the test might be expected to show bidirectional rather than unidirectional causality.

The test of the relationship between the balance of trade and the effective exchange rate was, for reasons discussed in the notes to Table 7.11, the most difficult to conduct. The test may be regarded as weak evidence in support of the hypothesis that the exchange rate affects the balance of trade – an appreciation of the exchange rate for a time marginally improving the balance of trade. The test provides no evidence of any effect from the balance of trade to the exchange rate.

Appendix 1: History of the European Agreement

1971

May   Floating of mark and guilder delays planned implementation of narrower margins as set out in the Werner Report.

1972

April   'Snake' established, with permitted margins between members of 2¼ per cent on each side of par.

June   £ sterling floated and United Kingdom leaves snake.

December   Italy leaves snake.

1973

March   Remaining members agree to float jointly against other currencies; mark revalued within the system by 3 per cent.

June   Mark revalued by 5½ per cent.

September   Guilder revalued by 5 per cent.

November   Norwegian krone revalued by 5 per cent.

1974

January   France withdraws from snake.

1975

July   France rejoins snake.

1976

March   France withdraws from snake; 'worm' agreement for even narrower margins between Benelux countries suspended.

October   Realignment within snake: mark revalued by 2 per cent; other countries devalue, leading to a net revaluation of the mark of 6 per cent against the Danish krone, 3 per cent against the Swedish krona and Norwegian krone and 2 per cent against Benelux currencies.

1977

April   Realignment: Swedish krona devalued by 6 per cent, Danish and Norwegian kroner by 3 per cent.

August   Sweden leaves snake. Norwegian and Danish kroner devalued by 5 per cent.

1978

February   Norwegian krone devalued by 8 per cent.

October   Realignment: mark revalued by 4 per cent against

Danish and Norwegian kroner and by 2 per cent against Benelux currencies.

December   Proposals for EMS drawn up; snake arrangements to be bolstered by borrowing facilities.

1979
March   EMS comes into effect.

References

[1] Box, G. E. P. and Jenkins, G. D., *Time Series Analysis: forecasting and control*, San Francisco, Holden-Day, 1976.

[2] Corden, W. M., *Monetary Integration*, Princeton Essays in International Finance, no. 93, Princeton (NJ), 1972.

[3] Helleiner, G. K., 'The less developed countries and the international monetary system', *Journal of Development Studies*, April–July 1974.

[4] IMF, 'The European Monetary System', *IMF Survey* (supplement), March 1979.

[5] NIESR, 'The European Monetary System', *National Institute Economic Review*, February 1979.

[6] Pierce, D. A. and Haugh, L. D., 'Causality in temporal systems: characterisations and a survey', *Journal of Econometrics*, May 1977.

[7] Sims, C. A., 'Money, income and causality', *American Economic Review*, September 1972.

[8] Williams, D. *et al.*, 'Money, income and causality: the UK experience', *American Economic Review*, June 1976.

8 Report of the Discussion

by R. L. Major

Introduction

The conference began by discussing exchange-rate questions, on the basis of first the econometric study by Beenstock and Burns (Chapter 5) and then Emerson's appraisal of the EMS (Chapter 4). The comparative merits of the exchange rate and protection as instruments of economic adjustment were next analysed in relation in particular to Neild's advocacy of protection (Chapter 2); the consideration of the issues raised by trade controls was then broadened in the light of Cable's paper (Chapter 3). Forsyth's paper (Chapter 6), concerned largely with the role of the capital account in balance of payments disequilibria, was the last to be considered. The discussions which took place around these themes are summarised successively in the rest of this chapter.

Effects of Exchange-rate Changes

The conference first considered the implications of the simulations by Beenstock and Burns of the effects on other key variables in the economy of an appreciation in the rate of exchange. It was, however, emphasised that the simulations should be regarded as a means of organising the discussion rather than as forecasts of what would happen in particular circumstances. There was, for example, evidence that confidence in particular policies could have important effects, via expectations and anticipation, in reducing the length of time lags, which appeared in any case to be shorter now than had been generally supposed. But average lags based on past experience had been adopted for the model. Moreover this was not the full London Business School model, which might give different results, but an experimental version.

With these reservations, it was noted that in the first three or four years the Beenstock and Burns results were in the main similar to those produced by the National Institute model. Both indicated that, other things being equal, an exchange-rate appreciation would mean lower prices, lower nominal wages, and a deterioration in the balance of payments after an initially favourable J-curve effect. Close comparison of the balance of payments consequences was, however, not possible. The National Institute's results were in terms of the current balance, whereas a large part of the effects recorded by Beenstock and Burns were on capital account, which their model did not differentiate in view of its close interdependence with the current account. In neither model was the level of output greatly altered by appreciation. The National Institute model produced an initial reduction in output which was later reversed, whereas the opposite sequence was implied by the Beenstock and Burns model. In the latter there was a conflict between the depressing effects of worsened competitiveness on the trade balance in real terms and stimulative real balance effects, operating partly through a lower savings ratio. The real balance effects came through the faster and were important also in the Treasury model.

Beenstock and Burns emphasised that the equations in their model were freely estimated and the consistency of the longer-term results with monetarist theories of the balance of payments did not mean that they were in any sense imposed. They were supported, moreover, by a substantial volume of evidence showing, in particular, that output tended to revert to trend in spite of booms and slumps and that, though actual prices differed from country to country, the proportionate relationships between them tended to be constant when expressed in a common currency. The real wage likewise could, in equilibrium, be regarded as fixed in the long term, there being no reason to expect the real variables in the labour market to be influenced by nominal variables such as the rate of exchange. In this model the balance of payments, which should be regarded as an intermediate variable rather than an objective, did not hinge on the real wage but on monetary policy.

Other speakers did not accept the Beenstock–Burns view of the determination of real wages and of the essential futility, except in the short run, of any attempt to control them in order to make a devaluation effective or limit the inflationary risks of expanding domestic demand. It was, however, generally accepted that it was not now possible, if indeed it ever had been, to operate effectively an exchange-rate policy with which monetary, fiscal and exchange-control policies were not consistent. Some speakers who favoured a lower rate of exchange believed that in the short run at least this could and should be brought about in both nominal and real terms by influencing the balance of supply and demand on capital account. This could be done either by relaxing controls on capital movements, which, it was suggested, had in any case been breaking down over the last five years, or by engineering a reduction in interest rates, which were well above the international average despite the rising rate of exchange. If the authorities opted for a policy of expansion, a fall in interest rates might be brought about by raising the M_3 money supply target, which in itself would tend to weaken the rate of exchange. Alternatively, however, it could be done by lowering the public sector borrowing requirement. The temporary inflow of revenue from North Sea oil, which was one of the factors responsible for the current strength of sterling, should help to make this possible. Though it was not disputed that the stance of fiscal policy was already restrictive by conventional standards of measurement, it was argued that there had been a switch from the more productive types of public expenditure to subsidies and transfer payments and that the overall effect was inimical to the successful working of monetary policy.

Although there was strong support for lowering the exchange rate, there was not unanimous agreement even that its rise during the North Sea oil boom should be restrained. A contrary argument was that the period of temporary balance of payments strength provided an opportunity for sterling appreciation which would help to bring down inflation. If the savings ratio behaved as in the Treasury model this would actually contribute to the growth of output. Model calculations indicating that exchange-rate changes affected inflation only for a short time tended to be based on observations of the impact of steep movements in the rate, whereas the German experience suggested that a gradual appreciation could exert a continuing anti-inflationary influence. In the longer term there was likely to be a particular need for this in the event of full British participation in the EMS, which would have implications over a far wider area than the rate of exchange. Not only would domestic fiscal and monetary policies be affected, but greater financial integration and liberalisation of exchange control would also be entailed.

The European Monetary System

Dixon emphasised that the EMS should not be thought of just as a semi-fixed exchange-rate system, but rather as a first step towards something wider. The case for monetary union in Europe was partly political, but it was also economically desirable in order to establish Europe as a feasible currency area which would be better placed than the present collection of open economies to come to satisfactory terms with the United States over the potentially disruptive role of the dollar. The aims of stability within the system and stability over a wider area were not in conflict, and both were highly desirable in view of evidence that fluctuations in exchange rates had been detrimental to both trade and inflation, the cost of insuring against them being relatively high. Informal consultations on policy were working well, despite the lack of formal agreement and recent evidence of unilateral German action on interest rates and the rate of exchange with the dollar.

In the discussion of the advantages and disadvantages of full British participation, it was generally assumed that the present strength of sterling was temporary; in so far as loss of freedom to vary the exchange rate would be entailed this would in effect be a loss of freedom to devalue in order to protect competitiveness in the face of relatively rapid inflation. In favour of participation it was argued, however, that this would not necessarily mean surrender of the exchange-rate weapon as an instrument of policy. There were signs that Germany would actually welcome devaluation of sterling to the extent that it might be necessary to maintain parity of inflation rates within the system in terms of a common currency. In any case the object should be competitiveness not at low but at high real wages. This could only be achieved by an improvement in productivity and the easy option of continuing devaluation would not help to bring it about nor to achieve a reduction in unemployment, which rather required a different relationship between the relative costs of capital and labour. The strict monetary control that might be needed if the necessity to devalue was to be avoided had already become a key element in official policy. Moreover it could hardly be argued that when laxer policies had been in operation, whereby the monetary authorities in effect ratified whatever wage increases the British worker secured, this had given him rates of inflation, unemployment or growth which his German counterpart would envy. But if the money supply was now to rise this year by only 8 per cent while wages were going up by 14–15 per cent, some kind of crunch in the coming winter appeared to be inevitable. Under these circumstances the EMS might have political attractions as providing a convenient justification for government policy.

Against full participation it was argued that a wage explosion would be precisely the kind of development which could make a diminution of freedom to influence the rate of exchange particularly costly. While the general principle of stability would be universally welcomed, there would be less general agreement that adoption of fixed but adjustable rates of exchange would be an appropriate first step towards its achievement. It was, moreover, important to be clear what type of stability was envisaged. Was it to be stability of competitiveness, of exchange rates, or of something else? There was a tendency for people of differing economic persuasions each to regard the EMS as providing appropriate conditions for the achievement of aims which were to a certain extent in conflict. Those who believed in expansionary policies could see in it a means of bringing about their adoption on a basis of European coordination and cooperation. Those who gave greater weight to monetary discipline could equally see it as leading in the direction which they thought desirable. But the greater the success of the intervention mechanism of the EMS, the more important and politically contentious would policy issues become. Past experience suggested that agreement would not be easy to achieve, as there were fundamental divergences of view between those who gave policy a minor role confined to monetary and possibly exchange control initiatives to control inflation and those who stressed the real side of the economy, whether domestic or European. Clearly the convergence that Germany contemplated was convergence on German rates of inflation and, though the rise in British prices could probably be slowed down by monetary measures, unless and until this was validated in money wages the result would be a squeeze on profits which would have damaging effects on output and investment and was unlikely to improve productivity.

If the real relative effective wage rate was wrong, with British workers receiving the same real wage as German workers despite their lower productivity, then exchange-rate adjustment would probably. do little to remedy this. Loss of the exchange-rate instrument might be unimportant also at the other extreme if real wages were wholly determined domestically by the competitive process and if Beenstock and Burns were right in believing that in the long run changes in the exchange rate would not alter competitiveness. The difficulty lay in between, when, as might now be the case, there was a movement towards international wage comparability while differences in productivity persisted. In Europe there was as yet no internationally redistributive budgetary mechanism of the kind which in the United States, for example, compensated for differences in productivity between one region and another. This made it all the more important that productivity should converge before real wages and not vice versa.

The Case for Protection and the Case Against
Neild explained that this was very much the kind of consideration that underlay the advocacy by the Cambridge Economic Policy Group (CEPG) of non-market mechanisms for checking the growth of imports. Its basis was despair over the efficacy of alternative ways of checking the downward slide of the British economy within a world environment which itself seemed prospectively rather unfavourable. He would make the same recommendation for any country where a balance of payments constraint could not be removed by devaluation, but the United Kingdom seemed to be the extreme example though others probably existed. Import controls were not for him the thin end of a *dirigiste* wedge based on dislike of the price mechanism. But he did not share the monetarists' faith and, even if devaluation could be regarded as an independent weapon, he did not see how it could be effective in this country in view of the apparent impossibility under present conditions of maintaining the initial squeeze on real wages which the shift to profits resulting from devaluation must produce. If the political means of avoiding real wage rigidity could be found he would welcome this, and, being little influenced by the 'cheap labour' argument, he would in these circumstances consider devaluation preferable to protection. He did not, however, believe that it could be done, as the possibilities of incomes policy had in his view been exhausted. If this was right, some instrument had to be used which would break out of the balance of payments constraint without infringing the real-wage constraint and so inviting defeat.

Direct measures to reduce import propensities would make it possible to reduce rates of taxation and raise real wages quickly, since higher domestic output would mean increases in tax yields and reductions in unemployment benefit and aids to industry. The precise method was to him a matter of secondary importance. Apart from quotas, one possibility was a general tariff, a second the coupon scheme described in his paper, and a third some combination of taxes and subsidies of the type for which Lal's commentary on his paper had indicated a preference. He had not been able to think of such a combination which would avoid depressing the real wage, except possibly the old and partially abortive Selective Employment Tax with a subsidy to manufacturing industry.

The tabular summary in his paper, in which the effects of protection appeared to contrast favourably in most respects with those of de-valuation, related essentially to the short term, but getting through to the longer term might not be easy. He was postulating throughout that there would be no retaliation. It was also assumed that labour and other resources needed for an increase in output were available and that British manufacturers would not take advantage of protection to raise their domestic selling prices.

Neild's gloomy assessment of British prospects was supported by Godley and Singh. Godley argued that, while the balance of payments problem was temporarily masked by North Sea oil, adverse trends in imports and exports of manufactures were producing a dynamic dis-equilibrium which would reach critical proportions in the 1980s. Singh added that the Stone model at Cambridge gave a similar picture to that of the CEPG, with British industry in long-term structural disequili-brium and the balance of payments in full-employment deficit even with 1972 terms of trade. This, he argued, was mainly because of the poor performance of manufacturing industry in spite of the competitive advantages which until recently depreciation of the pound had been providing. Protection seemed a necessary condition for improvement, but controls should be supplemented on the supply side, in particular by a strong competitive antitrust policy and economic planning co-ordinated on a European basis. An example of successful planning of trade was provided by Comecon, which had managed to combine high rates of employment with low rates of inflation.

Speakers' arguments against the CEPG case fell into three broad categories. First, it was suggested that it was based on an excessively gloomy view of future prospects under present policies. Secondly, it was argued that a number of adverse consequences which could be expected to follow from protection had been ignored or under-rated, while others had been specifically assumed not to operate, and that partly for this reason the relative merits of protection and devaluation had been wrongly assessed. Thirdly, it was pointed out that even if there were deep-rooted British economic problems in the medium term which measures other than protection would be unable to solve it did not follow that further interference with free trade or free currency arrangements would mean an improvement; the key problems appeared to be real-wage rigidity and inflation, for which the solution probably lay in the long term through improvements in productivity and industrial relations or the abandonment by the British people of attempts to live at a standard compatible only with high unemployment.

There was little evidence that the ratio of United Kingdom growth to that of competing countries had fallen recently to any marked extent and, it was suggested, the time trends in imports of manufactures were less alarming than they might seem. They were not confined to this country and could be explained. The Kennedy round of tariff reductions had produced a general upsurge of imports which had coincided with the estimation periods of a number of models and, while world trade in manufactures had subsequently been less buoyant in relation to output, imports (and to some extent exports) had been stimulated between 1972 and 1975 by British membership of the European Communities.

It seemed very doubtful whether membership would make common protective measures easier to organise than common expansionary measures had proved to be, and in any case the success claimed for Comecon might well be attributable less to trade controls than to wage controls. The Soviet satellites would probably not be very enthusiastic about the way in which trade controls had worked; they had not been conspicuously successful in Australia or New Zealand either. Their advocates tended to make insufficient allowance for bureaucratic failure due to inadequate information. Because of increased interdependence any selective controls would be much more difficult to operate now than in the immediate postwar period and the machinery for their operation which then existed in this country had long ago been dismantled and would be hard to re-create. Furthermore, despite the logic of the argument that the growth of imports must somehow be checked and other countries should be fairly indifferent as to the method, experience with the import deposit scheme suggested that it would be impossible to maintain a unilateral system of protection without retaliation.

In further discussion about the relative merits of protection and devaluation it was agreed that if the problem of real-wage rigidity could be overcome in the transitional period, the requisite external balance could thereafter be achieved at a higher level of trade with devaluation than with tariffs. Doubts were expressed, however, about the likely response from British industry if faced with an increase in domestic demand as a result of restraint on imports. As regards the scope for raising output, stress was laid on the inefficiency of the labour market, as revealed in frequent reports of specific shortages at a time when the general level of unemployment was exceptionally high, and also on the fact that investment was discouraged by low levels of profitability. In a world of multinationals and price-takers production took place where it was most profitable. As regards prices, it was agreed that the assumption that these would not be raised by protection except to the extent that the cost of imports rose was crucial to the CEPG case. In support of the assumption it was argued that, though exchange-rate changes had had substantial effects on import prices, there was no evidence of a shift to profits under these conditions. The opposite conclusion was, however, drawn from experience in the United States, where a 10 per cent devaluation was believed to have resulted in a 2 per cent rise in prices, of which only $\frac{1}{2}$ per cent was directly attributable to higher import costs and the rest to higher charging by domestic producers.

It was pointed out that devaluation was equivalent in its effects on the economy to a uniform tariff combined with a uniform export subsidy. Whether this subsidy went overseas or to the British export sector depended on whether exporters changed their foreign currency prices or their sterling prices as a result of devaluation. Since not all prices could be changed immediately, some initially adverse J-curve effect was inevitable, but given the presumption that this would be relatively short-lived any balance of payments deficit that was entailed could be financed from the reserves or overseas borrowing. It was questionable whether it would call for measures to reduce domestic demand, although such measures had been the normal concomitant of devaluation in the past. In the slightly longer run Britain probably had little power to influence its terms of trade in a world in which prices of manufactures tended to be set by the larger economies of the United States, Japan and West Germany. Thus the effect on the terms of trade of either a tariff or devaluation was likely to be fairly small. As there should be increasing returns with either a tariff or devaluation, this implied that the question of domestic income distribution was in fact the crucial one.

With a devaluation it would be open to the authorities, should they wish to do, to use the proceeds of a tax on the export sector to compensate for the fall in the real wage which would result from higher sterling import prices in the interim period before the income effects of higher output materialised. The distribution of income would then be essentially the same as with the CEPG proposal to use the proceeds of the tariff in a similar way. But this would militate against the relative expansion of tradeable output which both schools of thought were concerned to encourage.

General Issues of Trade Control

As the CEPG school and most of its opponents shared a common preference for market mechanisms, protection had up to this point been discussed mainly in terms of tariffs rather than direct controls. The conference then moved on, however, to a brief review of the issues raised by increasing control of trade in general as described in the papers by Cable and Mrs Page. (It was suggested that the term 'management' was a misleading expression as there had been a move away from management in any true sense. Control, however, was undoubtedly growing, though its extent was hard to measure partly because of problems of definition.)

Cable remarked in opening the discussion that the main conflict over policy in this field tended to be between the economists and the policy-makers, on whom all the pressure came from sectional interests. There seemed in fact to be little disagreement among the economists present despite some difference of opinion over the scope for management of commodity markets, where it was suggested that the price movements necessary to evoke a supply response were excessive and the industrial countries might be well advised to provide greater stability in return for security of supply. The point was also made that there might be scope for bilateral deals between the weaker advanced countries and the developing countries. The NICs would, however, have to generate more domestic demand and more trade between one another if their rapid export growth was to continue in face of trade union opposition in the advanced countries.

Britain did not appear to be especially vulnerable to imports from the NICs, and in the OECD area generally it was not true that these imports were responsible for high unemployment. They still accounted for only 2 per cent of consumption of manufactures, though their share was rising fast. At present they were at a stage of development comparable with that of Japan in about 1953. But unlike Japan, whose difficulties they attributed to its past mercantilist policies, they encouraged imports on both economic and political grounds and they could not collectively be characterised as surplus countries. They would provide rapidly rising markets for industrial countries' exports and it was only in the sense that a high proportion of their imports came from Japan that they could be said to be contributing to balance of payments disequilibrium in the industrial countries.

The Problem of Surplus Countries

Forsyth suggested that whether or not Korea, for example, would become a surplus country in the Japanese sense largely depended on whether or not it continued to rig its capital account and hence to develop vast surpluses of capacity as a result of high profitability. A current surplus must have its counterpart on the capital side and if this took the form of official rather than autonomous private flows sustained differences were possible between levels of profits in different countries. This could be illustrated by the case of Germany. The Deutschemark had not been allowed to rise to the level at which the current surplus would have been either reduced or cleared by private capital exports. High domestic real interest rates had brought high savings rates and a very high level of profitability, which had encouraged German companies to invest at home rather than abroad, and effectively the whole of the aggregate current surplus from the end of 1970 to late 1978 was added to reserves.

The United States and the United Kingdom had followed the opposite policy of propping up the exchange rate by controls, thereby raising the relative profitability and attractiveness of overseas investment. This had militated against domestic corporate investment and in his view had led to a deficiency of capacity, which meant that British industry would be unable to fill the supply gaps which protection would leave. The problem of an over-high exchange rate had been aggravated by the violent swing in the oil balance, a tight monetary policy and the high real interest rates entailed by the size of the public sector borrowing requirement, which had sucked in short-term funds from overseas. The burden of adjusting to the improvement on oil account and the gain in terms of trade so that the foreign-exchange market could clear had therefore fallen ineluctably on manufacturing industry. If present policies on the capital account and intervention were maintained, protection could improve one part of the current account only at the expense of a worsening in another part. If on the other hand capital account policies were changed, then protection would become unnecessary.

There was some difference of opinion as to whether a current deficit was or was not a bad thing in itself. The view that it mattered what form was taken by the capital counterpart was also questioned. On the latter point Forsyth reiterated that the structure of the capital account could not be a matter of political or economic indifference. At one extreme direct overseas investment by a country in current account surplus helped in the adjustment process; at the other, the German authorities' purchases of United States Treasury bills were financed by the German long-term capital market so that the United States authorities did not need to borrow on their own market. Thus long-term rates were driven up in Germany and down in the United States, with the unwelcome result that international borrowers turned to the latter rather than the former. Other speakers agreed that financing via private capital flows was preferable to financing by official accumulation of foreign assets as in the case of OPEC. The aim of current account balance was regarded by Forsyth as a dangerous shibboleth and some support was given to this view on the basis that if Germany was prepared to use its savings to finance the supply of goods and services to other countries they had no reason to object. Other speakers disagreed, however. In the British case in particular it was suggested that some surplus on current account was desirable, at least while North Sea oil was available, both to improve the international balance sheet and to maintain a non-oil base which could help to bring about a satisfactory trading position thereafter.

Index